THE DECLINE
OF INTELLIGENCE
IN AMERICA

THE DECLINE
OF INTELLIGENCE
IN AMERICA

A Strategy for National Renewal

SEYMOUR W. ITZKOFF

PRAEGER

Westport, Connecticut
London

Library of Congress Cataloging-in-Publication Data

Itzkoff, Seymour W.
    The decline of intelligence in America : a strategy for national
renewal / Seymour W. Itzkoff.
        p.   cm.
    Includes bibliographical references and index.
    ISBN 0–275–94467–0 (alk. paper)
    1. Intelligence levels—United States—History—20th century.
    2. Intellect—United States—Genetic aspects—History—20th century.
    3. United States—Intellectual life—20th century.   I. Title.
    BF431.5.U6I87   1994
    153.9′0973—dc20   93–5416

British Library Cataloguing in Publication Data is available.

Library of Congress Catalog Card Number: 93–5416
ISBN: 0–275–94467–0

First published in 1994

Praeger Publishers, 88 Post Road West, Westport, CT 06881
An imprint of Greenwood Publishing Group, Inc.

Printed in the United States of America

The paper used in this book complies with the
Permanent Paper Standard issued by the National
Information Standards Organization (Z39.48–1984).

10 9 8 7 6 5 4 3 2 1

Dedicated to
Jules and Coleman,
and their generation

Contents

Acknowledgments

A number of student research assistants, along with Smith College library staff, were of great help in gathering together much resource material that went into the writing of this book. Special recognition must be given to Deborah Kershner and Suzanne Brendle for their devotion to the task. Pat Stroman, as always, critically supervised the editing and the manuscript's organization. From the Greenwood Publishing Group, wise guidance was received from John Harney and James T. Sabin. My thanks to them for keeping me on a sober track, considering my deep concerns with the subject matter.

Part I

DECLINE

Chapter 1

Introduction: Truth and National Survival

> Men are not more zealous for truth than they often are for error, and a sufficient application of legal or even of social penalties will generally succeed in stopping the propagation of either. The real advantage which truth has, consists in this, that when an opinion is true, it may be extinguished once, twice, or many times, but in the course of ages there will generally be found persons to rediscover it, until some one of its reappearances falls on a time when from favorable circumstances it escapes persecution until it has made such head as to withstand all subsequent attempts to suppress it.
>
> John Stuart Mill, *On Liberty* (1859)[1]

The argument of this book is simple: The United States is declining as a nation. This decline can be confirmed by any of the criteria that historians have ever used to measure the state and condition of a nation and its people.

Examine our economic and labor problems. Take a look at our educational achievement scores in the international context. Finally, think about the social pathologies that we are being forced to accept as inevitable, perhaps because we are helpless to interdict, much less reverse them.

The fundamental cause of this growing weakness, I believe, is rooted in the overall decline of our nation's intelligence capital, its level of thought and behavior which neither additional educational monies nor social work efforts will be able to improve significantly.

The generation coming to maturity today in the United States, either presently in school or now coming into the workforce, does not have the educational, vocational, or cultural potential comparable to that of earlier generations who participated in the building of our nation. Nor is it competitive with large portions of the developed and developing world.

We are bombarded with discussion in the media, Congress, everywhere, with regard both to cause and cure of our decades-old decline. Such discussions end, predictably, in placebos and soothing words. They may calm the waters at the beginning of a new presidential administration, especially during a momentary economic up-tick—no nation's decline is without its breathing spells. The high-end jobs are still disappearing, however.

It is important to state here that my argument is not directed toward any of our "colored" minorities. Indeed, it is true that by any of the current measures—I.Q., educational achievement, or social disorganization—these minorities are heavily over-represented in the scale of vulnerabilities. There are achievers and disasters in all our ethnic groups, including the white majority. The real problem is our changing demography.

The new generation in all our populations is coming from the lower end of the intellectual, and thus the social, scale. We are creating a population of permanently poor Third World Americans. My concern is with proportion and population, not with individuals, about whom nothing can be stated until one encounters the actual person.

Some will protest that the argument from nature is too deterministic. Their tired rationalization is that we still do not know the precise relationship between nature and nurture. Therefore, we apparently are honor-bound to try, yet once more, a new and more efficient set of environmental amelioration programs, even after the failure of all the others. For many, choosing nature over nurture seems so final, so hopeless.

This argument is heard over and over again because people have not considered the true relationship between nature and nurture in the raising of a child, or in the rearing of a society. Think of a baseball game. The person at bat has to get on base. He hopes that he can go all the way around the diamond to home plate and score a run. The more runs, the greater the possibility that his team will win. But he has to touch first base at the very beginning if he is to get a run. Even if he hits a home run, first base still has to be touched.

Think of second, third, and home bases as the environmental fulfillments of a society's victorious *élan*. In the end, however, it will all come down to touching first base before anything can happen. First base is high human intelligence. Following that, a good family, education, and a rational political and economic structure will constitute what an individual and a nation need in order to succeed.

If things do not happen in the United States to bring about improvements in that trinity of economic prosperity, educational achievement, and social stability, even after all the programs, fine tuning, and media propaganda, I hope that the reader will be willing to consider more heretical explanations of the causes of our national decline, and will perhaps even consider some practical and realistic proposals for a long-term cure.

The issues are truly profound, worthy of the consideration of responsible intellectual and political authorities in our society, as well as by the citizenry at large. It will necessitate that we abandon our ideological zealotry, the infantile search for demons that might simplistically explain our sad loss of hope.

Throughout the world, for almost a century, we have searched for political and social programs to lift the evil spirits of poverty and human degradation from us. In the East, the fruitless politicization of the problem of inequality led to ever more horrible despotisms, all in the name of that ephemeral vision, classlessness. It is ironic that this ideal has since been largely achieved in various nations of the world through the normal democratic and market processes involved in modernization. Western Europe and Japan are the clearest contemporary examples.

In the United States, we have invested our inheritance of wealth and philanthropy in an attempt to dissolve the barriers, to extend a helping hand. The universally acknowledged failure of all these programs, after almost forty years and the expenditure of over five trillion dollars, has not dissuaded ideological liberals.[2] We see the old knee-jerk responses in the present Democratic administration. Ever a familiar refrain: more summer programs for "needy youth," make-work jobs for the urban poor, a few $89,000-per-year jobs for a year, temporary "infrastructure" jobs to repair our city streets. All these in the face of decisive theoretical and experimental evidence that no amount of tax monies is going to change the situation.

Intelligence is part of each individual's inheritance, as much as are one's height and personality. Intelligence, high or low, is not fixed for any one race or ethnic group. Because people of similar ethnic backgrounds have usually bred together, it is inevitable that they will share an intellectual and personality profile. This group profile, however, can change in a relatively short time. It all depends upon who in the group will have the children and thus create the next generation.

The scientific evidence for the biological roots of our social behavior continues to accumulate, and with incremental speed. Simultaneously, our disenchantment with these never-ending visions of social amelioration increases, along with the taxes that we are paying to subsidize these bureaucratic pipe dreams.

Yet we are paralyzed into inaction by our frustrations with failure. And our nation falls ever more deeply into risk. Why?

Truth. This mysterious, germinal concept forever remains the essential challenge to any leadership group. If a nation bars or places restrictions upon the public examination of any issue, it will inevitably foreclose any possibility for the attainment of truth, and thus the instrumental possibilities for reform and renewal.

That is precisely what we are doing to ourselves. The intellectual leadership of the great public media institutions and the universities has effectively handcuffed our elected political representatives, preventing them from considering solutions. The taboo word is, of course, *race*. Because so much of our internal tragedy does involve the minorities of color, the stereotyped excuse is that discussions about biological intelligence and the variable behavior that it elicits will militate against the interests of these minorities.

This is not true. And it is one of the purposes of this book to explain why it is in the interest of all Americans, of whatever ethnicity or race, to think deeply about this reality of variable human intelligence and whether there might be a connection between this issue and the fact that our national profile is sinking so rapidly.

One of the pieces of evidence that I will try to place before the reader is that, parallel with all the so-called ameliorative social programs and the torrent of wealth that has subsidized a great governmental bureaucracy in administering this largesse for the poor and degraded, the condition of these minorities has steadily worsened.

Were we to put aside the rhetoric of ostensible friendship that white media and academic liberals and their politically opportunistic allies have regurgitated to pat the backs of these "victims'" heads, we could make a case that these so-called friends have truly felt only contempt toward their so-called wards. Why else, for all their honeyed words, would their policies have resulted in such ghastly horrors for the intimidated recipients of this philanthropy?

It may already be too late for the United States. The power czars controlling our institutions of information and communication have successfully engaged in a conspiracy of silence, a quiet attempt to maintain the status quo that guarantees their power and perks, even if it means the destruction of the American middle class. The generation that will come to maturity in the early twenty-first century is already in place.

Never in history has a society that has blocked the open search for truth survived to prosper. Yet in their smug assuredness, amidst the steady decline and tidal expansion of human degradation in this supposedly free United States, these pampered and privileged "knowledge" elites continue to violate one of the sacred canons of our democratic constitutional legacy of freedom.

This moral injunction to search for truth ought to be the foundation of their own most deeply held professional commitments!

The smugness and assurance of their power positions, the wealth and notoriety that come with monopolistic control of the "truth," seem to explain it all. Perhaps we are asking too much of these pampered "yuppies." Truthfully, it has often been this way. Cartelists always fear the new, the unknown, and thus the threatening. Thomas Jefferson's urgings in 1787 for a revolution every generation or so—"The tree of liberty must be refreshed from time to time with the blood of patriots and tyrants"[3]—must be applied to those who control the national destiny. This new "knowledge"class has a potential for power accumulation over the lives of the masses far in excess of our elected officials. Media intellectuals today have the power to create the ideas and values out of which will flow the legislation and the judicial decisions of tomorrow.[4]

When one has for so long fabricated and shaped the "truths" that people believe in and act upon; when one's power is predicated on the stage, sets, players, and lines that our political servants have mimicked for so long—do not expect these mind-shapers to lightly give up the well-controlled verities for new and perhaps revolutionary ideas. Such ideas might open the way to a wholly new group of intellectual leaders. In the process, such a change in national perceptions might cause the American people to arise and throw "these rascals off the air and out of print." What then would happen to the good life in which the media elite presently wallow?

One does not lightly make such a revolutionary suggestion, revolutionary only because we as a nation have denied ourselves the knowledge that could clarify our unsolvable problems. It is deeply saddening to assert that nothing in the way of social programs will ever permanently ameliorate the tragic twentieth-century civilizational circumstances of our most vulnerable inhabitants. I testify regretfully that the facts will confirm these assertions.

To the liberal orthodoxy this will be labeled "racism" or some other epithet. It does not daunt them to be apprised of the fact that racial and ethnic groups other than white Anglo-Saxons, even many blacks, are doing very well throughout the world, without the philanthropy visited upon them by these liberal ideologues.

To consider that biological factors of intelligence passed down through heredity and the generations can be so implicated in the fate, for good or ill, of individuals and ethnic groups is hateful given our century-old moral commitment to environmental amelioration.

We must accept this alternative reality. But it may be literally impossible for many intelligent human beings to admit to the possibility of error. For indeed, if they have been wrong, they will have to reevaluate countless beliefs and behaviors around which their normal mental, moral, and social life has revolved. This is asking much for those who live by ideas that are unfortunately held semireligiously and not as scientific hypothetical views that ought to be subject to emendation with the ever-shifting weight of evidence, of facts.

Our nation is falling apart around us because the leadership is either frozen into fear of such considerations, or else finds habit and privilege too precious to abandon. Yet such a revolution of ideas is what our nation was at its very inception, a precipitous venture of a leadership brave enough to set off on the high seas of the unknown.

This book is an appeal to the brave few who may feel, as I do, that the circumstances of our beloved nation are too fragile for them to continue to endure patiently the explanatory nonsense and hypocrisy that emanate from the intellectual power centers. If you have any feelings for the ordinary working person, intelligent, industrious, with family, mortgages, and dreams for the future, then you must help throw off the cant and lies that are destroying a once-great nation, our United States.

The reader should know that I have been researching and writing about these ideas for many years. At first, it was with questions of fact, of the reality of these biological intellectual differences, and the reasons that these differences are part of our human evolutionary heritage. From this study came four books on the evolution of human intelligence.[5] These helped to explain the larger meaning of this absolutely central human intellectual issue.

The second phase of my writing is now devoted to an explanation of the contemporary significance of these truths.[6] This volume is the third in this series of writings.

I hope that this book, concerned as it is with the fate of our own country, will reach and perhaps persuade more people of the fundamental importance of the issue of variable intelligence in humans, of the manner in which this subtle dimension of human nature and behavior can change, as no other factor can, the destiny of nations, indeed of the human race itself.

Chapter 2

Nations, Powerful and Wealthy

QUESTION

What makes a nation powerful and then wealthy? You will answer, of course, that it is the people of the nation that determines its fate. And you will be correct. But how do we create a great people?

We Americans need to understand the meaning of power, wealth, and above all national greatness. In order to know the extent of our loss, we have to envision in a new historical setting what is possible for our nation. Many out there—comfortable purveyors of scaled-down aspirations for you and me—will still be enjoying their perks as the rest of the citizenry settles into poverty and impotence.

Certainly there is more to a great nation and a great people than conquest. No one would call the Mongols a great people despite their monumental military campaigns. To many, they were destroyers, the civilizational fruits of their conquests nowhere to be seen by history or the world community.[1]

Mohammed, for all the loss of life in his campaigns and those of his followers, gave us an important religious and cultural tradition. Its consequences are still profoundly within the consciousness of humankind. What the ultimate future judgment of the world community will be of Arab civilization no one can predict. And that, of course, is the rub about the meaning of the power of nations and, ultimately, of the wealth of their people.[2]

The meaning of power and, ultimately, wealth, lies in our mind's eye. It is a matter of values. There is no external test by which we can measure power or wealth except by the judgments about social preferences contemporaries imply by their behaviors.

We would have to be completely blind to the fact that the power that our rivals, the Japanese and the Germans, have recently accumulated is due to the eagerness of a world community, which judges these matters by deciding how to spend its valuable wealth, to purchase what the Japanese and Germans have to trade to the exclusion of the products of other nations, such as ours. "Why don't they buy Chrysler cars?" weeps Lee Iacocca, when the Mazdas they purchase as "Japanese" cars are practically replicas.

He might just as well ask why I and many others spend precious dollars to travel to Vienna to retrace the steps of Beethoven, in his various domiciles, each replete with an authentic Graf pianoforte upon which he composed the "Moonlight" Sonata? Why, instead, don't we visit the city of Detroit?

HELLENIC GENIUS

Go to Athens in Greece, an ordinarily poor southern European nation that stays afloat economically by dint of the worship by millions all over the world of that stony hilltop of disintegrating temples. Why have people clambered devoutly about the Acropolis for so many generations now like so many gesticulating praying mantises?

The creation by any nation of a profile of power or wealth is truly an expression of the ability of its people to mine deep within our human nature an important dimension of what we value in human experience and action. The "high city" in Athens is certainly one of the greatest religious, civic, architectural, engineering, and artistic enterprises that any people has created.

In addition, however, it represents perhaps the most powerful culture ever, not solely because of its military and economic achievements, epic in themselves. This unique monument symbolizes a level of creative activity in every conceivable area of human social behavior—scientific, philosophical, literary, political—that we consider the core of what is valuable in human existence today.[3]

The world knew and appreciated this achievement then, as we do today. When the Athenians had at last capitulated to the Spartans and their allies at the end of that tragic Achilles-like military/political debacle, in 404 B.C., after an almost thirty-year "world war," their neighbors, Megara and Corinth, appealed to the dominant Spartan leadership to do as the Persians had once done, burn the city and pull down the temples. The Spartans, who prided themselves on their Homeric resoluteness and educational integrity, considered this plea. During the discussions, a voice from somewhere broke into a musical rendering of a passage from the renowned Athenian poet Aeschylus, who himself almost one hundred years earlier had fought against the Persians at Marathon, a great victory for the Athenians, and much admired by the Spartans, then their allies.

The Spartans refused to destroy a city that had meant so much to the spirit of the Hellenes, which they now intended to lead. Only the defense walls would come tumbling down, and to the flute-playing of the local "priestesses."[4]

CIVILIZATION IS POWER

The reader no doubt has a favorite exemplification of great and powerful peoples and their significant achievements. Isn't it puzzling that whatever a powerful nation or people can garner in the way of a value consensus in our own minds will be a nation that is powerful both in the mental or civilizational as well as the physical sense? There seems to be an unending stream of tales in which the powerfully creative and interesting also become wealthy in the material sense.

You may protest that it is the other way around. First come the wealth and the power that flows from this wealth. After all, even the Mongols had their herds of horses, sometimes as far as the eye could see. Unfortunately, they lacked something in their national character, in their individual personalities and mental attitudes, perhaps, to be fair, in their historical readiness. The Mongols themselves in the early Middle Ages, or their Hunnic predecessors, after their conquests, seemed to have eventually melted into the indigenous populations, Hungarian, Russian, or Chinese, in the latter case taking on the language and culture of the more developed Chinese civilization. Perhaps ethnic self-consciousness is also a requirement for civilizational power.[5]

My argument is that what we admire in the people and the nations of great accomplishment and power, almost always of great wealth too, is what we call *civilization*. The building blocks of every civilizational enterprise are constituted by the substance of what we define as high human intelligence.

EVOLUTIONARY LESSONS

To get a perspective on this crucial contemporary issue we have to go back many millions of years of human life and behavior, to the "eoliths" of *Homo habilis*. This human group living on the plains of Africa some 3 to 4 million years ago shaped these fragments of granite, shale, and flint into barely discernible utilitarian shapes, to scrape, puncture, perhaps even to slash a human or animal prey.[6]

We believe that these diminutive ancestors had culture. But we cannot know the full shape of their expressions, religious, linguistic, or artistic.

These latter are ephemeral. They do not provide evidence as do the stone tools, the eoliths. However, we have never known of a social group of humans who made tools without having the whole panoply of social and cultural institutions.

As we go forward in time, the tools that we find are closer to the surface of the land. Our scientific understanding and intelligence tell us that this means they are more recent in fabrication. When we examine them we notice that the tools are more clearly shaped in terms of what we presume to be their purpose. Here again our analysis is made possible because of a human intelligence that has created the complex scientific discipline that allows us to draw such conclusions.

These later so-called Acheulean tools were usually fabricated out of harder rock, granites and marble. They were increasingly faceted, chipped into shape by a very conscious human maker. There is no question as to their purpose. The shapes announce themselves as they would to a contemporary builder or carpenter who enters a local Home Depot store.

Because the fossilized skulls that we find associated with these tools have larger within-the-skull dimensions than the *Homo habilis* skulls that we find with the earlier eoliths, we can draw the conclusion that the makers of the "Acheulean" tools were more intelligent creatures. We have labeled them *Homo erectus*.[7]

We can call their improved (by our contemporary analysis as to what constitutes "improved") tools a product of a more intelligent people because we see this process of bigger skulls and more "refined" tools having a trajectory right up to our contemporary time. We can refuse to label these differences in ability as differences in intelligence. But since we are analyzing these facts in order to bring mental order from the chaos of so much sensory data, itself an act of thought, abstraction, knowledge—or intelligence, call it what you will—we will have to define the relationship between within-the-skull capacity and the character of the technology that these ancestors of ours have left behind. Common language use throughout the world will force us eventually to say, yes, intelligence.

It is fair to say that individuals of such-and-such intelligence made those tools. The factory system had yet to be invented on the various continents of the Old World, including Africa, from which humans had migrated by about one million years ago. But as they migrated they moved, by and large, in groups, not as solitary and vulnerable individuals.

The "band" is the smallest social grouping that the intellectual scholarly mind has defined. It usually consists of several extended, interbreeding families, with a very informal political structure of leader/follower. Perhaps as few as twenty or so people made up a band, enough to provide for protection against natural animal enemies and predatory humans, likewise in small groups. Also, the bands were capable of moving on and living off the land without subjecting local resources to much attrition.

Their tools, their language, their rituals and beliefs would have been as unique as they probably were undeveloped. In constituting an interbreeding unit, the groups would certainly share all the values of family life, the glue of familiarity and similarity. Our belief is that as time, variability, and natural selection operated on the human genome, increasingly intelligent humans created increasingly complex social arrangements, and the band evolved into the tribe. Here was a much larger and more efficient social unit, often still of a migratory people, but with more highly developed political, economic, and military wherewithal.[8]

CONFLICT OF COUSINS

An important example of the relationship of communal intelligence levels to the meaning of social power and wealth comes from the end of the Ice Ages some 35,000 years ago. The Cro-Magnon and Neanderthal peoples were similar Caucasoid *Homo sapiens*, products of apparently devastating environmental and climatic challenges that destroyed many transitional erectine/*sapiens* types.[9]

Both groups had large skulls and large brains, with one important difference. Cro-Magnon was tall and delicate of bone, with a brain structure similar to ours. Indeed, he was a northern European, someone who would seem at home in Copenhagen or Warsaw. Neanderthal was shorter, heavily boned, similar to the original *Homo erectus* prototype that had existed throughout the world for almost a million years, but slightly taller and with a very large and primitive brain.

Both groups of *sapiens* made their living primarily by hunting. There is evidence that both groups coexisted in western Asia for a good interval, with the Cro-Magnons seemingly moving into western Europe at a later time and rapidly expanding in numbers as well as settlements, from Spain to the Ural Mountains that separated European and Asiatic Russia.

The diligent flint-tool technological industry of the Neanderthals attests to their social cohesion. They buried their dead with ceremony, the graves often being decorated with flowers. They also showed philanthropic feelings in that one group apparently kept a crippled youngster alive until he died in middle age of a separate accident. Most probably their social organization was of a band-like character. It is probable that they had semi-permanent home sites in the protective setting of caves from which they went forth on their various hunting expeditions.[10]

The Cro-Magnons may have been one important step beyond the Neanderthals in social organization. Their cultural products and residence sites, which they had inherited from the Neanderthals, have a much richer ambience. Outside the caves one often finds deep ditches in which vast quantities of animal bones are found, evidence of a high standard of cuisine, with much meat protein. The artwork in the interior of the caves needs no elaboration here except to note that it is unequaled in many important technical and aesthetic respects by anything that has since followed. Their sculptures of the many Venuses are famed. Not as well known are delicate female faces that were carved, perhaps by loving husbands, again revealing similarities to modern European faces.[11]

One senses that we have before us groups of a complex tribal structure with a certain amount of specialization, given not only the painstaking artwork deep in their cave cathedrals, but also the numerous seemingly chronometric markings on bone and stone that hint at attempts to symbolize abstractly the tantalizingly mysterious regularities of their world.[12]

That the Cro-Magnons and the Neanderthals encountered each other is probable. There seems to be no more than a five-thousand-year interval between the general occupation of home sites by the Neanderthals and their replacement by Cro-Magnon tools and fossils. When they did meet, the bows and arrows, spear throwers, and harpoons made of bone and stone had their effect. Not too many realize that the Cro-Magnons had learned how to fire-harden pottery. Who taught them how to create a culture with so many innovations, innovations of a complexity that approaches that of the River Valley civilizations created some 25,000 years later?[13]

The medical researcher A.T.S. Simeons describes one such imaginary encounter between these racially similar but intellectually different human groups:

One can imagine Neanderthalers watching from the edge of a cliff how the Cro-Magnons hunted in the valley. To the brutish, fear-ridden Neanderthalers these almost hairless giants with jutting chin and towering forehead must have appeared to be superhuman spirits. He saw them using a miraculous technique which was utterly unfathomable and incomprehensible to him. He saw the animal herds from which he had for thousands of years picked what he wanted being ingeniously rounded up and driven into traps, over precipice or through a narrow gorge into the fire, the clubs and the spears of the hunters who jabbered excitedly and made strange cries while they waited for the bag. As he gazed at the elaborate preparations they made for the chase, Neanderthal Man must have felt an eerie terror and a sickening weariness at the futility of his own poor efforts. He must have realized that against these—what we would call God-like—beings he had not the slightest chance to compete. More and more he must have drawn away from such terrifying creatures, not because they violently threatened his life, but simply because their miraculous powers were too much for him to contemplate and filled him with primeval panic.[14]

The culture and tribal life of Cro-Magnon lived on for over 20,000 more years, slowly evolving and deepening in its creative richness, even amidst an icy and forbidding environment. The Cro-Magnons were a powerful and dominating people, their genes gradually spreading throughout the world, to Africa, East Asia, and beyond. With this relative wealth, and the leisure that came with it, also came this explosion of creative energy, innovation in every area of human experience, and no earlier precedents to build on. It was, indeed, a product of their brain and its intelligence.

Eventually even this well-contented quasi-civilization had to break up. It was the withdrawal of the ice to the north and the beginning of a new climatic environment that reshaped this way of life. The trees moved north, into the new forests the herds disappeared, and the stable encampments had to be given up. A new life on the move made the art, the technology, much more difficult. Soon new civilizations would become possible, now in the river valleys and the oases of the south and the southwest.

SYMPATHY

In addition to high intelligence in a national group, an element that will determine both the power potentialities of the nation as well as the wealth of its people is a group's mental superego, its philosophy or ideology. What we have inherited as part of our evolutionary mental structure is an ability to turn off the natural tooth-and-fang survivalistic qualities that thrust human beings of high intelligence into dominance at the expense of less able humans.

I have often wondered about that lonely Cro-Magnon fossil that was found amidst the tools of the Neanderthals. How was such a thing possible?[15] There have been many explanations, but is my speculation any less possible? Consider:

This fellow was a sympathetic hunter and warrior who would often return from the hunt or even a fighting skirmish with a bedraggled Neanderthal captive or two, perhaps even a young maiden as concubine or slave. Gentle soul, he could *not* get himself to see every good Neanderthal as a "dead Neanderthal."

Finally, as with all of us, this good fighter, hunter, and happy human met his ultimate fate. An illness, accident, or even battle cut his life short. His fellows thought it appropriate, even his just reward, to bury him in an abandoned Neanderthal camp site, to the eternal bedevilment of anthropologists![16]

Along with sympathy come mental understanding and the need to intercede against our immediate gut reaction, to plan out our lives to align with a vision of what we humans are, or can be.

SUICIDE OF NATIONS

For many thousands of years, religion and the priests' interpretation of the voice of the gods directed human behavior, often with bizarre and counterproductive results for the nation or the people. Armies often went out into suicidal encounters on the basis of such "wisdom."[17]

The Persian emperor Xerxes in the year 480 B.C. had defeated a succession of Greek naval and land armies, including the Spartan holding force at Thermopolyae. The Athenians were forced to abandon their city, and watch it burn from the ten-mile-long island of Salamis two miles across the strait of the Saronic Gulf. The Delphic oracle had told the Athenian delegation that "a wooden wall will defend you." This enigmatic statement they interpreted to mean that they should rely on their navy to defend them.

In an earlier century, the Lydian King Croesus sent an emissary to Delphi to find out if he would succeed in a war against the Persians. Naturally the priests at Delphi were showered with magnificent gifts. The answer given by the oracle was that by going to war, Croesus would destroy a great empire. The empire that was destroyed was his own.[18]

THE ROAD OF REASON

In our own time ideology has taken the place of traditional religious guidance. Ideology guides people when they think they understand deeply simple truths about complicated issues. So they set forth to create public policies for their people in the light of "true belief," as did the Communists on the basis of the "wisdom" of Marx and Lenin.

Unfortunately the power that was mustered over the lives of their intimidated citizens was such that even when these "truths" were contradicted by simple factual experience, the power brokers were not deterred. "Full speed ahead to utopia," they enunciated; that is, until the waves came crashing down around them in the chaos of their people's misery.

Certainly the American people, while not held in the thrall of totalitarian coercion, are being seduced to follow meekly the path of an ideological mapping of reality that is seriously out of kilter with reality. The Europeans and Asians, who have lived in this mental concentration camp for so many decades, are still the civilizationally talented if historically undeveloped people that they were before the communist usurpation. They may well show the United States the way to dominance in the next century.

They will then be back on track with a realistic vision of the road toward power and wealth. But will we? Will our national actions prove to have been far more debilitating to the long-term renewal of our society? Will our pseudo-philanthropic ideology prove to be uniquely disastrous, no comparison with the actions of that lone benign Cro-Magnon?

In our subsidization and implicit encouragement of the less intelligent quadrant of our nation, will our leaders have committed an even greater violence against our civilizational heritage than that of the communist vision?

Chapter 3

America's Greatness

UNDER THE BOARDWALK

History was made under the boardwalk at Coney Island. Okay, only a boy's history, a wee bit of memory held by one who lived through those seemingly ancient days of denial and struggle. For the United States, the 1930s were a down moment in that juggernaut once called the American century. For city kids like me, it was, as are all historic moments, both mysterious and exciting.

Never mind what was happening out on the beach, or on the boardwalk itself. Under the boardwalk, even when there was no twilight darkness to mask the entwined lovers a kid would sometimes stumble over in his explorations, there was always some kind of action.

The events that made history for me, albeit only now that I look back on it from a perspective of over fifty years, were the gang fights. But so different from today. And so symbolic as to how our nation has changed.

The "bath house gang wars" was how it was described in those days. Mostly weekend gangs of ethnics, as they came together in different combinations of individuals all during the summer. From one bath house came the "micks," from that one, the "wops," down the boardwalk a few blocks were the "kikes." On occasion, arriving seemingly from nowhere on the IRT were groups of "spics" and "niggers." "What the hell were 'they' doing on 'our' beach?" Come to think of it, such remarks were applied indiscriminately to any and all of the other ethnic beach gangs when push inevitably came to shove.

And push and shove it was in those days of depression, tension, unending and pent-up rivalries. Whose fault was it that we were poor? Naturally, the blame fell on those noisy, pushy bastards over there on the sands playing beach ball with their molls. Eventually a ball would fly into the midst of the *others*, else some "Charles Atlas" would come running by to catch a ball or chase a maiden, pitch some sand over the *others*' maidens and the battle was joined—under the boardwalk.

Kids of my age felt the electricity of battle like an underground tremor. "Fight, fight" came the excited whispers, and by the dozen we zipped away from our mothers' aprons. Off we went, under the boardwalk, to witness American history in the making.

It didn't matter which groups were involved. The rules, as with the gladiators of Rome, or the feudal knights of medieval Europe, were completely stylized and *de rigueur*. Fists only. But the blood came with ferocity. To a little punk like me, it was horrible, nauseating, and deeply stirring.

A world was being shaped and decided upon, under the boardwalk. Which ethnic group would prevail, ours or theirs? In the balance was the future of the United States. Eventually, some "chicken" would call the cops, and the action would dissolve in a blink as the wounded were quickly hustled back to the anonymity of the masses huddled under their beach umbrellas, or enveloped in their blankets to be quietly succored by one of their own bathing beauties.

"Wait till next time" was the weekly message. It was always too indecisive for us kids. Probably one of the girlfriends finked on the fight. No one really got "killed" this time, as we regretfully compared notes: a mildly mangled face, perhaps a half-mouthful of detached teeth to be spat out onto the sand under the boardwalk. Next week the action might be more interesting.

I do not recall ever hearing about knives, clubs, or, Heaven forbid, guns being used in those battles, only fists, arms, legs, and heads, all bare and vulnerable.

Friends on occasion whispered seriously to me about a battle that they understood to have resulted in an ambulance, also much weeping and vengeful anger. But I never personally experienced such a result of the weekend ethnic wars.

One summer, it was over. Instead of action under the boardwalk, it was on top where a whole new scene startled young eyes. There, in navy whites and army khaki, they strolled proudly with their girls. I couldn't tell the difference, wops, micks, kikes.

The December before, the Japanese had attacked, and we were now united in war. Already victorious in battle, seemingly everyone was in service or working important defense jobs. Our country could never again come undone to repeat that divisiveness, a momentary past that I will always want to forget, "under the boardwalk."[1]

AMERICA, THE BEAUTIFUL

The rest is history, as they say. For about forty years the United States appeared to be not only the most powerful, but also the most free nation in the world, a democratic wave of the future that we thought would endure forever. And it would pull the rest of the world, traditionalist, authoritarian, and class-ridden, even the totalitarian enemies, eventually to be our allies.

The economic expansion and prosperity that came with the end of the war was breathtaking. Between 1950 and 1965, a span of not even one generation, we increased our gross national product, the value of all goods produced within our borders and the monies that flowed back into the United States from overseas investments, as much as this gross national product had increased from 1620 to 1950, in equivalent dollars.

America was Levittown, and all its kin throughout the land. Owning one's own home in the suburbs was a real possibility. Decent housing, from between $8,000 and $15,000 with a 4.5 percent GI or FHA thirty-year mortgage, made all our dreams possible. Instead of ethnic wars under the boardwalk, the ethnics met each weekend on their crabgrass lawns, the instruments of cacophonic strife now the interminably roaring gasoline combustion mowers.[2]

The dollar was king, and we, the formerly poor, slid into the middle class, many of the old-time socialist types even voting Republican for war hero Dwight Eisenhower as president of the United States. In the process a great and liberal-spirited attempt was made to right historical racial and ethnic wrongs, to bring all of our citizens under the banner of the new and modern economy of corporate America.

The *Brown* desegregation decision of 1954, coupled with the Civil Rights Act of 1964, expressed the urgency of this need for national reconciliation and nondiscrimination. In the public mind these measures were equivalent to the New Deal legislation of FDR in the 1930s, emergency measures to attempt to right the ship of state.

If both sets of governmental actions essentially failed to achieve their goals of both social and economic equality, perhaps because such actions and goals, as we now sadly understand better, are beyond the reach or the grasp of governmental prescription, then it was at least a powerful liberal rallying cry that tempered the unbelievably powerful economic expansion with a dose of humanitarian concern.

We fought wars for democracy, freedom, and humanity in Korea and Vietnam during this period, and armed ourselves and the world to the teeth to defend against the Cold War. And, of course, we tried to help the needy of the world. The total cost, only a few trillion here and there. But then, we had the money.[3]

From the time of Lyndon Johnson in the mid-1960s, we have spent that 5.1 trillion dollars on internal welfare programs, in addition to the many billion previously spent during the immediate post–World War II period to attempt to give a tangible upward hand to the politically, socially, and economically disfranchised. And still we roared off to ever headier standards of living, even as the rest of the world began to recuperate and attempt to emulate us.[4]

It was what we had wanted. We, the United States, would fly point for the rest of the world. They, gasping behind in delirious appreciation, would gradually pull themselves out of their ancient reactionary habits. This was the American century, wasn't it?

WHAT HAPPENED?

Of course it hasn't happened. And the American people want to know why. Those enemies that we defeated in war, whose cities were destroyed with both fire and atomic bombs, have come back to lord it over us. It is estimated that 80 percent of the submariners in the German navy went to the bottom of the ocean, permanently; 50 percent of the Luftwaffe pilots were shot out of the skies never to see the clouds again. The Japanese officer corps, too, suffered mightily. The cream of both nations.[5]

After all the horrors they caused the human race for their aggressive megalomania as nations, as people, it is ironic that almost fifty years later the Germans and the Japanese sneer at us as a declining nation. At one time, we produced over 100,000-per-year of the finest warplanes that the world had ever seen. The Soviet army toward the end of World War II survived on U.S. food and material supplies, all while we fed our own and all the Allied population as well.[6]

Things don't just happen. A nation does not rise up to be one of the most powerful the planet has ever seen, able to give a vast majority of its population the richest standard of living that any people have enjoyed, and to do this for over a generation, without real reasons, reasons that can be identified and understood objectively.

The skeptic will smile and say, "everything that goes up . . . " Yes, but the laws of gravity apply to all physical objects, and if it applied to Germany and Japan, they should not be where they are today, not after their previous attempts to subjugate the world. After all, we did churn them into the dust.

Fifty years after the city gangs of my own youth fought their battles for dignity, pride, and group solidarity, very different youth battles are being fought in our city centers. No longer under the boardwalks, the streets themselves are now being claimed by automatic weapons; the losers, now "dead on arrival." It may be pride that underlies the bloodshed, but it is also crack cocaine.

They say that if there is no memory, there will be no civilization. To the reader I say, "I remember. I hope you will, too!"

OBJECTIVITY

We must not be mesmerized by patriotic rhetoric. Indeed, we were a great nation, between 1890 and 1970. Before that, we were an alluring symbol of frontier and progress. Today, when most of the world is in even worse trouble than we are, hurtling out of control into demographic free fall, it is not surprising that the poor are chancing everything to get within our borders as "illegals." The hopeful migrants still see us as a land of great opportunity. Once inside, they will gain government-mandated welfare and educational privileges far beyond their dreams in the home country. They will be "home safe."

It is important to understand what it is that allowed the United States to become not merely the greatest economic and military force for a major portion of the twentieth century, but also to provide, for a period of nearly two generations, for its citizens of all ethnicities a standard of individual material pleasures and amenities the likes of which have never been seen on this earth.

I think all objective persons would have to admit that the conditions were special, perhaps never to be duplicated in the history of our planet. This is not to say that other nations will never be able to equal our standard of living. In some ways, the special allure that the United States held out for humankind will remain unique.[7]

The following points will, I believe, allow me to continue the argument. It is not merely our greatness that is in question but our current decline, and the possibility of a more precipitous fall. On the other hand, Japan and Germany, now even China, have certainly made dramatic recoveries in our century. There is no law of history that says, "8, 9, 10, America, you're out forever!"[8]

My argument will focus on the following five areas—the political, the economic, the land, the people, and history.

The Political Dimension

Our revolution and independence from England was obtained in a "clean" war. We were discovered and colonized during a period of great material and intellectual change. The victories of the English over both the Spanish and the French symbolized the victory of a modern political way of life over more traditionalist forms of political association.

Parliamentary England gave the American colonies and their largely English-speaking inhabitants an endowment, which even in revolution and eventual breaking away was a precious inheritance. The freedoms that the enlightened English middle classes had grasped for themselves were transferred to their English counterparts overseas. Our Declaration, and the Constitution that followed, were framed from the most advanced thinking that existed about the natural and social world.

We were the products of the scientific revolution that gave us creative minds such as Thomas Hobbes, John Locke, Isaac Newton, James Watt, and Joseph Priestly, the latter a refugee to the new United States. Otherwise we would not have had the likes of Benjamin Franklin as a home-born citizen.[9]

As a nation without embedded royalty or a class of aristocracy, with so much openness for dissidents and innovators, our political system of division of powers in the federal government, of limitation on the power of this government over the people and the states, personified in the Tenth Amendment, started us on our historic political journey as a free people.[10]

In the late eighteenth century, ours was the most modern, most rational embodiment of the existing knowledge of the day. Some, such as law professor Richard Epstein of the University of Chicago, argue that in falling away from the intent of the founding fathers during the period starting with the New Deal of Franklin Roosevelt and into our own time we have expanded the power of government, not merely taking and redistributing the economic and social fruit of our individual endeavors, but inevitably compromising those basic political freedoms promised to us in the Declaration and Constitution by those thinkers who shaped the principles upon which this nation was built.[11]

Economic Freedom

The time is coming when we will view Adam Smith as the preeminent social and political philosopher of freedom of the modern scientific era. A native of Scotland, he taught at the University of Glasgow, where his professorial chair was in moral philosophy. Indeed, we are rapidly coming to see in his advocacy of the free marketplace, unconstrained by statist mercantilism, or, more recently, statist totalitarianism and redistributionist egalitarianism, his true contribution to human freedom. Sadly, this latter constraint involves *taking* by government through the tax system and forcibly redistributing it to the so-called oppressed needy.

Mercantilism in Smith's own day constituted the efforts of nations and their merchant and producer surrogates to grab or protect markets for their products, or the sources of raw materials that would allow their manufacturers and traders to profit by this colonial control. It led to tariffs and other barriers being placed against the products of other nations, as those effected by the English against the Dutch cloth manufacturers in the sixteenth century, and against our own colonial monopolies, which in our case led to revolution. We did not want to have to purchase English products derived from their other dependents, such as Indian tea, and at a mark up, and then be taxed additionally for the privilege.

Smith's *The Wealth of Nations*, published in 1776, developed the idea that free trade and the marketplace of goods as well as ideas would always and eventually balance itself out, without the overt and manipulative hand of the political power structure. These power manipulators presumed to act in the interest of the greatest number, but in effect their intrusions usually were in the name of special privilege, always to the long-term detriment of the citizenry.[12]

By the time our Constitution was being written, the impact of Smith's ideas was being felt; that document is certainly compatible with the philosophy that all forms of institutional restraint on free trade, especially as exemplified in later nineteenth-century antitrust legislation, harmonized with the ideas of Adam Smith.[13]

Simply, we came into being as a nation at a time when there was an awareness that trade and the marketplace were as important arenas of freedom as were the halls of legislature, the courts, and the schools. The Constitution does not mention the regulation of our economic lives or our educational decisions, which were reserved to the initiatives of the people and the several states and local communities.

The struggle of which we have increasingly become aware in our own century is revealed in the preempting role of government as it intervenes in nonmonopolistic or cartel-like settings of economic relations. The government alone now attempts to decide what the national good requires in terms of social welfare, police powers, and the pacification of society.

The Land

Can there be any doubt that the land mass of the United States, now including Alaska and Hawaii, is one of the most blessed pieces of real estate that this earth has ever seen? Little needs to be added here except to reiterate that coming at a time of rapid industrialization, the openness of opportunity, the richness of natural resources, the temperate climate which by and large saved us from the ills of the tropical world, constitute a bonanza that added immeasurably to the political and economic freedoms that we inherited from our eighteenth-century intellectual leadership. What more coincidental luck can be found than in the discovery of oil in Pennsylvania in 1859, the simultaneous exploitation of the vast Minnesota iron ore deposits, and the profligate abundance issuing from the ten feet of black loam under the Illinois prairie?

Hucksters of patriotism will extol our political ingenuity and the economic enterprise that flowed from this bounty, or else the wonderful people that made it happen. However, these people were largely the same, as I will note below, as those who remained behind in Europe. The latter are now showing us that despite the debacles of revolution and the death of so much talent in two world wars, they, too, can work, produce on an international level, and still maintain the democratic compact.

They did not have our land, its climate, resources, or variety to stimulate and challenge with its open, raw, virgin temptations. Only as we lose those advantages of underpopulation and resource plenitude will we begin to appreciate the truth that God gave the American people an enormous initial advantage at an opportune moment in time.[14]

Our descendants may one day judge that we squandered their futures.

The People

"The prison ships from London transferred the human garbage from their streets onto our shores. Until the Revolutionary War intervened and Australia became a new dumping ground, the American colonies were the preferred destination for the internal cleansing of the human detritus of eighteenth-century England. Unpredictably, what the English were really creating was an incipient revolutionary elite, which would one day permanently sweep 'them' from 'our' shores."[15]

Thus my young and enthusiastic history professor intoned. This was at a former YMCA college in Hartford, Connecticut, then attempting to redefine itself as a full-fledged liberal arts institution. It was housed in a vast abandoned elementary school in one of the oldest and most rundown areas of that city. I came there as a music student attempting to get my share of liberal arts elevation.

The name was Hillyer College, now the University of Hartford, and it was blossoming in the distant suburbs. The students, then working class, multiracial and multiethnic, aspiring veterans, and mostly part-time, knew that they were not in the same league with the students at Episcopal and upper-class Trinity College across town. The irony is that many decades later Trinity still stands on its lofty hill, but now in the middle of a new urban ghetto!

I loved football. And Trinity was then the name of the game. I used to watch the home team against the Wesleyans, the Amhersts. I watched these elite young men, ruddy, strongly built, with crew-cut towheads and, above all, a sense of destiny. There they went, I thought, the children of the dregs of the prison ships, now the elite. If them, why not me?

The United States, in its incipient and ultimately realized glory, was a European nation, planted in a new hemisphere across the ocean. Immigrants, largely from various European nations, and mostly voluntarily relocated, gave our country an ever-widening infusion of new blood. In its melting-pot ambitions, the United States was on its way to creating a new person, a new citizen, immune to the burden of debts to its past that Europe had to struggle with.

I do not mean to slight the Africans brought to these shores in bondage nor the Amero-Indians who suffered the fate of many native peoples, including the Africans, of not being prepared for the turns of history that determine power and destiny. (The irony may be that the largely European United States of the twenty-first century may itself be bypassed by history's thoughtless indifference.)

Just as whites were sold into slavery by whites to other whites in Europe in earlier days, Africans were the losers from the Middle Ages on. Their fate was to be sold by other blacks into slavery under whites, first to Arabs, then to Europeans for the American "market."[16]

Culturally, educationally, perhaps even intellectually, these native peoples had remained vulnerable. The Amero-Indians were decimated by disease and war. In Central and South America, they were eventually absorbed into the oncoming Spanish immigrants. In the West Indies, the Indians were exterminated, replaced by African slaves on the agricultural plantations.[17]

In the United States agricultural slavery worked, if not as famously when compared with the productivity of the free white farmers of the north. It was a sharply altered African-American population that struggled forth after emancipation to take its place in a gradually opened-up setting of economic and political enfranchisement. Partially white, and even under segregation developing an indigenous elite, this minority was moving upward toward full equality into the middle of the twentieth century. This upward movement continued until the incubus of social amelioration intervened, the unintended but ultimate result being the destruction of community cohesiveness, in the process seriously wounding the national fabric.[18]

There can be no question but that the character of the people, their intellectual capacity as well as their philosophical outlook on human experience, determines the future of a nation. For two hundred years, by following the initial mandates inherent in our political and economic system, our nation flourished. The people met the world-class challenges that confronted them. They struggled against and defeated an all-powerful eighteenth-century British imperialism.

Almost two hundred years later we had the scientific, educational, and industrial wherewithal to save a dying Old World liberal tradition challenged by ideologically berserk totalitarianisms armed with the most modern weapons that science and industry could produce. Our land produced the resources, our educated men and women in the factories fabricated the finest military hardware that our engineering and scientific talent could design, our armed forces utilized these weapons with efficiency and coordination. With our productivity, we fed and clothed the world, and cleansed the seas of raiders.

Could our people rise to such a challenge today? Yes, we can go up against a tyrant like Saddam Hussein of Iraq, who had a third-class military operation, even with the modern weaponry provided him by other producers. But could we defeat twenty-first-century Germans or Japanese?

History

There is a time for prosperity, and a time to bide and wait.

The Veneti, an Indo-European people from what is now the coast of Croatia, moved into the area of their later prosperity in early republican Rome to take advantage of the trade opportunities opened up with the taming of the sub-Alpine Gauls. Later Julius Caesar, on his way north to pursue his campaign in Gaul proper, detoured momentarily to disconnect the Veneti from their sphere-of-interest pretensions and bring them under the sway of Rome.

There they remained and prospered until Rome slowly broke up. Then Attila the Hun in the 5th century A.D. frightened the now-pacified citizenry out onto the swampy mounds of the Rialto. There they gradually carved out a new empire of trade throughout the Mediterranean, first with the Byzantines, then with the Ottoman Turks, until Europe began to look westward toward the Atlantic.

Still they maintained their prosperity, if not their dominance, well into the eighteenth century, only to fall victim once more to the imperial pretensions of larger powers. Again, fallow decay, until they were rediscovered, this time by the yearnings of the European and American industrial elite for the antique, to be followed by an avalanche of tourist dollars and marks.[19]

In this way, one can trace the highs and lows of Holland as its industrious and talented people carved a country out of the North Sea swamps, a nation below sea level. Traders, craftsmen, fighters for liberty and national independence, the Dutch more than once opened their doors to talented refugees from all over Europe. In the seventeenth century, with such refugees as Spinoza and Comenius, Holland became the affluent democratic civilizational beacon to the world.[20]

Somewhat bypassed by the industrial era of nineteenth-century prosperity, then dependent on abundant natural resources of which the Dutch had few, they have once more backed into affluence, again revealing their great business and technological skills, as always built upon extremely high educational and cultural standards.

But they are concerned that this prosperity, now flourishing in the midst of a world of the poor, including the few colonies that they had retained and with whom they maintain a sentimental historical relationship, not seem arrogant. This moral sensibility demands of the Dutch leadership that the people once more share their freedom, wealth, and cultural *élan*, now with the world of the poor, with the culture of "liberty," drugs, prostitution, AIDS. It remains to be seen whether, having added a whole new non-European population and a culture of permissiveness, the Dutch will both retain and build upon the prosperity and freedom they wish to share.[21]

OUTCOME

Every nation, because it cannot control nature or human events, is subject to the vicissitudes of change. Even a continental power such as the United States occupies only a small percentage, less than 7 percent, of the land mass of the earth, or borders on only so much of the open seas.

We are moving into the twenty-first century. Already a new international situation has placed us at a disadvantage. Nations such as Japan and Germany, which, fewer than fifty years ago, were on their collective knees for genocidal brutality, then burned out, suffering from the drain of millions of their finest young men killed or maimed, at the mercy of and subject to the overlording charity of their conquerors, have returned to the fore in less than the blink of an historical eye.

They now sit atop the international mountain, dictating the rules of the game. Is it all an accident of history? Are there any laws that can explain this odd turn of events? Can the United States learn from the past so that it may once again see the future as real possibility instead of genuflecting, repeating the empty rhetorical slogans that deceive no one, about our once and future greatness?

Chapter 4

Economics: Is the Sleeper a Giant?

If the route to success is inventing new products, the education of the smartest 25% of the labor force is critical . . . If the route to success is being the cheapest and best producer of products, new or old, the education of the bottom 50% of the population moves to center stage . . . If the bottom 50% cannot learn what must be learned, new high-tech processes cannot be employed.

Lester Thurow (1992),
Dean, Sloan School of Management, MIT[1]

The planes had returned to the carrier Nagato. The commanding pilot of the corps proudly reported to Admiral Yamamoto, supreme officer of the flotilla. The squadrons had had a dazzling success over Pearl Harbor. They had achieved the almost unbelievable destruction of the entire U.S. Pacific Fleet. As the pilot left the bridge, the admiral looked out over the rolling seas and spoke quietly to his aide, "But we have awakened a sleeping giant."[2]

The Japanese commander was correct. The United States would stir itself from its depression lethargy. The productivity of the land and the people would rapidly approach tidal wave proportions. Within six months, after the April 1942 victory at Midway in the Pacific, and the subsequent suppression of the German U-boat submarine menace to the convoys and supply lines to Britain and the Soviet Union, the inevitable outcome would never be in serious doubt.[3]

PERSPECTIVE ON DECLINE

The question is, What happened? How in those twenty-five years after 1945 did we produce this vast proliferation of goods and services for our people all the while in the 1960s and 1970s laying the seeds for our oncoming economic decline? Why did we not hear even a whisper of concern from those in our political establishment, those supposedly committed to the care and long-term prosperity and stability of the nation?

The explanation for our prosperity is clear. Considering the state of knowledge, technology, and natural resources in the international scene at large as well as in our own national consciousness, we were an undeveloped nation. World War II revealed to us the potentiality that existed within these borders. Unstated, but perhaps even more important, were the latent educational skills of the citizens coupled with an enormous energy and hunger to utilize all those assets that had made and would make us the great world power that we were.[4]

The decline was symbolized in part by the Vietnam War, which escalated throughout the mid-1960s. As will be discussed below, it could also be traced to the small, cheap, and efficient Toyotas and Hondas that started to be exported to our shores about the same time. First came the Corollas from Toyota; soon after came Honda's improved Civics. The disappearance of British-exported autos—once the post-war rage—in the face of this competition should have warned us of things to come.[5]

The 1970s also saw the virtual elimination of our consumer electronics industry—cameras, household appliances—and the erosion of market share in our domestic auto industry and textiles. These events should also have provided advance warning of more serious economic challenges in the future. Remember, we were in not merely a hot war in Vietnam, but also a cold war with the Soviets and the mainland Chinese. Our arms industry provided much employment and the confidence of continuing technological fallout to maintain our domestic future.[6]

The United States was still an expanding economy, with aerospace, computers and software, memory chips, pharmaceuticals, financial services, farm machinery, and telecommunications industries still holding leadership positions. We had plenty of oil and access to world petroleum as well as other international natural resources, and still at bargain prices.

The oil crisis of 1979 sent the U.S. economy into a tailspin. Interest rates flew up, President Jimmy Carter spoke with sadness of our need to come to terms with limits, to scale down our appetites and pretensions. The unbelieving public turned to Ronald Reagan who lowered interest rates and, through a monetary legerdemain dubbed supply-side economics, boosted military spending to counter the "evil empire." He also set off a burst of deficit spending that with the help of George Bush and the Democratic Congress quadrupled our national debt to $4 trillion in the 1980s.[7]

We now know and understand how our Reagan years' prosperity was paid for. It was not, however, all government spending and the printing of borrowed dollar bills. The private sector went through its own final speculative binge. In 1979 total public and private debt was 150 percent of the gross national product (GNP). By 1990 it had risen to 195 percent of the GNP. In 1979 private debt was 69.5 percent of personal disposable income. By 1990 this ratio had risen to 87.7 percent of personal disposable income.[8]

The October 19, 1987, collapse on Wall Street was a sobering symptom of speculation amid inflated equity values. The junk bond speculations and manipulation epitomized by instant billionaire *cum* convict Michael Milken, along with his colleagues, was one aspect of these unthinking investment speculations that symbolized the problems of the private sector. Wall Street did recover, reflecting reality therapy in this portion of the business community.

Real estate speculation, especially commercial real estate overbuilding in every city and suburb, imposed huge pressures on the banks and insurance companies that overfinanced many impractical projects. Early in the 1980s, the collapse of the Latin American debt load further weakened the American banking system.[9]

Congress' reform of the income tax system in 1986 had a not surprising, but unintended consequence. The elimination of the tax exemption for multiple residences, for those properties for which one did not have a proprietary management risk, for investment real estate posing as third or fourth home, or for other tax deductible property investments, hurried the collapse of the savings and loan institutions that had funded these speculations. It also revealed enormous bank fraud by insiders, epitomized by Charles Keating of California's Lincoln Savings and Loan. The tab for all the 1980s banking extravaganza, not known yet, may well reach $500 billion before the files are sealed on this episode in our progressive economic collapse.[10]

By the early 1990s, despite George Bush's preoccupation with international conferences and patriotic exhortations, including the frustrating "Desert Storm," it was clear to the American public and all economic and political pundits in between that a momentous change had occurred in the state and power of the United States.

As we are aware, Desert Storm could not have been undertaken had not the rest of the world underwritten the financial cost, somewhere between $50 billion and $60 billion. In effect the American forces had acted as a mercenary army for the free world, now prosperous enough to pay for this expedition.[11]

The underlying factor in this growing international perception of American weakness was partially economic, but it also entailed complementary pictures of ourselves from the educational and social worlds. The private sector had shrunk enormously. Lloyd Bentsen stated in 1991 that at least 3 million high-paying jobs had been lost since 1979.[12] This would represent a loss of 15.6 percent of the manufacturing jobs out of the total number of jobs in non farm employment, between 1979 and 1992.[13]

However, the cleansing of the private sector excesses, the fact that foreigners purchased at least 12 percent of the federal debt of $4 trillion plus a good portion of our state, municipal, and corporate bond debt, reaching 16 percent of the total debt, indicated a measure of confidence within the international community that the United States was not passé. However, this does represent over a three-fold increase in only ten years in the amount of debt held by foreigners.[14]

Part of this confidence was due to the "lean and mean" slimming down of American industries, a process that continues to this day. Using Japanese efficiency models in both organization and production, which had been learned decades ago from American efficiency experts, U.S. businesses have shed much overhead and dead wood to become the leading edge of an American renaissance in export efficiency.

We are today making money abroad due to the frontierlike leanness of both small and large corporations. The rub is that these companies have become competitive and profitable by shedding many workers and executives. Their jobs are no longer there.

In June of 1992 the U.S. Labor Department reported that there were 18.2 million manufacturing jobs in the United States. At the same time 18.6 million people were on the nation's federal, state, and local government payrolls, up from 16.4 million in 1980. These latter jobs are paid out of the taxes of ordinary Americans. ("Manufacturing jobs have gone overseas," says Kathleen Camilli of Maria Ramirez Capital Consultants. "Government jobs, on the other hand have not been exported."[15])

CURRENT ACCOUNTING

Where do we stand now? With the federal debt over $4.5 trillion, the interest on this debt comprising 14 percent of the yearly federal budget, the 1992 deficit $290 billion, and the fiscal 1993 budget deficit estimated to be over $350 billion, the freedom of the federal government for fiscal stimulation of the economy is sharply limited.[16] A series of disasters in the early 1990s revealed how vulnerable we were. The bloody, destructive racial/ethnic riots in Los Angeles, hurricanes in 1992, and floods in 1993 only added to this debt.[17]

How many government bonds could we sell to pay our public bills, how many pieces of real estate or businesses could we sell to maintain the solvency of corporations? Foreign ownership of U.S. assets has quadrupled from 1980 to 1990, to $2.2 trillion.[18] When one analyzes our current account—the total value of our trade exchanges with the world, the property we own abroad and from which we receive income, minus the bond interest and income earned by foreign investors in the United States as well as the value of U.S. property and equity owned by these foreigners and returned to their homelands as interest on investment—the news is not good.

From being one of the great creditor nations in the world up to about 1970, we have slowly slipped in our current account so that we now are behind 1990, to the tune of $361 billion. We are the world's largest debtor nation.[19] Jeffrey Garten figures our current account deficit to be increasing by as much as $100 billion per year in the mid-1990s.[20]

The reader should ask what the value is today of all the Marshall Plan dollars we spent abroad to assist the world in getting back on its feet after World War II. Add to this the foreign aid to the Third World over the past four decades. Finally, what about the defense of Germany, Japan, and the rest of the free world? Whose money and men were expended in Korea, in Vietnam, to defend allies who did not bear such a burden? Included in this statement would, of course, be the cost of stationing our troops in Europe, under NATO, as well as defending other parts of the world. One could argue, and I believe rightly, that this current account deficit would look somewhat different if we sat down with now-wealthy nations, our military clients for so many decades, and asked for a just measure of restitution.[21]

Interest rates at the beginning of 1993 had declined to the lowest level possible without either destroying the dollar or risking a run on our stocks and bonds. The stimulation that these lower interest rates were supposed to give to the economy—loans for new and cheaper housing, investment in new enterprise—began to show itself early in 1993 with the appearance of some revived economic activity.[22]

What was supposed to be a recovery, however, was modest at best. The banks apparently found few qualified borrowers in either area, real estate or low-cost housing, preferring to invest in the higher interest payments of government bonds to profit without risk from the low payouts that their savers were receiving.

Unemployment is probably the key to understanding any nation's prosperity. At the end of 1992, a 7.8 percent unemployment rate pointed to about 10 million people officially looking for jobs. Perhaps equal numbers were not looking or had given up the search. Certainly another 15–20 million people were employed part-time. Their omission from the statistics does not contribute to a clear understanding of the gap in middle-class jobs.[23] Also, we ordinarily do not compute statistically the out-of-school adolescents, and the adult underclass that exists on food stamps and welfare, a severe brake on the entire economic system.

Enormous job cutbacks, amidst corporate contractions at IBM, Sears, Digital, General Motors, United Technology, Boeing, McDonnel-Douglas, and other corporations, highlighted an economy on the mend from the limited perspective of corporate efficiency and viability, but not an improved job market, considering this loss of 150,000 high-wage jobs from these corporations alone in 1993. Here, what was clearly needed was the growth of widespread entrepreneurial efforts, new businesses and services moving into the breach of shrinking older industrial forms.

The end of the Cold War and the political possibility of reducing the defense budget by from $60-90 billion of expenditures per year over a five-year period promised by both 1992 presidential candidates should also be evaluated from the standpoint of jobs. We are certainly speaking here of 500,000 jobs lost, 315,000 by the end of 1992 alone.[24]

In addition, the scaling down of the armed forces will release hundreds of thousands of men and women into an economy whose job-creating ability is quite different from that in 1970, when the first impact of the loss of the manufacturing sector to overseas competition, the consequence of the free trade philosophy pursued by successive American presidents, began to have a negative effect on the growth of the economy.

WHY DID IT HAPPEN?

Explaining the events and factors that led to our economic decline would be a step in the direction of reversing the trend.

The first shock leading to our descent should have set off alarm bells. After World War II, we were producing at least 90 percent of our own consumer electronics and appliances. The names Philco, Zenith, Hotpoint, Wollensak, Emerson, Argus, Dumont, and Electrolux trigger memories of American innovation in the same way that the late, lamented Pan American Air does.[25] Some of these names survive on a variety of products. More likely, however, these particular items are today made in Mexico, Taiwan, or Singapore.

Explanations are many. For some, the patents were sold off to the Japanese because the American companies thought that they could do better in other enterprises. In other cases innovation had to be procured at the price of much company/union conflict and uncertainty. The Japanese came in quickly with cheaper versions, their wage rates being quite primitive in the 1960s.

In other cases, domestic management was simply too venal or complacent to look ahead. After all, an older generation can remember that the brand "Made in Japan" had a stigma of inferiority. Recall the famous 1953 statement by Charles Wilson, chairman of General Motors: "What's good for General Motors is good for America." Put slightly differently, his comment would have made sense. It sounded, however, as if he were putting the interest of his corporation ahead of the nation. And, of course, the way management and the UAW made cars in Detroit, they assumed that the American market, if not the world, was theirs forever.

Perhaps the decline of the U.S. industrial base was best epitomized in the automobile debacle, which, interestingly, as compared with television, audio electronics, and cameras, is still in the balance. Autos are low-tech, and the Japanese have proved to us with their U.S. production of Sentras, Accords, and Camrys in Ohio, Kentucky, and Tennessee, respectively, that with well-made components, engines made in Japan, and fine designs, the American worker—in this case a non-union, often a "non-minority" worker—can assemble cars that compete on the world market.[26]

The contrast between Japanese cars and GM cars made in Detroit during the 1970s, when one was warned never to buy a Chevy that was made on Friday or Monday—the rumor was that you would chance a missing air filter or discover a wrench in the fuel tank—was stark. On the other hand the Chevy Nova, in reality a Toyota Corolla with a Chevy exterior, manufactured in California, has been celebrated as one of the most successful and reliable cars made in the United States.[27]

Some would attribute this decline in U.S. productivity to structural errors that can be traced back to the 1960s. They point to the enormous investment by the Japanese in research and development as compared to the United States. We on top of the economic hill reveled in our superiority, intent on redistributing some of this wealth to the poor, but in general perpetuating a lazy and contemptuous corporate culture with inflated perks.

The Japanese engineers were down on the production floor with their designers and production workers correcting flaws as soon as they showed up, and there were many. The Japanese workers, hungry for a better livelihood, endured working conditions that our workers would consider fit only for abject slaves. Using their essentially junior high school education, the Japanese were trying to create the finest product they could given their existing technological skills. Those at the top knew that those on the bottom could deal with every new qualitative productive advance. And they supped together as fellow soldiers in an economic struggle that they had to win.

This was "a war that we would not lose," according to a Japanese executive sent over to manage Honda U.S.A.[28] The key was to live and work lean, invest every bit of profit in ever more technological refinements, produce an increasingly well-educated workforce that could master the challenges of any new technological process or innovation that was productively conceivable.

Great profits amid high union wages and benefits was our rule. We were living in a world in which the United States and its internal domestic political, social, and economic agendas stood alone. This was, after all, the American Century. Our political leaders had told us so, and the American people were content and smug about the future. We had encapsulated the Soviet and communist threats. We were the leading world military power. Our economy, even if challenged, seemed to be expanding in ever new directions.

The irony is that even amidst a seriously wounded international economic profile, the political rhetoric in late 1992, in a presidential election, still sounded the old themes of unlimited power and wealth, redistribution forever. The enormous burdens, regulatory, legal, environmental, and the taxation under which the private economy had to labor—for the private economy is the ultimate source of the wealth—must be seen as partial causes of our economic decline. Add to that the 12.4 percent of the GNP that we spent in 1990 on health care. All these have discouraged entrepreneurship domestically and caused the flight of jobs offshore.[29]

It is not completely fair to say that complacency ruled. Great research and development efforts were involved—in computers, IBM; telecommunications, AT&T and its Bell Laboratories; pharmaceuticals; aerospace, Boeing, McDonnell Douglas. In fact, our university centers—MIT, Harvard, Cal Tech, Princeton, Stanford, University of California, and others—still produced ever-new revolutions that were picked up both here and abroad, biotechnology being the most recent, where our leadership is still supreme.

In fact, in computers and memory chips the Europeans, including the Dutch, Germans, French, and Italians, have withdrawn from the competition. It is only the Japanese who now give us a strong run for our money in computers, chips, and microprocessors. As with biotechnology, computer software is an American industry—Microsoft, Borland, even IBM.

The Japanese have begun to set up their own research laboratories in places like Cambridge, Massachusetts; Princeton, New Jersey; and Palo Alto, California, in an attempt to tap into the creative scientific research still being produced as by-products of these university graduate programs. What they can do that American corporations and universities cannot, especially considering the over 50 percent drop in the value of the dollar against the yen in the last five years, is to pay the extremely inflated salaries and benefits that the Japanese are offering to the best young minds.[30]

On the other hand, the United States is a leader in the export of commodities, with the exception of petroleum and some other minerals—a mixed blessing, to be sure. Our farmers are still world-class, and, creditably, are enormously efficient and productive. We do export, to Japan and to the world, mostly raw lumber on the stump, and pulp. Our metal junk goes to the Japanese. It has been argued that we are becoming a semi-colonial nation in that our earnings are increasingly from unfinished products. Our natural heritage is being exported overseas.

But so are the jobs. Perhaps the most infamous example of this tide of "off-shoring" is the *maquiladora* agreement with Mexico whereby American industries can fabricate their products below the border at Mexican wage and benefit rates, along with Mexican pollution and environmental standards and costs. Following that, without that vast U.S. proliferation of anti-discrimination and other regulations, the industries can then merely truck the finished work back into the United States without tariff restrictions or costs.

This practice will soon be institutionalized on a much larger scale if and when the North American Free Trade Agreement is signed into reality. No American worker would be allowed to work and live under such conditions considering that these jobs pay from $30 to $60 per week in U.S. equivalents. It is great money for Mexican workers who have achieved a decent elementary school education. Equivalent salaries in the United States are anywhere from ten to twenty times as high.[31]

Mexico is not the only nation that has inherited American jobs. The rising educational levels in parts of the Third World over the past forty years has produced a cadre of literate peoples who can do semi-skilled or unskilled assembly and fabrication work as well as if not better than their American counterparts. The boredom and drudgery associated with this kind of labor in our own political and media environment of the "good life" breed discontent, which leads to poor quality products, our own counterpart to what happened inside the communist bloc after World War II.

Of course, the Japanese were subject to the same kind of dynamic pressures. As their own worker skills improved, and with them the conditions of labor and salaries, cheaper goods from Korea, Taiwan, Singapore, and Thailand began to appear. The Japanese with their newly acquired capital could easily go offshore themselves. This they did in a big way, such that much of the clothing, shoes, even utensils, bearing the names of these nations, now including the Philippines, Malaysia, and Indonesia, are in reality from Magna-Japan.[32]

More recently, Hong Kong has begun to take over southern China for manufacturing, as it prepares for the unification with China. Taiwan has made significant investments along the coast of Fujian Province and the city of Wenzhou, home of many immigrants to Taiwan in centuries past. Who will take over whom in the next decade remains to be seen.[33]

The reality is that each of these northeast Asiatic off-shoring colonial investment strategies has not left the home country bereft of its industrial base. Quite the contrary. As with the assembly of Japanese cars in the United States, largely supplied with their more complex parts manufactured in Japan, these countries are attempting to secure for themselves the high value-added manufactures which produce maximum profits. The more complex and technologically avant-garde, the greater the requirements in the workforce for high intellectual and thus educational skills—these advantages the three great northeast Asian ethnicities, Chinese, Japanese, Koreans, feel they have.

In Europe the Germans and the Dutch have followed this practice. In fact, the Netherlands, population 15 million, is the third-largest holder of American assets after Britain and Japan. And the French are continuously increasing their investments in the United States. One can understand what these monies, coming from the United States to the Netherlands, do for the value of its *guilder*, its current account, and thus for the domestic standard of living of the Dutch.[34]

EXPLANATIONS

What is wrong with our economy? Two kinds of criticism seem to dominate, one from the standpoint of our domestic situation, the other in its international context, here arbitrarily labeled micro-analysis and macro-analysis. I will use the writings of several contemporary economists to illustrate these two areas.

Micro-analysis

A current exponent of micro-analysis is Lester Thurow, dean of the Sloan School of Management at MIT. Thurow is the author of *The Zero Sum Society* (1985) and *Head to Head* (1992), the latter an analysis of the U.S. competitive situation vis à vis the Japanese and the Europeans in the early twenty-first century. Thurow is a strong believer in the reality of the coming of a common marketplace in Europe under the aegis of the European Economic Community.

Robert Reich's *Work of Nations* (1991) also reflects on the global changes in competition and the fact that we can no longer view our domestic problems from a strictly national perspective. There is virtually no legislation or public policy that will not bear on international competitiveness.

Both scholars are political liberals, Thurow having been a close adviser to Michael Dukakis in the 1988 presidential campaign, Reich having been a fellow student, transition adviser, and Labor Secretary to President Clinton. Reich was a lecturer in political economy at Harvard's John F. Kennedy School of Government.

To Thurow, the economic future hinges on the educability of our workforce, on its ability to rise to the challenge of those new value-added technologies that will decide which nations will be the prosperous leaders of the twenty-first century. No longer, he argues, do national financial wherewithal, natural resources, even the invention of new products and technologies, become critical to the power of nations. Rather, economic power lies in what he calls process technologies, the ability of a nation to react quickly to new developments and bring to market, and thus profit from, their lead over rival nations in getting these products to the paying middle classes of the world.[35]

While Thurow grants the international nature of markets and corporate entities, it is the workforce in the largest sense—and Reich strongly agrees with this premise—from engineering and design, financial management, marketing, production, maintenance, and quality control, that will determine the relative position of nations. As he sees it, the competition lies in the three great competitive spheres, Europe, Japan and eastern Asia, and North America led by the United States.

The future prosperity of each of these competitive areas will depend on their positions in seven crucial technologies: semi-conductors and computers; commercial aircraft; consumer electronics; materials and chemicals; textiles; motor vehicles; and machine tools.[36]

To Thurow the skills of the lowest 50 percent of the workforce are critical here. The significant gains in productivity reflected in the successful export industries of the United States are constructed from the changing skill requirements of all the employees. At one time, so Thurow's argument goes, the top 20 percent in any corporate enterprise, the designers and engineers, the various layers of corporate bureaucracy, might have been seen as crucial to an industry's success. Given the efficient use of computers by the now-educated "secretarial" staff, which has access to all information within the corporation, this top 20 percent of the white-collar middle-management bureaucracy is gradually being peeled away.

Thurow agrees that corporations are much leaner. Computers and robots have taken the place of unskilled and uneducated workers. The "I.Q." of the computers and robots approaches that of the production worker with no worry about medical benefits, overtime, or grievance wildcat stoppages. A new breed of educated human factory "workers" have in reality become members of "quality teams."

What the Japanese learned in the way of integrating all levels of management and fabrication into what the U.S. space program under Wernher Von Braun (the former Nazi scientist whom we hired to overtake the Soviets and their *Sputnik*) had labeled the *production team* would mandate highly educated workers at all levels in this new corporate structure.

Two indications of the social and economic consequences of raising minimum achievement levels in a national workforce come out of the two leaders, Japan and Germany.

The Germans probably have the richest salary, benefits, and vacation contract of any group of workers that we have seen—six-week-long vacations, family leave, total health benefits, and extremely high productivity and salaries in a partially socialized national educational and cultural system. The German pay differential between top executives and production workers is about 12 to 1.

The Japanese have a ratio of earnings from the top executives to on-the-line workers of about 15 to 1. In the United States it is almost ten times as large a spread. Another important statistic is that Japanese workers with a high school education on average earn salaries not far below college graduates as a group. This small disparity is attributed to the high universal educational achievement of that 96 percent plus of high school graduates.[37]

In the United States, the income spread between high school and college graduates has increased about 25 percent in the past twenty years. Again, this statistic supports the argument that the new world economy will put a premium on a highly able and educated workforce at all levels of the economy. The old American assumption that the lower 50–80 percent of the workforce can easily master world-class technological skills constitutes the great economic question raised by Lester Thurow.

Robert Reich's argument in *The Work of Nations* is similar. He is very much against protectionism. Reich rejects even the possibility that there is such an animal as a national corporation. Internationalism is the rule, and the new criteria for living standards of populations around the world depend upon their ability to participate in the institutional structure of this world economy.

The "symbolic analyst," Reich argues, represents the person of the future. This person, even when employed by a corporation or institution that is nominally rooted in a nation, still has intellectual skills, allegiances, and ambitions that transcend borders. These are individuals who work with their minds rather than with their hands, deal with larger conceptual issues, whether in the financial markets, engineering, or teaching.[38]

They will have left behind the person who parks your car at a restaurant, who rings up the sale of your shirt at a department store, who repairs your car at the garage. Their allegiances are less with the other social classes in their communities. Their affluence takes them into protected suburban enclaves. Their children often attend private schools or, at the least, exclusive suburban public schools. The future they anticipate lies in the corporate and institutional structure of the world community, that distant entity that nevertheless shares their knowledge, values, and commitments.

While Reich sees the nation as being wounded by such educational and social class separations, he is aware that the nation is destined to be the center-of-life allegiance for the foreseeable future. Thus his emphasis is on redistributing the wealth of this top 20 percent and resocializing the "symbolic analyst" back into the community through civic commitments and a sense of philanthropic duty, to contribute to the well-being of those for whom education did not function as it was expected to, economically and socially.[39]

Macro-analysis

The macro approach, while not ignored by Thurow and Reich, is central to the writings of Robert Kuttner and Jeffrey Garten. Kuttner's *The End of Laissez Faire* (1991) illustrates that the free market ideals of the United States for the world economy is increasingly an illusion when compared to the practices of the various nations.

Here the Japanese are especially notorious in their intention to have it both ways. First, they protect the development of technologies that are crucial to their maintaining the lead in those highest value-added products. At the very beginning of their thrust to dominance in the 1960s, the Japanese saw the need to maintain an environment of sacrifice at home to discipline both their workers and consumers. They excluded the goods of foreigners, protecting their home market while developing equally good or better products that would be priced competitively on the international market.[40]

At the same time, the Japanese concentrated, through their Ministry of International Trade and Industry (MITI), on methods for penetrating markets that were ostensibly claimed either by the home nation or by other foreign exporters. In the United States they quickly displaced our own consumer electronics industry and undermined the German and English auto imports to the United States. They competed successfully with the Germans in cameras.

They did not necessarily engage in the cartelization of competition, for a number of Japanese companies were always competing, such as, for example, Minolta, Nikon, and Canon in the camera area. This form of national competition for domestic and foreign markets provided the internal discipline for corporate Japan. However, the financing and marketing of its products were carefully monitored and guided by MITI.

As Clyde Prestowitz has demonstrated, what the Japanese achieved was a great unified national effort that clearly envisioned a managed trade program whose ultimate intention was to short-circuit free trade. It was a well-planned strategy for economic dominance.[41]

Jeffrey Garten's *A Cold Peace* (1992) envisions the future similarly to Thurow, but with a united Germany as the centerpiece of the European economic competitive bloc, along with Japan and the United States. The argument is roughly similar to Kuttner's in that the competitive focus would be built around national entities. These nations would not merely lead with their economic chins. Their futures would be determined by the entire national profile, social, educational, and economic, thus comprising the stuff of future international competition.[42]

Simply, and as with the Japanese, the external competitive profile that a nation presents to the world, Garten argues, is already and will increasingly be determined by the internal social and educational *élan* that allows for the success of certain policies and not others.

For example, many options in the U.S. competitive profile are already undercut by the enormous federal debt, the continuing trade deficit, and the extremely low interest rates that are thus necessitated, weakening the dollar vis à vis other currencies and their investment clout, if strengthening our export industries.[43]

Toward the end of 1992, the already weakened economies of Britain and Italy, the latter due to completely irresponsible fiscal policies in running up an internal debt greater than the United States in terms of GNP, ran into even stormier waters.[44] The German need to control inflation in its expansionary absorption of the eastern provinces necessitated higher interest rates. This action on the part of the economically strongest European nation undermined the currency of the two weakest of its partners, Britain and Italy, necessitating a sudden increase in interest rates to stem the currency outflow, which further slowed down already limping economies, finally crashing their respective currencies.

Both Kuttner and Garten warn that a free trade philosophy in one country, while the others are manipulating trade by keeping out the goods of foreigners for one reason or another, is the long-term name of the game. This will not result in a trade or physical war. The methods for regulating trade are highly complex today, which explains the number of international conclaves, such as the General Agreement on Tariffs and Trade (GATT), which is attempting to order and stabilize the competitive game, and the Maastricht Treaty, which represents an attempt to create a unified European currency.

THE NEW ECONOMIC REALITY

These economic commentators and many others reiterate the new realities of our time. International competition in technological, economic, and cultural values is here to stay. The educated classes of the world, the symbolic analysts of Reich, will increasingly share more skills and ideals with their confreres around the globe than they will with their modestly skilled and educated fellow citizens.

Any nation that pretends to world leadership will have to purchase its leadership role with the power engendered by the productivity of its people. This productivity will have to merit a world-class income by persuasive sales to other populations of "symbolic analysts," in terms of those lifestyle products and services that those populations covet and that might not be available at home.

This means, as both Thurow and Reich point out, that a high proportion of the national citizenry, certainly much higher than 20 percent of our population, has to be able to make the claim of equality with the best of the world in order to promote national prosperity. The Germans and the Japanese can both claim that at least 90 percent of their people are engaged in economic activities with the requisite skills that reward them with world competitive incomes.

Garten and Kuttner would argue that we need to protect our own newly innovative or reforming industries until they get on their feet in the international competitive sense. This is what is called industrial policy. The fear by many is that if the federal government gets involved in such subsidization (such as the Sematech consortium based in Austin, Texas, to redevelop our microchip industry), it will lead to the politicization of what in effect will be a jobs program, pitting one industry against the other, or one section of the country against another.

The success of industrial policy—now called "strategic trade"—has been mixed. The French have been jealous of their independent industrial capacity, and have officially entered such waters. In the case of the international consortium AirBus Industrie, which includes Great Britain, Spain, and Italy, it was a success, with a market share that hovers around 30 percent, a real challenge to Boeing, and a veritable destroyer of McDonnell Douglas, the two important U.S. rivals of AirBus.

On the other hand, Groupe Bull, the French computer giant, has not made a profit since 1988, and then only a small one. This company presently shows losses of 7 billion francs in 1990, and over 3 billion francs in 1991.[45]

Kuttner has conceded this difficulty, and has argued that at the very least the research participation of the government ought to mirror Japan's and Germany's investment in the development of frontier industries (lecture, Smith College). Certainly much of our industrial leadership in the past, aerospace as one notable example, was a by-product of our government's defense research and production strategy.

Yet even Japan has had costly failures, among them multi-billion-dollar equivalent losses in steel and aluminum in the 1970s. More recently, Japanese taxpayers have been the big losers in artificial computing intelligence and high-definition television.[46]

THE BOTTOM LINE

In the end, both the micro and macro approaches to the challenge facing the United States focus on the general innovative productivity of the economy, underlined by the ability of the American population to produce goods and services in design and quality demanded by the middle classes around the world.

It is not enough for a nation to prosper if roughly 20 percent of its people are working successfully at this international standard, while the remaining 80 percent are dependent on handouts from the government—charity derived from high taxation on the productive minority, which was President Clinton's economic strategy in early 1993.

The question ultimately concerns the causes behind this economic decline. On one hand, there are many situational reasons to explain the disappearance of high-end productivity. According to an old proverb, there are a million reasons to say "no." A "yes" only requires one friend.

In our case, that friend is high educable intelligence. With it, we can find an unlimited number of highly creative entrepreneurs to create frontier industries. Then we will find, as have the Japanese, Germans, Dutch, Koreans, and soon the Chinese, the workers to fabricate goods with the aid of sophisticated machines and computers requiring autonomy of decision-making, care and delicacy of response, rapid use of information, complex symbolic integrations. No industry can allow one "weak sister" into the loop of production, no matter how seemingly semiskilled a task may be involved.

Our research knowledge about the intellectual potential of the American workforce is at present largely inferential, based on educational achievement levels and some I.Q. testing, carried out by companies for whom such testing can lead to life-or-death product efficiencies and quality. The issue is repressed by both official and informal censorship. Thus knowledge has gone underground, else the companies flee our shores.

The overpowering economic fact is that at present some 50–80 percent of our workforce is not able to work and produce at an internationally competitive level, and thus is not able to earn an income commensurate with the rest of the developed world.

For example, in 1989 it was estimated that approximately 800,000 of New York City's seven-plus million population were keeping the city going economically, educationally, and culturally.[47] In 1993, given the declining state of this city as well as others, the number of productive residents probably has since decreased accordingly.

According to the great majority of economists, the future of economic modernization in the United States depends ultimately on our educational achievement levels, and thus on the productive efficiency of the American public school.

Chapter 5

Our Educational Wreckage

CRISIS

There are few American economists who do not link our structural economic decline with the correlating decline in educational standards and achievements of the public schools. We probably would not be as aware of the linkage of these two domains had it not been for the fact that educational achievement, and the curriculum that it reflects, has become an international index of relative progress in a nation's modernization.

It is ironic that just at the time that schools and colleges of the United States are enveloped in an orgy of "multiculturalism," the entire world has gone over to the European/North American standard of knowledge and cultural values. It is even more ironic but not unexpected that the Japanese, well on their way into the European model of education and industrialization, as well as militarism and imperialism, are now the world standard when it comes to education up to the eighteen-year-old level—secondary schooling.

We have experienced a decade of frenzied fulminating at our educational descent since a presidential commission published "A Nation at Risk" in 1983. The hysteria started with experiences such as that reported by the Chemical Bank of New York, which had to interview 50,000 high school graduates to find 2,000 entry-level workers. Unfortunately Chemical Bank still sends its daily records by overnight air express to Shannon Airport in Ireland to be entered into the computer by Irish workers, ostensibly because they can't get enough reliable New York City high school graduates to do this work.[1]

Again, the president of Pacific Telesis in Los Angeles in late 1992 stated that fully sixty percent of the high school graduates applying for entry level positions at his corporation could not pass the qualification exam, which was set at the seventh grade level.[2]

Robert Woodson of the Afro-American Neighborhood Alliance, a leader who stays close to his inner-city brethren, notes that the $6–8,000 per child expended for each inner-city child's education is well above the nationwide average, and close to expenditures per child in the best suburbs. For example, Massachusetts averages about $4,500 per child per year in its public schools. But, Woodson adds, the achievement levels have remained as dismal as ever.[3] Kansas City has invested $240 million since 1990 to redo the inner-city schools as magnet schools. So far, the academic results are not encouraging.[4]

RECENT HISTORY

Let us get some perspective on this debacle. The United States won World War II largely because its productivity as a nation was world-class. The military hardware, the men and women of our armed services, the coordination of a vast two-front distribution and fighting system revealed a nation equal to any.

The educational level of about 50 percent of our citizenry was at the twelfth grade level. We were the best, the model for a national educational system around the world.[5] After the war, we set about not merely to extend and strengthen this public school structure, eventually to desegregate it racially, but also to develop a world-class system of higher education for every American youngster.

The California model under the leadership of Clark Kerr was followed by the rest of the country. For every high school graduate, a free community college education would be available, providing two more years of education for those who did not aspire to the highest levels of knowledge or preparation (comprising about 50 percent of the graduates of the public high schools). Another 33.3 percent would go on to the four-year state college system and receive their bachelor's degrees. Beyond that were the great research campuses of the University of California at Berkeley and Los Angeles and a number of other very fine campuses that then existed or were added later.

This concept was the "multiversity," a system in which the talents and potentialities of every citizen of California were to be integrated in the development of new knowledge in this postwar revolution that Clark Kerr saw taking place: "Knowledge has certainly never in history been so central to the conduct of an entire society. What the railroads did for the second half of the nineteenth century and the automobile for the first half of this century, the knowledge industry may do for the second half of this century: that is, to serve as the focal point for national growth. And the university is at the center of the knowledge process."[6]

This was a prescient statement considering when it was written. Years later, looking back at the entire process of university building and the enormous growth of our economy and the prosperity that enveloped our nation and its consciousness, Kerr would argue that the generation that returned in 1945 from "The War," and that of the following several decades, constituted the finest generation of students and leaders that this nation has produced in the modern era.[7]

These were the culminating years of the American educational system. Up until the mid-1960s and the "counterculture," the campus rebellions against the Vietnam war, the struggle against segregation, and the humanistic education and free-school movements in the lower schools, our school system seemed to be striving in the direction of ever higher intellectual and academic standards. In all fairness, this search for comprehensiveness and all-inclusiveness, a universal vision of equality of educational opportunity and achievement, warped the institutional capacity to deliver.[8]

And then it gradually began to break down. Why this happened has puzzled all subsequent reformers. Reform has followed further reform, each raising much dust and then promptly forgotten, soon to be followed again by yet another. Now, several decades later amid a wreckage that still has not been sorted through, the reforms are as mysterious and spurious as ever.

EDUCATIONAL ROOTS

To hope to make some sense out of the process of decline and the realities of contemporary frustrations it is necessary to recall briefly the background for the creation of this once-mighty system of democratic education.

The Constitution does not mention education. Education is one of those powers reserved to the several states of the union and to the citizens. The founding fathers in the context of late eighteenth-century individualism felt that institutional education, important as it was even in those days and still largely in the hands of the Church, was yet a responsibility of the individual, certainly not of the State.[9]

The kind of knowledge necessary for basic living and the obligations of citizenship was easily available to the family from a variety of parish and community schools and at little cost. For those interested in higher forms of schooling a number of private secondary schools existed, along with a number of colleges such as William and Mary, Harvard, Yale, Kings (now

Columbia University), and the College of Philadelphia (now the University of Pennsylvania).

The ways to rise in society were many, even with the simplest literary competency, the kind that Abraham Lincoln obtained from his stepmother, Nancy Hanks. The Constitution did not forbid what had existed since the earliest seventeenth-century settlements, schools sponsored by local communities and supported by voluntary assessments. At this point there were no state laws mandating compulsory education or taxation.

State laws setting up systems of education began to be enacted in the 1840s, coincidental with the spread of industrial urban life and the requirements of the new technologies. Also, increased immigration brought in large numbers of non-English and non-Protestant poor. The states could no longer depend on purely private initiatives, especially as the frontier rolled west.[10]

By the 1880s the modern American public educational system had grown out of the earlier Common School. In the midwestern states the idea of the *kindergarten* (introduced by German immigrants), together with the spread of public high schools, had created the reality of a universal educational system, free to all children, and supported both by local property taxation and supplemental state tax revenues.

It was this system that had to absorb millions of the abject poor who arrived on our shores at the same time that the United States was undergoing a rapid industrialization and reaching out to the world at large in trade, commodities, as well as industrial products. At this time, we had at hand not only an independent sector in the lower schools but also a number of important private research universities, now being joined by important public universities in Michigan, Illinois, and California, as well as urban public colleges in New York, Cincinnati, and elsewhere.

The only significant challenge to this evolving pattern of public/private symbiosis was the so-called Oregon Decision of 1925, *Pierce v. Society of Sisters*. This decision grew out of the attempt by the state of Oregon to mandate attendance of all school-age children in the public schools of the state. The decision, which was based on the "takings" principle of the Constitution, disallowed the mandated law as an expropriation of the property of the Catholic schools which had appealed the decision.[11]

That this system of education functioned efficiently for the United States was proved by our international involvements in two world wars. In both cases, especially between 1940 and 1945, U.S. power and productivity were decisive. The United States throughout the ferment of the twentieth century remained politically stable, optimistic, and inviting to the outside world, excepting the immigration laws of the early 1920s that shut off the spigot of unrestricted immigration.

The reader has to compare our educational achievement during this period with what was happening in the world at large, especially Europe. Germany, the Soviet Union, Japan, and Italy had fallen under totalitarian control. The former two had engaged throughout the 1930s and 1940s in a vast genocidal campaign against their own and Europe's most intelligent and educated minorities. In the process they destroyed much of their own young talent. In the postwar period they and the entire world lay shattered and in educational disarray. Yet we were whole, relatively untouched. By 1950 we were graduating from high school 58 percent of our white youth and about 25 percent of African-Americans.[12]

France had inherited a universal system of education, one that was highly elitist, as well as profoundly traditionalist in its subject matter and approach to education. Britain was still sponsor of a class-ridden educational structure, epitomized in the 11-plus exam, and was unenthusiastic about extending educational opportunity to all its citizens.

After 1945, from Japan to Europe, the world community hurriedly began to create educational systems based on the American principle of universality and modernity, meaning extending the educational franchise through the secondary level and on into higher technological as well as liberal arts programs.[13] As they did in the economic sector of this postwar period they, too, learned from us, and well. The results I will attempt to describe below.

ASSESSMENT

The Scholastic Aptitude Test (SAT), given since 1926, has become by now a rite of passage for those sectors of our society who seek upward mobility through education. The national averages have been published since 1952. Universally, colleges evaluate these scores as indicative, together with grades, of an individual's academic potential. The tests have been designed to reflect a similar level of difficulty over time despite new knowledge, changing curricula, and lifestyles. As such they have become a yardstick by which we measure our national educational achievement as well as the success of our schools and cultural life.

The SAT is probably the bridge academic testing procedure between I.Q. and achievement tests, which are also given in a high school student's senior year in the various subject matter disciplines. Those usually covered throughout the high school years: specific sciences such as physics, chemistry, biology; foreign languages; English; the several disciplines of mathematics, algebra, geometry, trigonometry, calculus; the various sub-disciplines of history, modern European, American, ancient.[14]

Even though the Educational Testing Service (ETS) of Princeton, New Jersey, has argued that the SAT is not an I.Q. test, its sub-components, the Verbal and Math sections, certainly are geared to discover aptitude and not specific knowledge. These components themselves mirror what most I.Q. tests dip into—verbal reasoning and math/spatial skills.[15]

Because the SAT, in its traditional, unrevised format, has a long-embedded reputation as an I.Q. test, it has long come under attack. Some argue that the test can be crammed for. This gives those with the economic wherewithal to take such courses the possibility of receiving better scores, which in turn qualify them for more selective colleges and/or more scholarship aid. Others have argued, against strong rebuttals by ETS, that the tests are biased against minorities and women.

James Crouse, with Linda Gottfredson, has written extensively about the SAT's lack of improved predictability for either college success or life outcome, as compared with accurate grading in high schools. Crouse's view is that the SAT, as do grades, usually reflects the "g" factor of intelligence, the ability to process accurately high-level academic material.[16]

But it is agreed that this critical educational predictive tool is necessary because of the average high school's inability to communicate reliable grades. Crouse would like to see a more heterogeneous use of pre-college admission tests: grade point averages, SAT-type tests, achievement tests. In this we would approach the practices of many developed nations.

Lloyd Humphrey, a well-known researcher at the University of Illinois, agrees that there is a way to get around the most controversial aspects of the SAT, its I.Q. test associations. His solution is to give seniors in U.S. high schools a battery of reliably constructed achievement tests.[17]

Humphrey's view is that all students should take the English and basic math achievement tests, plus three others of their own choice. Such a testing procedure, even including the Graduate Record Examination (GRE), would allow us an equally predictive equivalent of "g" for general intelligence. Such test results, moreover, might not provoke the usual "bias" accusations leveled at the SAT.

SAT DECLINE

Probably the most discussed set of educational statistics is the quarter-century decline of SAT scores. In 1962 the mean Verbal score was 478, the mean Math score was 502. In 1990, after a gradual but consistent decline, these figures stood at 424 and 476 respectively, showing an 11 percent plus drop in the Verbal and a 5 percent plus drop in the Math SAT.[18]

In 1990 African-American scores continued a small recent year-by-year increase, while the white scores continued to fall. The African-American increase might be attributed to the slight percentage decrease in the number of seniors of this ethnic group taking the test, the increase in percentage of females taking it, or perhaps even in the smaller absolute number of African-American students entering college.[19]

Still, the 1990 total scores show that Caucasian, non-Hispanic SAT scores were 933 and African-Americans 737 out of a possible 1600, still an almost 200-point differential for the best of our high school college-bound seniors.[20] And while there has been a steady increase in the total number of African-American youngsters reaching college age, the proportion of African-American college students in the entire cohort has fallen from 9.4 percent in 1976 to 8.6 percent in 1986, even with large amounts of scholarship and recruitment assistance from both the public and private sectors.[21]

In the number of above-600 Verbal achievement scores for the SAT, the percentage of whites over African-Americans has ranged from six to eight times. In 1984, out of 71,177 African-Americans taking the SAT, 283 scored over 650. Only 66 scored over 700, out of a total of 9,392 at this level. The average African-American Verbal score was 350, well over 100 points lower than that of whites. It should be noted that about 15 percent of students taking the SAT do not clearly identify their race or ethnic background.[22]

Donald Rock, of ETS, has attributed the general decline in the scores to a change in the demographic origins of the Caucasoids who take the test. Many, he argues, now are peripheral academic students from rural and southern backgrounds pressured by ambitious mothers to go to college.[23]

What he does not mention is that even in a cohort that is increasing in size, such a drop, given the relative stability of African-American scores, would not have been possible without a significant drying up of the top talented and academically proficient Caucasian students.

A puzzling dimension of this decline is the absolute reduction in high scorers, especially in the Verbal section. In 1962, which represents the postwar apogee, 19,099 students scored 700 or above in the Verbal section, out of a possible perfect score of 800. On the Math scale ranging from a perfect 800 to 200, the lowest possible score on each section of the SAT, 40,644 scored over 700.[24]

By 1983–84, as noted above, only 9,392 scored over 700 in the Verbal section and 32,469 in the Math. The number of students taking the test had gone from 912,204 in 1962–63 to 964,684 in 1983–84. At the very top of the scale, above 750, 1962 produced 2,673 who achieved that level on the Verbal, 8,628 on the Math. In 1983–84 the numbers were 1,588 and 7,002 respectively. In 1988, 986 students scored over 750 in the Verbal![25] In 1992 total SAT scores improved microscopically, by a point or two.[26]

High School Debacle

General academic achievement up to the high school level also reflects this abysmal trend. Studies in the late 1980s in reading comprehension, mathematics, and science proficiency, using world-class standards of what seventeen-year-old students should know, even in comparison with achievement levels of high school students two generations ago when the high school was usually the concluding educational experience for American youth, reflect this crisis of contemporary achievement.

As reported by the Department of Education, reading comprehension scores in 1983–84 were arranged in five levels of difficulty, from rudimentary to advanced, the latter presumed to be the kind of material that these seventeen-year-olds would face in their first year in college. One step back, at level four, or "adept," the students were expected to be "able to find, understand, summarize, and explain relatively complicated literary and informational material," presumably reasonable ninth and tenth grade readings. The percentages at level four were: white, 45.1 percent; black, 15.5 percent; Hispanic, 19.9 percent.[27]

At the higher pre-college level (level five), which required that students be "able to understand links between ideas even when those links are not explicitly stated and to make appropriate generalizations even when the texts lack clear introductions or explanations," the results were: white, 5.8 percent; black, 0.8 percent; Hispanic, 1.5 percent. The overall percentage of American seventeen-year-olds who could comprehend pre-college reading materials was 4.9 percent.

These results were duplicated in independent tests of science and mathematical ability. At the same advanced pre-college levels in science the scores were: white, 9 percent; black, less than 1 percent; Hispanic, 1 percent. The overall percentage of seventeen-year-olds prepared for good college-level science courses in 1986 was 7.5 percent.

In math, at the so-called 350 level of good pre-college preparatory skills, the results, in 1986, were: white, 8 percent; black, less than 1 percent; Hispanic, 2 percent, with an overall level of achievement at 6.4 percent. Naturally, at lower achievement levels one finds higher percentages of achievement in all the ethnic groups. The radical falling away takes place, as it does in the traditional curve of I.Q. scores, as we go higher in the test of the requirements for abstract thought. However, we are here only asking for basic pre-first-year college skills. What equivalent level of I.Q. would be indicated for success in these subject matters?

For example, the commonly noted differences in science achievement between boys and girls show this statistical effect. The 300 level, or good junior high skills in science, is reached by 50 percent of the seventeen-year-old males, 33.3 percent of the females. The 350, or advanced pre-college level, is reached by 10.5 percent of the boys and 5 percent of the girls.

Overall, in math, the evidence is that fully 49 percent of American seventeen-year-olds did not attain to the 300 level—good junior high achievement—in 1986. It is not difficult to understand the workforce problems that Pacific Telesis or Chemical Bank is experiencing when we look at these internal U.S. educational achievement levels.[28]

The real test of the meaning of these internal educational achievement levels takes place when we compare the educational achievements of the various nations on our planet. The world is increasingly bound together in a scientific/technological embrace. When it comes to the above learnings—reading comprehension and interpretation, writing of clarity and fluency, mathematical understanding and scientific sophistication—we leave the realm of cultural diversity. All nations who would make a claim to modernity and middle-class standards of living in the twenty-first century realize that the grammar of economic survival is constructed from the above educational skills.[29]

INTERNATIONAL COMPARISONS

The most comprehensive international comparative study of educational achievement, the Second International Mathematics Study, addressed itself to the mathematical sophistication of eighth and twelfth grade students, seven thousand and five thousand in number respectively, in twenty countries, including the United States. The study was carried out in 1981–82, the full results published only in 1987.[30]

Our twelfth graders, the most revealing of the achievement levels of the two age groups, were in the bottom 25 percent of all the nations and the lowest of all the so-called developed nations. In terms of teacher preparation in mathematics and in class size, we stood quite high. In the type of courses offered and in the emphasis on mathematics in the curricula, the American pattern seemed to be one of "spiral" return to basic math, with much review, repetition, and rote learning.

The Japanese emphasis, by contrast, was on algebra; the French, on geometry. Only 15 percent of our high school students took advanced mathematics, a proportion similar to that of several other nations, including

Japan. But in those nations, all advanced mathematics students took calculus, compared with only 20 percent (3 percent of our total high school student population, itself 75 percent of the total age cohort) of the advanced high school math students.

Ross Perot, in his 1992 presidential campaign tract, *United We Stand*, added an interesting confirmation of this dismaying U.S. tale of educational laxity. He reports that today five million young people are studying calculus in Russia, whereas in the United States the number is five hundred thousand.[31]

An interesting statistic follows that may be an augur for the future. In 1981–82 about 82 percent of our seventeen-year-olds were still in school. Today, in 1993, about 72 percent of our seventeen- to eighteen-year-olds receive diplomas. At that time, 1981–82, 92 percent of the Japanese were in school. Today, about 95 percent of Japanese youngsters will graduate from high school.[32]

Among the Japanese seventeen-year-olds, 12 percent took algebra, attaining an average score of 78 (the highest average, and equal to a select group of Hong Kong seventeen-year-olds). The U.S. percentage of seventeen-year-old students taking algebra was 13 percent, and scoring 42.[33]

Hungary was a participant in this study. In 1981–82 under an educationally conscientious communist regime, only about 50 percent of seventeen-year-old Hungarians were in school. All seventeen-year-old Hungarians who had continued on in school (50 percent of the total cohort) were required to take algebra, scoring 44, higher than the 13 percent of Americans who took algebra. As it is phrased in certain quarters, this Hungarian statistic connotes a thick layer of high educability. It is not surprising to see Western corporations streaming into Hungary to take advantage of this educated high intelligence.[34]

The following comparisons taken from the top students were chilling from the U.S. perspective. For example, in functions and calculus, the top 5 percent of American students of the small number that take such courses scored at the 51 percent level; our average calculus student scored at the 43 percent level. Larger proportions of Finnish and English students who take these courses *averaged* at 52 percent and 55 percent respectively. The Japanese students, who consistently scored the highest of all those populations that reflected a non-selective group of students (students from select Hong Kong schools scored the highest of all the nations), scored in calculus at the 58 percent level. The very top 1 percent of those American students who took calculus scored 60.5 percent, again compared with the *average* Japanese calculus student who scored 58 percent.[35]

One is reminded of the story reported by George Gilder. At a Japanese-owned semi-conductor plant opened in the southeastern United States (perhaps Atlanta, Georgia), it was necessary to hire graduate students (perhaps from the Georgia Institute of Technology) to do the statistical quality control functions performed by high school graduates in Japan.[36]

A more recent international math and science study, supervised by ETS of Princeton, this time involving twelve populations totaling 24,000 twelve- and thirteen-year-olds, has confirmed the general results of the earlier research. Published in 1989, the study took place in February 1988, of children born during the calendar year 1974. They are now either entering college or the workforce.[37]

The South Korean and British Columbian children performed consistently above the other groups, including the United States. It should be borne in mind that a large proportion of British Columbian students are of Chinese ethnic background.

In intermediate math, the so-called 500 level, the percentage of Koreans was 78; French Quebec schoolchildren, 73; British Columbia, 69; United States, 40. At the higher, 600 level of understanding concepts, the Korean percentage was 40; British Columbia, 24; French Quebec, 22; United States, 9.

At the most advanced, the 700 level, the Korean percentage was 5; British Columbia, 2; French Quebec, 2; United States, 1. This was the only area where the U.S. thirteen-year-olds were not at the bottom. Ireland, French Ontario, and French New Brunswick scored lower at this level. However, it should be said that only 1,000 U.S. children were involved, half the average (2,000), and from 200 schools, double the usual number of schools chosen from other nations to be included. Thus our students might have been more select.[38]

In science, the British Columbia students were slightly ahead of the Koreans, with students from the United States not quite at the bottom, in ninth place.[39] The gender gap in science was significant, especially among the Koreans.[40] Ireland and Spain reported the highest amounts of homework; the United States was average here. Two-thirds of American students thought they were good at math, whereas only 23 percent of the Koreans believed they were good.[41]

MEANING OF EDUCATIONAL DECLINE

It is interesting to note at this point that this motif of unreality extends throughout the internal U.S. studies. African-American students consistently report their enjoyment of math and that they think they are good at it, even when their actual achievements do not measure up.[42] Clearly, the psycho-sociological cult of "feeling good about oneself" as being the key to achievement has here been tested and found to be ineffective. The correlation both of the internal U.S. educational achievement levels and the international comparisons fit entirely and consistently with the internal American and international I.Q. data.

What anomalies exist can be interpreted in terms of the 20 percent to 50 percent indeterminacy in the variability from person to person or group to group. The one caveat that can be made with regard to the above statement is that it is clear that U.S. Caucasians, in scoring much lower educationally than their European and neighboring North American counterparts while at the same time producing I.Q. profiles that are roughly equal, may be telling us something about the effectiveness of our educational system, that is, our serious underachievement.

On the other hand, the evidence seems to be that I.Q. scores of African-Americans, in the 82–85 range, over-predict actual school and college results.[43] This phenomenon, over prediction, does not apply to achievement test scores. The immediate question that comes to mind is, Are teachers and professors evenhanded in their treatment of African-American students? To date, studies have shown no differences in the results of African-American elementary and secondary school students whether taught by African-American or by white teachers.

The other question revolves around the further success or failure of minority students when they leave school for the various workplaces in our country. As noted earlier, I.Q. and aptitude tests seem to predict more accurately the success of candidates for a wide variety of jobs.

Since 1970, the total number of students, kindergarten through university, has leveled off to about 60 million per year. Yet schooling expenditures have continued to rise in constant 1986 dollars to the point that, as of 1986, we were spending $309 billion per year, about 7.5 percent of the GNP. By 1990 that figure had reached $405 billion. Considering that many nations lump health, cultural, and other expenditures under "education," the United States is investing an enormous amount of its wealth in an institution that is realizing ever more futile results for the additional dollars expended.

An important contemporary confirmation of the futility of the "expenditures-for-education" argument comes from the latest ETS-sponsored International Assessment of Educational Progress, of thirteen-year-old seventh graders in math, from around the world. The study was undertaken in March 1991 and published in February 1992.[44]

It is useful to remember that from Lewis Terman's famous longitudinal studies of over 1,500 talented young Californians (starting at about thirteen years of age—Terman called them "geniuses"), which began in the 1920s, to the Johns Hopkins Study of Mathematically Precocious Youth, from the early 1970s, thirteen-year-old educational achievement has been a significant milestone. It marks the beginning of reliability in predicting an individual's future educational and vocational possibilities.[45]

The leading mathematical achievement scores came from mainland China. But because 49 percent of their thirteen-year-olds are no longer in school and another thirteen percent are in grades lower than the seventh, their scores must be set in context. The population from which the scores were drawn was 425 million out of a total Chinese population of 1.15 billion.[46] These young Chinese mathematicians scored 80.[47]

The next highest scorers were Korea with 73; Taiwan, 73; Switzerland, 71; Soviet Union (then in chaos), 70; Hungary (also in revolution), 68. The United States was far down, at 55, below Ireland, at 61, and tied with Spain, for Catalonia—its most highly developed province—was not included.

Interestingly, the United States was recorded as spending at 7.5 percent, the second highest proportion of its gross national product, on education. Israel spends 10 percent. The mainland Chinese spend 2.7 percent on education. The Koreans spend 4.5 percent, the Taiwanese 3.6 percent. The U.S. per capita gross national product was $19,789; Switzerland was higher and first at $27,693. The mainland Chinese figure was $356. It is recorded that schools in Beijing spend about $54 per year on a middle-school pupil, compared with the about-$5,400-per-child expenditure in most large U.S. cities.

This relative educational decline in comparison with other nations begins early in the schooling cycle. Competency in reading comprehension, mathematics, scientific literacy, and geography require little in fancy equipment or teachers with doctoral degrees, or even small classes. Math class size in Japan at the eighth and advanced twelfth grades averages 40 and 43 pupils per teacher respectively, whereas in the United States it is 26 and 20 respectively.

In the above example of the 1991 international comparison of seventh-grade math achievement it is instructive to note that average U.S. class size is listed as 23; Korea, 49; Taiwan, 44; mainland China, 48.

ROOTS

John H. Bishop, writing in the March, 1989, issue of *The American Economic Review*, asks, "Is the Test Score Decline Responsible for the Productivity Growth Decline?" He reports:

The test score decline between 1967 and 1980 was large (about 1.25 grade level equivalents) and historically unprecedented. New estimates of trends in academic achievement, of the effect of academic achievement on productivity and of trends in the quality of the work force are developed. They imply that if test scores had continued to grow after 1967 at the rate that prevailed in the previous quarter century, labor quality would now be 2.9% higher in 1987, GNP $86 billion higher.[48]

Bishop confirms the now-accepted fact that the decline was larger for whites than for minorities. The declines, as reported above, were larger for higher level skills such as inference and problem solving than for the basic skills such as computation. Obviously these higher-level skills require higher intelligence levels in individuals. Interestingly, Bishop cites a U.S. research report on educational achievement (1986), authored by D. Koretz, which also reports no visible decline in achievement at the earliest grade levels, through the third grade.[49] The same conclusions can be drawn from the growing consensus about the non-existent long-run impact of Head Start beyond second or third grade.[50]

This last evidence can be explained by the heretofore puzzling fact that reading ability levels between children begin to diverge significantly in terms of comprehension at the third grade, eight-year-old level. The reason for this is now clarified by psycholinguistic theory, which explains that in the early years it is surface-structure facility in letter and word identification, sight or sound/phonic skills, that help or hinder children in their decoding reading skills. Around third grade, children go over to encoding, or deep-structure fluent reading, which involves prediction and understanding. These latter skills are synonymous with intellectual, cognitive ability.

The demographer Daniel Vining has translated these declining educational achievement levels into an approximate 4 to 5 point drop in average I.Q. relative to our past, and compared with other nations such as Japan, which does not seem to have experienced such a decline.[51]

It must be borne in mind that James Flynn has reported worldwide rates of I.Q. score enhancement, though the relative position of nation to nation, ethnic group to ethnic group, has remained neutral.[52]

Vining's research certainly correlates with the U.S. educational and economic decline relative to our past and to the rest of the world. If this largely hidden internal decline of I.Q. is correct, it could explain the observable decline in our general international position vis à vis the Japanese since the end of World War II. The Japanese I.Q. superiority over American whites is in the range of 3 to 5 points.

This may seem like a small amount. But, as Richard Herrnstein has noted in an article, "I.Q. and Falling Birth Rates" (see below), a small average differential in I.Q. leads to an enormous advantage at the extremes of the range. Thus, a 5 point average differential between one group and another would result in a 60 percent increase in the number of scores of over 130 I.Q. in the higher group and a comparable increase in the number of scores of below 70 I.Q. in the lower group.[53]

Let us estimate that in the U.S. population of 250 million persons there are 12.5 million with I.Q. 130 and over. In Japan, with half our population but with an I.Q. advantage of 5 points, the number of persons with I.Q. 130 and over would be about 10 million. Given the same distribution of talent and standard of deviation at about 140 I.Q., a point where we should expect to find extraordinary talent, the Japanese, half our population, should exceed us in absolute numbers of these highly intelligent and productive individuals.

However, recent research of the Japanese intellectual profile, published by Richard Lynn as well as by Daniel Vining, and reported by Daniel Seligman, indicates that the Japanese standard of deviation in their I.Q. profile is slightly less than 13 points as compared with the U.S. Caucasian 15 points. What this may indicate is that the Japanese curve is similar to the American female and the African-American profiles, which exhibit a more compact range of scores. At the upper end of the intelligence scale, the Japanese intellectual advantage might not prove to be decisive.[54]

This hypothesis might explain the Japanese desire to tap the creative scientific and technological talents of our best minds by setting up research laboratories in places like Princeton, New Jersey (NEC), Cambridge, Massachusetts (Mitsubishi), and San Francisco, California (Matsushita).

A fall 1993 bulletin and research report on adult literacy in the United States, published by the Department of Education, states:

Some 90 million adults—about 47 percent of the U.S. population—demonstrate low levels of literacy, according to a nationwide study released today by the U.S. Department of Education. However, according to *Adult Literacy in America*, most of these describe themselves as being able to read or write English "well" or "very well."

"This report is a wake-up call to the sheer magnitude of illiteracy in this country and underscores literacy's strong connection to economic status," U.S. Secretary of Education Richard W. Riley said. "It paints a picture of a society in which the vast majority of Americans do not know that they do not have the skills they need to earn a living in our increasingly technological society and international marketplace."

This report also notes that the literacy achievement of adults fell by 4 percent from the last study, which was carried out in 1986. Only 4 percent scored at the highest level of literacy (5), which approximated the skills of a college preparatory high school senior or first-year college student. These were overwhelmingly white, with black and non-Cuban Hispanics at less than 0.5 percent of this high literate group. By contrast, close to 79 percent of the respective populations of black and non-Cuban Hispanics scored at the first two levels, essentially illiterate for the modern economy.[55]

CONCLUSION

It is not possible to blame the wreckage that constitutes American secondary school achievement levels entirely on the tired and bloated bureaucratic public school establishment. For one, the teachers within their classrooms are as devoted a group of humans as one can expect, if not quite the relative caliber of their predecessors from leaner days.

Furthermore, there is no reason to attribute the falling off in achievement levels to instruction and equipment, of which there are more than enough. Compare the achievement levels of our thirteen-year-olds with those of much poorer nations and peoples.

The diminishment of achievement at the top, given the assiduous search throughout the nation for talent wherever it may be found, provides an even broader hint of what has gone wrong. In the next chapter, the evidence from the social domain, especially the demographic surge from the bottom of the social scale, will further buttress an increasingly compelling argument that even radical educational reform, one piece of which will be outlined in a later chapter, can go only partway toward reaching the achievement levels in the developed world.

Educational achievement is the second of the three bricks from which national prosperity can be constructed. Our hope for an economic renaissance is predicated on the availability of an educated workforce of highly skilled and competent production and service individuals. At the top of the educational pyramid, given the existence of this basic talent, should appear the creatively gifted. They will be able to utilize their dreams and ideas to create what does not yet exist, thence to employ that major labor constituency having the high-level basic skills to fabricate and distribute the resultant new products.

Even beyond, and perhaps fundamental to the realizations necessary in the above two institutions, the economic and the educational, is the social realm. For it is from here that the possibilities for producing a population able and willing to forge itself into a national unity will be decided.

The question is, What kind of society are we creating, given present-day international requirements?

Chapter 6

The Social Bond Unravels

MEMORY

Little did the Romans perceive the anomaly. Here, in the middle of Rome, a great arch was in process of construction—the Senate's contribution to honor the greatness of Emperor Constantine's victory over Maxentius at the Milvian Bridge in Rome, A.D. 312, and subsequently over the many powerful pretenders to the Imperial throne. Yet the arch was being decorated with sculptures taken from monuments built centuries earlier that commemorated ancient victories.[1]

If they had had an historical sense of the decay of Roman greatness the citizens of this period would have understood the meaning of the lack of artists creative enough to meet the challenge of earlier Roman genius. This falling off in the quality of Roman life augured an end that would come a century later despite Constantine's bluster and pretensions. Perhaps this surrender to the reality of change was to be seen in Constantine's reluctant conversion to Christianity, a mystery religion from the non-Roman eastern world of Jews and others.

SOCIAL DISINTEGRATION

There are signs today that our national *élan* is fading. Every study of the perceptions of the American people about the future of our nation reveals a deep unease. The political leadership appears impotent. No wonder that no presidential candidate in 1992 received a majority of the votes cast. The economic palliatives are all short-run and seem merely to touch the surface of the problem.

The statistics presented in the previous two chapters tell a story of structural decline that a few tax breaks or public works programs, or even traditional vocational training, seem unlikely to reverse. The injustice is that those striving today for office and its attendant perquisites will, like Constantine, yet fully share the heady brew of political and economic power. In time, one of these "leaders" will have the privilege of witnessing the entire edifice cave in, an Honorius brought down by some barbarian Alaric.[2]

The people have been bullied and brainwashed to avoid asking the necessary tough questions. Call someone "racist," "homophobic," "elitist," and all questioning will stop as the "politically incorrect" individual runs for cover. The media elite and the academic community are most responsible for this malfeasance.

One small example: Andrew Hacker, a well-known liberal professor of political science at Queens College in New York City, reviewing in the *New York Times* Sunday Book Review, discusses the book *Wake Up Little Susie, Single Pregnancy and Race Before Roe v. Wade*, by Rickie Solinger:

In 1950, only 1.7 percent of white babies were born to unmarried women, compared with 16.8 percent of black babies, or 10 times the figure. But by 1989, the most recent reporting year, the respective rates for the races had risen to 16.1 percent and 66 percent. While two-thirds of black births now occur out of wedlock, the accompanying fact is that the proportion of black births had declined from 10 to 4 times that for whites. Indeed, the white rate is where the black figure was 40 years ago. So *even in an age of racial division, we may be coming closer to a consensus where sexual behavior is concerned*. (Emphasis added)[3]

We presumably have lifestyle choices in the 1990s that we did not have in the 1950s. One of the results of this easing of morality has been a decline in parent commitment and family formation. In the United States today, the percentage of babies born to unmarried mothers is steadily arcing upward toward Sweden's 50 percent. But these Swedish mothers are middle class and have family support.

Consider also the 1991 report of the National Commission on Children, headed by Senator John D. Rockefeller IV of West Virginia. According to this report, more than half of fifteen- to nineteen-year old youngsters are sexually active. More than a million teenage girls become pregnant each year. Two million adolescents were arrested in 1990. Sixteen million children, one out of four, now live with only one parent, usually a mother.[4]

In 1991 a group of 250 business leaders, comprising the Committee for Economic Development, in *The Unfinished Agenda: A New Vision for Child Development and Education*, reported: "Between 1970 and 1987, the poverty rate for children increased nearly 33 percent. In 1989, close to 25 percent of children under the age of six lived in poverty."[5]

It is interesting to note how these figures mesh. The illegitimacy rate for the nation at large is now about 28 percent. One in four children now lives with one parent. One in four children now lives in poverty. But liberals will affirm that America is going through a great lifestyle change; women are being liberated. Never mind that over 25 percent of these "liberated" women without husbands live in poverty![6]

The National Center for Health Statistics has reported that the 1992 rate of 9.3 marriages per 1,000 people is the lowest since 1965. Today, 22.6 percent of Americans have never married. This compares with a 16.2 percent level in 1970.

From 1970 to 1991, the percentage of households with a married couple and a child or children has fallen from 40.3 percent to 25.9 percent, an almost 40 percent reduction, this despite massive infusions of funds into public programs.[7] Thus did our leadership accomplish the destruction of the nuclear family. This may not have been intended, yet it has been the unambiguous result.

Interestingly, the Census Bureau, which has reported these statistics, notes that countries in which more than 33 percent of the households were married couples with children were inhabited primarily by Hispanic, Mormon, or Indian families, in Appalachia, and in some suburbs.[8]

Harold Hodgkinson states: "In 1955, 60 percent of the households in the U.S. consisted of a working father, a housewife mother and two or more school age children. In 1980, that family unit was only 11% of our homes, and in 1985 it is 7%, an astonishing change."[9]

The U.S. recession, which continued through 1992, catapulted many more millions of individuals and families below the poverty line—$14,000 per year for a family of four. The figure was 12.8 percent for the population as a whole, but 35.9 percent for female-headed households, again the lifestyle of preference according to middle-class liberal media, academic, and political "progressives."[10] In 1992 a record 25 million people were on the federal food stamp rolls.[11]

NEW YORK CITY MICROCOSM

In New York City a survey of that metropolis's progress in the twelve years since 1980 was undertaken just prior to the Democratic Party Convention in July 1992. The city's population had increased during these years by approximately 250,000 to 7.322 million. Those on the welfare rolls had increased from 868,200 to 1,005,210, over half children, an increase of

137,000, approximately 16 percent, compared to about 3.6 percent population increase for the city as a whole.

The New York City jail population showed a greater increase, from 7,000 to 21,000 between 1980 and 1991. Homicides went from 1,826 to 2,154 per year during this period. Families in temporary housing (homeless) increased from 1,500 to 5,200. The number of children in foster care (homeless) also increased, from 20,953 to 48,924.

Perhaps the most striking indications of change in the cultural climate were the AIDS statistics. No cases were reported in August of 1980. In July 1992, 6,763 new AIDS cases were reported.

Despite the increase in population, and the supposed boom in the Reagan-Bush years, which should have helped the financial markets in the city, total employment in New York City had actually dropped during these twelve years, from 3.3 million to 3.25 million, but with the loss of about 400,000 high-paying jobs.[12]

These statistics ought not be thought to imply merely the decadence of this once-greatest cultural, financial, and educational center of the Western world. Certainly New York City is outpaced by Los Angeles, Miami, Washington, D.C., and Detroit when it comes to per capita homicide statistics.

CRIME

The statistics for the United States in general convey a larger sense of our changing social climate. In murders, the rate per 100,000 Americans has increased from 5 to 9.2 from 1960 to 1990. Rapes have increased from 10 to 41 per 100,000 in the same period; robberies from 55 to 252 per 100,000; aggravated assaults from 90 to 425 per 100,000. The number of in-place residential security systems has risen from about 9 million to 16.5 million from 1986 through 1992.[13] The statistics bear out the sense that the average American is intensely aware of being inundated by an epidemic of violent crime.

The 1992 riots in Los Angeles, estimated to have caused $1 billion in destruction, saw the looting of many gun stores. The subsequent flood of violent crime created a secondary wave of gun purchases by private citizens to defend themselves if and when the police were rendered incapable. It probably sounded the death knell for any comprehensive federal gun control law. And, of course, Congress appropriated, and the president signed into law, another billion dollars of national debt to do penance for that criminal atrocity. No sober social analyst would predict that such monies will alleviate the ongoing conditions that produced such events.

A study authored by Dr. Allen Beck, one of the staff demographers of the federal Department of Justice, showed that 52 percent of juveniles imprisoned in state institutions have immediate family members who have also been incarcerated. The study also found that in populations of 400,000 inmates in city and county jails, approximately 35 percent have close family members who have been incarcerated. For a population of 771,000 prisoners in state prisons, the percentage of family members who are or have been jailed is 37 percent.[14]

The challenge to the theory of social causation for criminal behavior is thus real. These figures support the growing acknowledgment throughout the world of the biological implications, if not causation, of violent behavior.

In 1992, a projected conference on the biological relationship of the propensity for violent criminal behavior, at the University of Maryland, sponsored by the National Institutes of Health (NIH) at a projected cost to the taxpayers of about $78,000, was canceled after protests by civil rights groups and the congressional black caucus. The accusation was that such a conference would be racist, since everyone assumed that a great disproportion of violent crime was being committed by young black males. In fact, as reported by David C. Rowe of the University of Arizona, 25 percent of African-American men, as compared with 2.5 percent of Caucasian men, are convicted felons.[15]

There are many explanations for the exponential expansion of our federal and state prison population. It may be that judges are more severe in their sentencing and parole is less easily granted, especially when the recidivism rate for released violent criminals is almost 80 percent. Perhaps it is due to the panic building program of jails that began in the 1980s in reaction to the flood of crime, especially related to drug offenses, that seemed to be inundating our nation.

Clearly judges and juries were less concerned about overcrowding in jails and acted with an awareness that one of the most deterring elements for criminal behavior was the surety, not necessarily of arrest by the police, but of actual imprisonment. At any rate, while in 1982 the prison population was about 225,000, by 1991 it had burgeoned to approximately 810,000.[16] (Some argue that it is well over one million.) Today the United States has more people per capita behind bars than any other country in the world, including South Africa and Russia.

An editorial in the *New York Times* noted that the prison population increase has far outspanned serious violent crimes, which from 1975 to 1989 stayed at 2.9 million per year. It further cited statistics showing that in 1989 only 12 percent of the 144,916 people arrested for violent crimes went to prison.[17] Perhaps the wrong people, drug users and petty criminals, were filling up our prisons while the true sources of this national plague of crime remained unapprehended.

There is no question but that in times of radical social change, in an era of greatly changing expectations, various forms of crime will show an increase. In 1993, with the advent of a new federal administration, the media were filled with discussions, associated with the confused selection of a new attorney general, that crime was an issue for the American people, second only to the economy.

Is it not plausible to view the enormous growth in violent crime as a product of a new and changing American demography incapable of coping with a world whose economic and educational requirements far outspan the intellectual capabilities of large segments of our changing society? These are human beings, so much like us in terms of desires and passions. But if their intellectual profiles are incapable of channeling these human drives through education and training into functional social pathways, can the alternative be other than chaotic and violent personal behavior?

DRUGS

Drug use by humans goes back to time immemorial. Few societies explicitly regulated such use, except in ritual and ceremonial circumstances. The individual was responsible for the consequences of his actions.

In the United States only the weakest laws existed in the nineteenth century to control the widely available cocaine, heroin, morphine, and opium. The 1960s and the affluence of the counter-culture brought marijuana into widespread use as a substitute for legal alcohol. By then strict laws had been enacted that controlled and prohibited the casual use of such drugs. As with so much of our social circumstances, the drug culture has exploded in its impact on our lives. The government has literally declared a war on the production, distribution, and use of all these drugs.

The federal cost has grown from several hundred million dollars per year in 1970 to at least $11 billion in 1991. The Federal Bureau of Investigation estimates that the number of arrests per 100,000 people has risen from 225 to 450 during this period, doubling in twenty years.[18] Is this rise in arrests caused by tighter law enforcement, or by more drug involvement in our society?

Doug Bandow of the Cato Institute puts the present yearly cost at $20 billion. Out of one million drug-related arrests, resulting prisoners occupy 75,000 cells, at a cost to the taxpayers of $3 billion per year.[19] Bandow's view, supported by many, including Baltimore's African-American mayor, Kurt Schmoke, would be to decriminalize drug use and thus withdraw the enormous law enforcement expense to the citizenry. Also, the streets would become safer simply because of the predictable decrease in violent drug-related crime.

Not only should drugs be available in public clinics, so the argument goes, but so too should treatment and prevention programs, along with education, be stressed. It is clear that cocaine, for example, has been given up by large sections of the middle class as a recreational drug of choice, simply because of awareness of the personal dangers that come with its use.

We have finally come to a consensus that alcoholism, a product of excessive personal use of a legal "drug," very often constitutes a physical illness. The desire for alcoholic drink, and its excessive use, constitutes a biological need to which many are susceptible.

It is not beyond plausibility that here, too, the tragic plague of uncontrolled drug use, similar to and associated with violent criminal behavior, arises in those poverty environments in individuals who are both intellectually as well as physically vulnerable. Obviously these arguments, still under philosophical interdict, require sustained investigation and study. This will never occur as long as we censor such research and burden its consideration by our moral and political obloquy.

DISEASE

Finally there is AIDS, an always fatal disease. Primarily a sexually transmitted disease, it can also be communicated through contaminated blood supplies or simply by means of medical laxity. There is also the blatant and growing reality of contaminated needles on the drug scene spreading the disease within inner-city populations.

What complicates the problem is the fact that in Western nations AIDS first reached epidemic proportions in the gay community. Because of the form of male homosexual behavior, the disease had easy access to individuals in this community. More recently, in Africa and other Third World areas, AIDS has spread wildly into the heterosexual community, along with the breakdown of traditional social restraints and the freedoms now associated with urban institutions and patterns of life.

The World Health Organization's AIDS program, headed by Dr. Michael Merson, estimates that there are approximately 10 million people around the world infected with HIV, the virus that causes AIDS. A Harvard University team has recently raised this figure to 13 million. The World Health Organization estimates that by the year 2000, 40 million people will be infected with HIV. The Harvard University group headed by Dr. Jonathan Mann is even more pessimistic. Its range of estimate runs from a minimum of 38 million infections to a possible 120 million people infected by the end of the present decade.[20]

Were this purely a medical problem dealing with a primarily sexually transmitted disease (STD), albeit one that is incurable and thus fatal once one exhibits the symptoms of AIDS, it would not have become as controversial a social and political issue in the United States, and thus one of the great cultural divides of our time. The tremendous political pressure placed upon our government by the homosexual lobby to obtain enormous expenditures to find a "cure" for the disease, expenditures now far outstripping research appropriations for cancer, is but one facet of the controversy. These federal expenditures have gone from several hundred million dollars in 1983 to $5 billion in 1993.[21]

In addition, with the impact of these one million North American HIV-infected individuals on our private health insurance system and the hospital system, in terms of both cost and competing demands as the systems cope with an exploding poverty class, as well as drug and criminal victims, it should be concluded that this is an undeserved and expanding burden that the citizenry is being asked to subsidize.[22] Today, the greatest increase in HIV infections comes from heterosexual populations and drug use, and always within the most impoverished classes.

AIDS has brought with it a wide variety of other illnesses. One of these, a new and as yet untreatable tuberculosis variant, seems also to be breaking out on its own as an epidemic, now associated with domestic poverty and impoverished immigrants, many of them "illegals," and thus spreading the disease beyond the control of our health authorities. The *New York Times* developed this theme in a front-page story.[23]

This plague is proving intractable to traditional public health controls, partially because these populations cannot be treated through traditional voluntary agencies. In 1991, in New York City alone, four thousand new cases of tuberculosis were reported. The total number of cases in this community as well as others throughout the United States is unknown.

The ideological struggle that came to the fore in the 1992 presidential campaign surfaced under the banner of "family values." The homosexual community, including lesbians who are less vulnerable to HIV than are male homosexuals, has made its pitch for cultural acceptance as an alternative lifestyle equal in social value to orthodox heterosexual marriages. It thus has laid claim to civil rights status in its demand for treatment as a discriminated-against "minority."

The 1992 Colorado ballot initiative that denied homosexuals special civil rights status has been countered by a massive boycott. Led by the gay community and its political allies in the media, this boycott, coupled with the political muscle exhibited in President Clinton's decision in early 1993 to attempt to fulfill his election promise and eliminate the ban on gays in the military, has resulted in an extremely polarized struggle. The media, in television and the major print organizations, now confront a grassroots phone-in and talk radio opposition. The result of this rancorous public debate is a compromise: "Don't ask, don't tell."

The gay community has been able to rally to its cause a large proportion of the bright and the powerful. "Stand firm" is its motto; the gay community is no mere STD-vulnerable group of deviants. Rather, it views itself as symbolizing the new sexuality in the modernist perception of the good American life. Martina Navratilova, the tennis great, a self-announced lesbian, has argued that it is her right to be able to adopt a child, perhaps including the right of all parents to inculcate their children with their values.

The claim is made that prejudice against racial or ethnic groups, as well as by "homophobes" who are prejudiced against homosexual behavior in its various forms—including so-called childloving—are all of a kind.

One is sympathetic to the calls from our political leaders for a mobilization of national purpose, a universal coming together to maintain that heritage of greatness that made the United States the magnetic attraction of the world for most of the American Century. But coming together to believe in what?

MIDDLE-CLASS DEFENSE

There is still a middle and a working class in the United States. And this middle America is, certainly increasingly conservative politically, as evidenced by the Reagan/Bush presidencies. The 1992 election, which was won by Clinton with 43 percent of the vote because of extremely weak opposition, gives evidence of a retained center. Here are demonstrated traditional family life; heterosexual marriages with children; ordinary community involvements such as the PTA, Girl and Boy Scouts, business and philanthropic groups; patterns of life that the ancient Egyptians on the Nile would not have found puzzling or incongruous in the context of their own values.[24]

The question is, considering the changes occurring in these various domains—economic, educational, and societal—what patterns of change can we see in the great center of society, now coming under increasing ideological attack? The answer is, quiet and resentful anger, combined with the traditional attempt by humans to maintain the social bond almost at all costs.

The middle and working classes are still having children and attempting to raise and educate them in the light of universal middle-class values as we know them at the end of the twentieth century. The publicity surrounding T.V. anchorwoman Connie Chung's recent (1992) publicly announced frustrated attempts to become pregnant now that she is in her early forties—sadly, for clearly she is a gifted woman—exemplifies the ancient human forces that are still operative. Ms. Chung sacrificed this dimension of her life for her career. Perhaps she now regrets this personal but stylish decision. Many other liberated women are now returning to "fundamentals" of this sort: husbands, children, sometimes even the surrender of great and powerful career ventures for the "mommy track."

OUR DISAPPEARING ELITE

The evidence for the drying up of abilities at the top is not as clear or dramatic as it is for the explosion at the bottom. Blatant pathologies do not appear at the top, merely subtle indications of a change in the number and character of the extraordinary humans coming forth from our cities, towns, and farms.

Heidrick and Struggles, a major personnel recruiting firm in Boston, state that in 1986 the average compensation for senior women executives was $116,810, not including stock options. Of these female executives, all presumably past their prime childbearing years, 53.7 percent had no children.[25]

An editorial of December 1990, in the *New York Times*, hailed the probable increase in the U.S. birthrate for 1990. The tentative estimate is that it will be at a rate of 2.1 children per female, the rate of national population stability. Our birthrates over the last several decades have averaged out at a rate of 1.8 children per female. This new rate contrasts with the extremely low rates of 1.3, 1.4, and 1.6 for Italy, Spain, and Japan, respectively, all traditionally high birthrate nations.[26] This is presumed as good news, since the media view births from all social classes as equally desirable. From which social classes is the increased birthrate derived?

It is difficult to obtain such social class–oriented statistics, except for the obvious examples of illegitimacy. The breakdown by race and ethnicity in the census statistics, on the other hand, is not surprising, since so much of our legal concern is race conscious.

A recent statistic concerning the Jewish minority is revealing. The Jews as an American ethnic group, rapidly disappearing, with an exogamous intermarriage rate of 52 percent in the current generation, once perceived as a discriminated-against, poor, and downtrodden group, have benefited from the openness and non-discriminatory character of our democratic tradition.[27] Out of the Forbes 400 wealthiest individuals in the United States, it has been estimated that 40 percent are Jewish. The Jews, observant and non-observant, represent, at about 6.5 million, about 2.5 percent of our population today. Their dominant roles in education, science, business, and culture have long been acknowledged.

Estimates of Jewish I.Q. scores range from Ellis Batten Page's figure of a combined verbal/math I.Q. of 109, to Robert Gordon's Jewish verbal I.Q. of 112.8, to Hans Eysenck's Glasgow (Scotland) state schools—not the private, elite Jewish parochial schools—of a combined I.Q. score of 117.[28] It is estimated that the Jewish birthrate in the United States is now 1.3 children per female. This should include the fecund "Orthodox."[29]

Jonathan Cole, provost of Columbia University. argued in 1989 that in the past decade, along with an approximate decline of about 11 percent in the enrollment of African-Americans in college, there was a 26 percent decline in the proportion of Ph.D.s earned by African-Americans in the physical sciences. In 1986, out of 3,003 doctorates awarded in physics, only 25 were received by African-Americans. This figure fits with the less than 1 percent number of African-Americans who place in the highest category of high school science and math achievers.

Cole reports that there has been an overall 25 percent decrease in the number of Ph.D.s conferred in the physical sciences in American universities in the decade ending 1989. By the year 2000 our requirements will be about 18,000 per year. It is expected that our universities will produce approximately 10,500 at that time—7,000 Americans and 3,500 foreign residents.[30]

William O'Hare of the University of Louisville, author of the report "African-Americans in the 1990s," estimates that the number of African-American families with incomes over $50,000 (presumably in 1989 dollars) rose from 266,000 in 1967 to over one million in 1989. Also, the incomes of college-educated black families now stand at 93 percent of the level of comparable white families.[31]

We are speaking of progress between two maturing generations. These talented individuals in the African-American community represent the past both in the sense of their own highly developed skills and in the special efforts of a nation at large to ameliorate the taint of previous discriminations. The question remains, what do the demographics say about future generations, even as we have put aside blatant racial and ethnic discrimination? In 1992, only 1 percent of all black prospective college students, 1,493, scored over 600 on the Verbal SAT, as compared with 8 percent, 55,224, of whites. These rare and talented black students are being courted by white colleges as they would court basketball talent.[32]

Robert Woodson, National Center for Neighborhood Enterprise, a conservative civil rights group, argues that over $2 trillion has been expended since 1945 to bring the poor into the middle class. Despite significant but small-scale successes, 50 percent of African-American children under the age of six lived in poverty in 1990. Ross Perot reports that 72 percent of black children born between 1967 and 1969 have been dependent on welfare at some point in their lives.[33] At the same time, the annual budgets of organizations in the "Civil Rights Plantation" had reached $5 billion.[34]

Where are the talented young people needed for our future to come from? At the very moment that the source of its most talented leadership potential dries up, the United States needs an even greater proportion of its citizenry to arise from these selfsame educable segments of society.

Walter Wriston, retired chairman of Citicorp, writes in a vein similar to all other writers on economic and social issues. He speaks about intellectual capital as becoming the great arbiter of national greatness in the next century. Educational power is the only truly transnational element of power, he argues, one that can more easily flow in and out of nations than their money and its value.[35]

A shift in the patterns of childbearing among the different social classes of a society as it surges into affluence is not new. Feminists during all periods of history have never had qualms about deserting childbearing, as it inevitably interferes with an individual's personal gratifications and freedoms. And, of course, it has always been the most educated, affluent, pampered females who have deserted motherhood. This has long been a worldwide phenomenon, going back at the least to ancient Greece and Rome, evidenced in the perennial laments of historians and philosophers.[36]

Prime Minister Li Kuan Yu of Singapore was accused of ethnic racism half a dozen years ago when he urged well-off and well-educated female Singaporeans (read "Chinese") to have more children and discouraged the less educated (read "Malay") females from raising families: "Levels of competence will decline, our economy will falter, our administration will suffer, and society will decline, because so many educated men are failing to find educated women to marry and are instead marrying uneducated [non-Chinese?] women or remaining unmarried."[37]

Certainly the feminist movement and the media's highly regarded homosexual lobby have done much to discourage the family ideal of many children as a model for modern life by the well-educated "Yuppie" generation. Patricia Ireland, the self-admitted lesbian president of the National Organization for Women (NOW), has referred to such "homemaker-mothers," as compared to President Clinton's first two candidates for attorney general (one child each, whereas the successful candidate, Janet Reno, has no children), as "unpaid child care providers."

The successful female executives cited above and, indeed, now several generations of highly intelligent men and women from all ethnic groups, have been lured and "blessed" by the powers that be to engage in lifestyles that literally disdain what the Japanese culture still approves of, if even at a moderate rate of 1.6 children per female.

In Japan, as Richard Herrnstein noted in the above *Atlantic Monthly* article, females are less liberated in their cultural expectancies. Educated, and now well integrated into a modern workforce, the Japanese woman will still most often retire to a home life of raising several children. It is important to note that this expectancy carries through to all social classes in Japan, an already highly homogenized society in social class, and thus in intellectual capabilities.

Compared to the U.S. overall rate of 28 percent illegitimacy, the Japanese rate is 1 percent. We need to ask whether there is a relationship between this apparent non-liberation of the Japanese female and the perdurance of Japanese nuclear families, of their scarcity of crime, welfare, drug abuse, AIDS, and homelessness, of the absolute superiority of educational achievement by the vast majority of their students, of the small economic differences between chief corporate executives and the workers on the line—as compared to our society—and of the overwhelming economic surge that has catapulted their nation to a dominant position in the world community.

Norman Mailer, wondering to himself, perhaps about himself and the new climate of literary mediocrity, stated: "There are no large people anymore. I've been studying Picasso lately and look at who his contemporaries were: Freud, Einstein."[38]

A 1979 study, entitled "National Longitudinal Study," reports on the high school class of 1972, four and one half years after its graduation. Already this points to a select group of youth, those able to graduate from four-year high schools: "As of October 1976, 36 percent of the men and 53 percent of the women were or had been married, about 10 percent of those ever married were divorced or separated, and 23 percent of all persons had at least one child. *Thirty percent of low-ability whites and 49 percent of low-ability blacks reported having children.*"[39]

The other part of the statistic was of even more interest and importance: "*Only 6 percent of the blacks and 10 percent of the whites in the highest quartile had had children. The estimate is that this proportionality would continue through the child bearing years.*"[40] This is one of the few pieces of concrete statistical information that we have confirming the growing demographic disparity in birthrates between the higher educational achieving and the less able segments of our nation.

Daniel R. Vining, of the University of Pennsylvania Research Center, confirms this dysgenic trend in the United States, which he argues is hurting the African-American population more than the white.[41] An interesting statistic from 1988 shows that 41 percent of new white mothers and 40 percent of white fathers reported that they had more than twelve years of education. For African-Americans who had had a birth in 1988, the figures were: mothers, 25 percent, and fathers, 16 percent.[42]

CONCLUSION

Societies do not unwind accidentally. Following World War II the Japanese and the Germans had to take stock after the horrors of aggression and defeat that they themselves created. So, too, do the East Europeans and the Chinese have to come to terms with their own forms of ideological madness, which led them, potentially talented like the Germans and the Japanese, into their own unique pathways toward defeat and chaos.

The dominating polarizations between the extreme right, represented by Patrick Buchanan, and the liberal left, in terms of abortion rights, homosexual lifestyles, the liberation and masculinization of the female, as well as a host of other social and moral issues, reflects the unraveling of the social consensus that existed in earlier, much less affluent and technologically developed eras of American life.

The crack in the existing national consensus as to what is right and wrong with regard to social behavior is widening. What shall we represent in our national moral and intellectual profile, and what should we fight to eliminate from our nation? These are the dominating questions that face the United States.

But more, it tells us that the leadership—intellectual, in communications, perhaps even political—sees the real tragic decline in the international profile of the United States from a very different perspective than those who see it from afar and have no interest in our success: quite the contrary.

For example, when the issue of family values is raised, the liberal community is concerned with more welfare assistance for single mothers and their children, more state-supported child care for working and professional women, mandatory unpaid family leave for those economically able to take off from their jobs, universal state-run health care systems to maintain the poor *in situ*.

There is an odd moral symbiosis and reciprocity between the expanding poverty populations at the bottom of society and those social groups at the top who sponsor and in effect expand this dependency. In the process, the latter apparently think that they can gain the ethical high ground in their war against historic human values.

No matter the widening social and economic gulf between these self-same "bright and beautiful" and those in increasing despair at the bottom. No matter the inexorable decline of their nation.

Chapter 7

Ebb Tide

If you don't know why the patient is sick, you can't cure him.

SOBRIETY

"America's Choice: High Skills or Low Wages," authored by a committee of distinguished, ideologically moderate economists and political figures under the direction of Ira Magaziner, William Brock, and Ray Marshall, enlarges the perspective of our contemporary situation.[1]

Focusing on the economic future of our nation as the key to our international position, the group was deeply concerned with the contemporary facts, and the future probabilities, unless radical improvement was inaugurated.

Real average weekly earnings have dropped more than 12% since 1969 . . . The highest earning 30 percent of American families increased their share of national income from 54 percent in 1967 to 58 percent in 1987, while the bottom 70 percent has been losing ground.

Over the past 15 years, the earnings gap between white collar professionals and skilled tradespeople has gone from two percent to 37 percent; the gap between professionals and clerical workers has gone from 47 percent to 86 percent.

Over the past decade, earnings of college educated males age 24 to 34 increased by 10 percent. Earnings of those with only high school diplomas declined by nine percent. And those in the work force who do not hold high school diplomas saw their real incomes drop by 12 percent.

Over 40% of new work force entrants will be minorities and immigrants, groups which are at disproportionately low incomes today.[2]

Harold L. Hodgkinson, in his "The One System," confirms these statistics. He notes that while African-Americans and Hispanics comprise about 17.5 percent of our population today, non-white minorities will constitute about one-third of our population shortly after the turn of the century. In about the year 2020 they will constitute over 40 percent of the population, given present birth and immigration trends. What is even more important is that they will dominate in the younger age groups.[3]

Magaziner and colleagues continue: "We can no longer depend upon more people working to give us economic growth. If productivity continues to falter, and real wages decline, we can expect one of two futures. Either the top 30 percent of our population grows wealthier while the bottom 70 percent becomes progressively poorer or we may all slide into relative poverty together."[4]

The author of an editorial entitled "The Rich Get Richer," in the *New York Times*, wrote of the glimmerings of an awareness of the economic consequences of our new internationalism that had finally touched the reality consciousness of our own liberal barons of the communications industry. The facts were definitive. Between 1977 and 1989 the richest 1 percent of the population received 70 percent of the increase in average family income. The richest 20 percent of the population during this period altogether took more than 100 percent of the growth in average family income. This was because the bottom 40 percent of the population lost ground during this same period.

Clearly a radical change had occurred in the national economy. Historically, all sectors of the national income profile had shared equally in the growth of the United States. The explanation of the *New York Times* editorialists was as follows:

Economists are increasingly persuaded that the rising inequality cannot be explained by anything as simple as greed, politics or foreigners. They look to something more deeply ingrained in modern industrialized economies—call it technology for short.

The days when high school dropouts could earn high wages in manufacturing are gone. Modern economies more than ever require educated, skilled labor. That explanation ought to jolt people out of traditional remedies.

For one thing tinkering with tax rates to favor the poor won't accomplish much. Studies show that even if Congress were prepared to jack up tax rates on the rich greatly while cutting taxes for the poor, the impact on income inequality would be trivial.

It is interesting to note that such redistributionist policies as "soak the rich" were exactly those presented in President Clinton's 1993 budget proposals. The Republicans were in unanimous opposition.

The *New York Times* solution was not too original: "Massive new commitments to Head Start, to primary and secondary education, to training high school dropouts and welfare mothers, to more higher education of different kinds, to workplace training."[5]

One could find a similar list from a wide variety of such editorials going back to the early 1970s. It hasn't happened before, so why should it happen now? The United States has probably spent more per capita on educational and welfare expenditures than any other nation. Today it is rapidly going broke, with a deficit that increases every year by at least $300 billion, which is on top of our pre-existing $4.5 trillion federal debt. The interest that we pay on this accrued debt has to come out of our federal budget each year, already severely in deficit.

REALITY THERAPY

The orthodox prescription for our economic malaise and thus the key to the possible remediation and reform of education—the hoped-for stemming of the social unwinding of our nation— is *productivity*.

What does that mean? It doesn't mean more government programs to put people to work. Nor does it mean additional congressional pork barrel programs to create a few temporary jobs for constituents. Nor does it mean pouring a billion or so dollars into the inner city, to provide "make work" jobs or to create "enterprise zones," so that the kids won't burn down the cities next summer with no guarantee about the summer after.

Simply, it means new jobs created in the private sector. Not minimum-wage counter-girl or stock-boy jobs. To create real "family support" jobs, what is needed is transnational entrepreneurship. This means individuals who will invest their time and money, and above all their skills and initiative, in thinking up new products or services that the middle-class *world* needs.

Since in today's international climate many nations are vying for the best-paying jobs that can be met by the skills of their workforces, we have to do that much better. This is because foreign workers outside Japan, Korea, and the off-shore Chinese nations, and Western Europe, are willing to work at pay rates that will not sustain a worker or his family in the United States.

Thus we are speaking about high technology in the widest sense. On top are those unique innovators with the education, the ideas, and the know-how to create, as did Ross Perot. Almost alongside these unique individuals are the people down on the assembly line, but now highly skilled, and therefore highly educated and, above all, with versatile intelligence.

Productivity is not an abstraction. A few billion dollars of additional vocational training fed into an already bloated and ineffective bureaucracy of education is unlikely to produce a magical transformation in an outskilled workforce. No innovative businesspeople are going to take a chance with the investment that is their survival, to undertake highly specialized and thus high-risk enterprises, unless they know that the possibility for success is commensurate with the risk. And the key to success is a truly educated workforce that is willing to engage in hard labor along with a regulatory environment that is not self-destructive.

Will the top 20 percent of our educated population, where the investment wherewithal and the high usable education lie, take a chance with the American labor scene? The evidence is that they are very reluctant to invest in the United States. While the corporations are becoming "lean and mean" by laying off hundreds of thousands of ordinary American semi-skilled and white-collar workers, new plants are being built overseas in both the developed and advancing countries, from Mexico to Indonesia. The cost of investment is less, the climate for risk and success is better.

BITTER TRUTH

Our problem is simple, but oh-so-difficult to discuss, let alone accept. We are a different people than we were fifty years ago. In truth, we are not the nation that we were. Relative to the rest of the developed and developing world, we probably no longer have the intellectual capital that can profit from the available educational resources.

As I will point out later in this book, we can do better with what we have. But for a nation now undergoing a population explosion from the bottom, now slated by the Census Bureau to have a population of about 385 million by 2050, as compared with a 1992 population of over 250 million, our present prospects are Third World, and in the lifetime of those already born.[6]

Our leadership has refused to listen to the few, if insistent, voices that pleaded for a chance to argue their case. The case: Humans vary in intelligence. This variability is not merely located in the person, from individual to individual, but also in communities. Thus while there is no racial test for high intelligence, it is true that ethnic groups who breed within the group tend to have a similar intellectual profile, which may be higher or lower on average than that of other ethnic groups.

Little did it matter to our leadership who had the babies. Thus, in the course of a generation or two, the welfare system, instituted by liberal intellectuals and politicians with the purpose of helping our people and our nation, has literally destroyed our intellectual potential.

Most tragically affected has been the African-American community that, even while it struggled against slavery, segregation, and discrimination, had come forth into the mid-twentieth century with great working- and middle-class resilience and a leadership that reflected a secular educational and political vision. It was ready to use *Brown v. Board of Education* (1954) to create an exemplar of what the struggle for freedom could do for its own members, and also of the power of its potential contribution to the country as a whole.

The flight of the educated middle classes from their traditional familial responsibilities of leadership, given that they were the recipients and beneficiaries of their country's good fortune, is perhaps the great historic crime of nation-destroying. Even today, liberal ideologists glorify that which is socially abnormal or pathological, to the detriment of the nation's survival. The protest is left to the extreme right-wing groups.

Of course, a scattering of individuals of high intelligence and creativity will appear. But ours is a quickly expanding population, now competing in an international arena of unprecedented educational demands. There is but an infinitesimal chance, given the existing evidence, that this nation could momentarily produce the number of creative minds necessary for the productive requirements of middle-class life, as defined by the twenty-first century, to benefit more than a small percentage of our population.

Ira Magaziner is correct when he envisions a sharply decreasing percentage of our population living middle-class lives. Unfortunately, this is a prescription for revolution and social chaos, the end to our democratic system.

Compare this situation with that of Japan. Here is a people 122 million strong, living on a barren series of volcanic islands with a total landmass equivalent to the state of Montana. The women by and large remain at home to raise their small families. The productivity of the entire population enables the Japanese to farm out the drudgery and all but high-value-added work to its sprawling colonial economic empire, now including the United States.

The key, of course, is the uniformly high intelligence of the Japanese, perhaps ten to twelve I.Q. points higher on average than the population of the United States, taking in all our various minority and majority groups.[7] From this intelligence of the Japanese come a disciplined social life, intact families, little crime or social pathology. From this stable social environment are produced extraordinarily high educational achievements for roughly 98 percent of the population. Finally, from the enormous productivity, technological ingenuity, cooperation, and planning, as well as equality of reward, arises a giant power in harmony with the coinage of late twentieth- and twenty-first-century national and international war—the economic struggle for survival.

FALLING NATIONAL INTELLIGENCE

James Flynn, an American political scientist who teaches in New Zealand, has recently called attention to the mysterious fact that over the past fifty years I.Q. scores have increased worldwide. This puzzling phenomenon has been widely discussed without a clear conclusion. It must be self-evident that humankind is not getting *absolutely* more intelligent. There is no theoretical basis for such a hypothesis or conclusion.[8]

On the other hand, the dissemination of information through modern communications has given humans throughout the world greater contact with the frontier of knowledge, information, and modern lifestyles, the grist from which I.Q. and achievement tests are constructed. Further, this rise in I.Q. scores has been uniform, with all sectors of world society seemingly rising equally with the tide of knowledge.

The tentative conclusion thus seems to be that this phenomenon is an artifact of a changing international environment and thus irrelevant to a comparative analysis. On the other hand, in the United States the SAT scores and comparative economic and social statistics have all been falling for the past twenty-five years.[9]

In 1938 psychologist Raymond B. Cattell published an article that summed up both his own early studies on this issue as well as previous writing that related intelligence levels to national character. It was entitled "Some Changes in Social Life in a Community with a Falling Intelligence Quotient."[10]

Cattell's research and analysis were based on his experiences in Great Britain, and thus they did not involve any multi-ethnic or multi-racial comparisons. His analysis was an extrapolation of British data that suggested a uniform drift downward in childbearing from class to class. Thus the lowered intelligence levels reflected a uniform slope in which those groups with the lowest intelligence levels had the most children and those with the highest had the least over a period of time.

Cattell summarized the consequences of this general societal decline in intelligence levels in eleven points, the first six of which are the following: "1. A fall in academic standards in the schools. 2. A change in the curriculum of schools towards less abstract and generalized studies. 3. An increased cost of education. 4. Increased unemployment in the less-skilled occupations. 5. Decrease in the average real earning power of the community as a whole. 6. A rise in the frequency of delinquency (unless there is a deliberate lowering of moral standards) and/or proneness to aggression between nations."[11]

Table 1
Black Income as a Percentage of White Income in 1987 among Persons Aged 25 or Over, by Sex, Education, and Employment Status

	No high school	Some high school	High school grad.	Some coll.	Coll. grad.	Total
All Persons						
Men	74.0	68.9	63.8	72.3	69.8	58.7
Women	84.1	84.9	98.3	98.9	100.9	85.8
Full-time, year-round workers						
Men	81.9	77.1	71.7	76.8	75.4	67.8
Women	91.4	87.3	91.9	86.2	86.2	85.5

Source: "Money Income of Households, Families, and Persons in the United States." 1989. *Current Population Reports*, series P-60, no. 162, Table 35. Washington, D.C.

One aspect of this decline that neither Cattell nor others discuss is the difference in male/female relations within a society. This issue becomes important because the difference in the standard deviation between the sexes is over 16 percent, males having a significantly higher standard deviation than females.

This means that the males have a wider range of differences in intelligence than females, who hover more compactly around the mean. Males are thus over-represented at both the highest and the lowest levels of intelligence. If a nation's general intelligence levels are lowered, one would expect females to be less seriously affected than males, who would be shunted more precipitously into the lower ranges. Females would become far more competitive in the job market, and in general social competence.

One wonders whether the surge into feminism in the United States in recent decades can be associated with this trend of declining overall intelligence levels, which impacts males most heavily; likewise the rise of homosexuality among women. In the case of the African-Americans with a mean I.Q. range between 80 and 85, it is clear to all observers that the African-American female is a survivor economically and socially. (See Table 1.) Much has been made by the African-American leadership of the tragic condition of males in this ethnic group. (See Table 2.)

Table 2
Murder Rate per 100,000 Persons, by Race and Sex (1950–1988)

	1950	1960	1965	1970	1975	1980	1985	1988
Whites	5.2	4.7	5.5	8.3	10.0	10.7	8.3	9.0
Male	3.8	3.6	4.4	6.8	9.1	10.9	8.2	7.9
Female	1.4	1.4	1.6	2.1	2.9	3.2	2.9	2.9
Blacks								
Male	47.3	36.6	n.a.	67.6	69.6	66.6	48.4	58.0
Female	11.5	10.4	n.a.	13.3	15.1	13.5	11.0	13.2

Sources: "Health United States." 1990. *National Center for Health Statistics*, Table 34: 181; 1979. *Statistical Abstracts of the United States*, 181.

CONSIDERATIONS

Other societies have undergone experiences similar to that of the United States. Rome was catapulted to international wealth during a similar period of expansion, conquest, and population growth. The first emperor, Augustus, in the early first century A.D. perceived a change in Roman demography as the founding Latin ethnics of the senatorial class renounced family life. Men and women both were liberated, and Augustus denounced them for undermining the greatness of Rome.[12]

Augustus understood what we have not. But Rome was more fortunate. It had extended the franchise to the other able Italic tribes. Hundreds of thousands of colonists had settled in Spain, Gaul, and Illyria during the late Republic. Thus there was available a new leadership class to take over, just as in the United States the various European ethnic groups, Irish, Italian, and Polish, supplanted the sterile New England elite at the end of the nineteenth century.

Our current situation is different. Blessed with welfare and death control, and without the understanding, discipline, and wherewithal to exercise birth control, an internal and external tide of people from the lower social classes is spiraling millions of the permanently poor over our borders to add to our resident poor. The intelligent and educated of their own homelands do not have to emigrate. They are becoming wealthy in their home nations even while these others sink into poverty and mass degradation.

"The aim is to make India a great country," said Kavel Ratna Malkami, the vice president and principal spokesman for the Bhaatiya Janata Party, the main opposition to the governing Congress Party. Mr. Malkami said his party was concerned less about population growth than about which segments of the population were growing faster. "Among Hindus," he said, "birth control was practiced by the wrong people . . . The so-called better-off classes practice family planning," he explained. "The so-called lower classes don't. This means a deterioration of the population."[13]

Chapter 8

The Free Market of High Intelligence

SUPERMEN

The White House had issued the order. October 1958, one year after *Sputnik I*. The discussions, arguments, even speculations, were now behind the nation. President Eisenhower had personally decided that future astronauts would be chosen from those who had graduated from military test pilot school and had had at least 1,500 hours flying high-performance military jets.

These astronauts would have to demonstrate the ability of humans to fly in outer space and return safely to earth; they would demonstrate that such space flight would handicap neither ordinary functioning nor the useful performance of a wide variety of physical and mental tasks; astronauts would act as a backup system to the various automatic control instruments of the spacecraft, thus providing extra reliability to the success of the mission; astronauts would have to act as scientific observers, supplementing the information, data, and knowledge provided by the instrumentation on board and the unmanned satellites.

Of approximately 500 test pilot candidates whose records were analyzed for suitability to be included in the initial phase of NASA's program, now titled Mercury 110 were tapped for testing. Of these, 31 were selected as finalists. By April 1959, the 7 Mercury astronauts were selected.

These men were required to have an enormously varied set of abilities, skills, and physical qualities, all in addition to what they needed to survive as test pilots. In addition to the stress and balance tests, there were tests to probe isolation sensitivity, reaction time, attention focusing, distraction resistance, personality and family stability, learning speed, and perceptual and space integration. They needed to demonstrate an intelligence that prepared them for the unknown, the accidental, to be able to make quick integrations of new information into old.

The subsequent success of the Mercury astronauts soon led to a new series of candidates, for Gemini, selected in September 1962, and for Apollo, selected in October 1963. For Gemini, 200 test pilots went through the selection process, of whom 32 became finalists, with nine finally chosen. For Apollo, the field expanded to 720 candidates; ultimately, 14 were selected.

We assume that test pilots, and thus astronauts, would be a highly unique and talented group of individuals, whose abilities for mastering the stresses and demands of high altitude flying, testing, and crisis management, all of which require instantaneous reactions, would be highly specialized.

One would assume the intelligence requirements for test pilots to be high, but not highly academic. The test pilots' 118.9 Verbal and 115.8 Performance I.Q. average on the Wechsler were high, equal to the average M.D., but a bit surprising in that the Verbal I.Q.s were higher than the Performance.

The astronaut candidates not selected for both the Mercury and the Apollo phases (Gemini data are missing) produced a full score I.Q. of 131–132. The I.Q.s of the chosen astronauts averaged 135, with a range from 127 to 140.[1] These scores of those with "the right stuff" are over two standard deviations above the norm of 100 I.Q. and thus qualify these individuals to be labeled intellectually gifted, if not geniuses, in the terminology of Lewis Terman's classic California longitudinal study of over 1,500 extremely talented youngsters.[2]

Importantly, the I.Q. scores alone did not qualify these men. As mentioned above, the men had first to pass the various physical, simulation, and psychological tests that subjected them to many "real life" situations, and that in themselves necessitated a functional distillation of their intellectual potential. It is interesting to note that the researchers viewed the Verbal I.Q. scores as most definitive and thus highly predictive of performance.[3]

WHY HIGH INTELLIGENCE?

The proven ability of these astronauts to handle both complexity and novelty, all in a crisis time-warp, illustrates dramatically the centrality of high intelligence in all dimensions of human experience. It is what makes us unique animals in the biological world. The variability of intelligence in the human species today constitutes a momentary way station into the future, a future that will see a far more homogeneous human genotype when it comes to intelligence, and at a much higher international level than today.

The reason this has to happen is that intelligence is our unique biological adaptation, and language is its primary specialized means for expression. Once on a road of specialization—ours is certainly 4 to 6 million years in the traveling—the only route is straight ahead to fulfill one's biological destiny with evolution.[4] Of course, a series of important mutational changes, coupled with alterations in our ecology and environment, could shunt us either onto another road through time or, possibly, to evolutionary oblivion.

What is the meaning or the definition of intelligence from the perspective of human or animal function? Simply, intelligent behavior is merely one of a number of adaptations that animals have used to survive over time. The first truly intelligent animals were the modern teleost fish, which came into being almost half a billion years ago. They swam in the mid-waters of the oceans and inland seas, moving around searching for sustenance, coping with their ever-changing environment, as compared with the starfish or snails inching along at the water bottoms.[5]

Intelligent creatures cast their fate with change and opportunity; they were faced with momentary challenges, but rarely with the cataclysmic unavoidable crises that passive creatures had to endure. In contrast to those creatures with rigidly fixed behaviors, intelligent creatures learn within a generation to cope with widely varying circumstances in time and place. The brain became the front and center of a "computer" that wagered on a tomorrow different from today. "Be prepared" was the motto. Stereotyped instinct gradually gave way to probing thought, the purpose of which was to organize new experiences into the web of meanings that constituted the sum of previous experience.[6]

Let us return to the astronauts and put them into this evolutionary picture. The modern human brain had exploded in size thousands of years ago to create a world of meanings and symbols well beyond the limits, even the safety, of animal life enmeshed within the preestablished boundaries of nature's security. The astronauts, well protected by systems themselves created by fine scientific minds to anticipate every conceivable challenge that theory could predict, given the existing scientific knowledge, yet had the opportunity to use their brains and intelligence to confront any malfunction of the preestablished systems, as well as to explore or analyze things which only an open, prepared, and curious mind of high intelligence could do, alone and far out in space.[7]

It can be said that the evolutionary adaptation of intelligence that has focused on one or two creatures in every animal group—sea gulls and starlings among the birds; cichlids among the fish; dogs, cats, horses among the higher mammals; and humans in the class of primates—has an ancient tradition in the great repertoire of animal adaptations.[8] But now we humans are out on the limb. We can't go back and live off nature as we did 100,000 years ago. Too much has been destroyed by *Homo*.

THE FOUR DIMENSIONS OF INTELLIGENCE

"G"—General Intelligence. The core of human intelligence, that which is measured by I.Q., is called "g," general intelligence. This is the capacity represented by the versatility of the astronauts to think abstractly, to reason. This is the same capacity required to organize large quantities of information into meaningful and useful systems, as that of the "symbolic analyst," a term coined by Robert Reich.[9]

In the field of vocational guidance the term *validity generalization* denotes those aptitude tests, given to individuals for jobs, which are not necessarily related to the actual tasks involved. It has been discovered by those in the field of vocational guidance and testing that no particular test of skills, whether it be parking cars in a garage, driving a bus, or repairing autos, predicts success as well as general aptitude tests.[10]

Tasks such as firing a tank gun accurately, or accumulating a fine record of achievement as a policeman or fireman, are best predicted by higher I.Q. scores. The reason is that while individuals may have what seems to be adequate skills for certain concrete learnings there is no job that involves merely a passive repetition of certain tasks. Every job requires that an individual adapt to a new slant—perhaps a smaller or larger car will have to be parked than was being driven the year before. A janitor may have to learn to use a new broom or detergent. General aptitude tests for "g" predict those who will have the intelligence to adapt to new challenges, to complete new tasks successfully.

Part of the battery of tests that every military recruit for the U.S. armed forces takes is the Armed Forces Qualification Test (AFQT). With the reduction of the armed forces in the late 1980s, the lowest scoring recruits on this quasi I.Q. test, those between 80 and 92 I.Q., were eliminated from the services.[11]

Daniel Seligman quotes the 1989 Defense Department report: "Service members with high scores on the AFQT and with high-school diplomas display behaviors that benefit the Armed Forces. . . . People with high AFQT scores are likely to achieve skill proficiency earlier in their first enlistment than those with low scores."[12]

The highest scorers continue to improve. "AFQT scores have been found to predict the success of soldiers performing operator maintenance on the TOW launcher, a wire guided missile system. . . . Category 1 teams [I.Q.

above c.105] scored 75% more tank equivalent kills using the M-60 tank than did category 4 teams [80–92 I.Q.]."

"P"—Postponement Factor. In addition to "g," general intelligence, the so-called postponement or persistence factor is important. It is a dimension of intelligence that is critical to functioning in a complex, dynamic environment.[13] In the film *One Flew Over the Cuckoo's Nest*, Jack Nicholson portrays a patient, unruly, scheming, who is subjected to a frontal lobotomy. The character retains his basic personality and intelligence, but he is now a human "vegetable," without will power or drive, no sense of a tomorrow to live for or plan for.

The frontal areas of the cortex, in contrast to the "g" or temporal/parietal parts of the brain, are thought to be the centers of drive, motivation, planning—the "p" factors. Coordinated with high abstract conceptual powers, they allow for the linkage of idea, to plan, to fulfillment. "P" without "g" is obviously a fearful endowment, the drive to succeed without the intellectual shaping of these human drives into intellectually rich and responsible patterns of thought and action.[14]

As yet there has not been developed a method of quantifying the variability from individual to individual of the "p." It is understood in the field of psychoneurology and in evolutionary theory. Testers of intelligence refer to the so-called Executive overseer in our mental makeup that guides and disciplines us in taking I.Q. or "Reaction Time" (RT) tests.[15]

Think of the many cases of individuals of all races and ethnicities who leave their homes and families to go to strange lands and take on formidable work or education assignments, so that in several years they might return to wives, husbands, and children to achieve the long-planned goals that had sent them on this mission of self-sacrifice.

Wayne Gravlin, an M.D., pilot, and flight surgeon with the air force and NASA during the early stages of Gemini and Apollo, was one of the first group of scientist/astronauts selected for the Shuttle Program.[16] Gravlin was convinced by his own background of achievements, and in his rapid move toward the select group, that only a few of those selected at each stage in the process were competitive with him in terms of qualifications.

However, he was amazed at the ability of many of these candidates to overcome their background limitations through pure grit and determination. Week after week, month after month, they applied themselves with enormous discipline. A number of them were selected who in his view had nowhere near the natural qualities and experience that had moved him so easily, but who had a real measure of personal ambition and effort. This proved to him the importance of the persistence factor, the drive to succeed linked with the intelligence to guide this drive for achievement.

Talent—The Talent Factor. The talent factor is often invoked in many seemingly specialized tasks from basketball playing to piano artistry to deep sea diving to mathematical genius. And we do know of the so-called savant syndrome, made famous by Dustin Hoffman in the film *Rainman*.

Savants represent a class of individuals who have mysterious talents in mathematical computation, verbal memory, musical performance, artistic skill, or other areas, but who lack the conceptual capacity to use these skills or talents to think through problems, to analyze, generalize. They cannot use these abilities for abstract thinking.[17]

Talent is thus a real, if mysterious, dimension of our intelligence. When linked to the intellectual genius of a Mozart or a Leonardo, a Leibniz or a Feynman, it can represent the crowning glory of what the human brain and its intelligence was destined for.[18]

Few would deny, because of the mysterious, often surprising personal origins of great talent, that it is probably a separate genetically linked characteristic from "g," or I.Q. As of now the exact neurology, or brain areas associated with these unique skills, is still an unknown.

Personality—The current assumption, as we will develop in the next chapter, is that only a small number of important genes contributes to "g." It is probable that the same is true of the "p" factor and of what we call "talent." It is difficult not to view personality as a more complex and diverse coming together of a variety of traits. These contribute to what we see as our individuality, the tonal coloration of personality and vitality that makes each person unique. Personality, some would argue, constitutes "the human core," the essence of our identity. Yet there still can be seen in any one individual such a complex concatenation of behaviors, drives, interests, and peculiarities that they can only reflect a complex genetic heritage.

In the research, the furthest we have gone thus far is an essentially anecdotal set of categories, such as extroverts-introverts, emotionals-phlegmatics, risk takers–home basers.[19] In all probability a large number of genes are involved in the sculpting of an individual's personality considering the enormous and often subtle variability in our personality profiles.

Much research in behavioral genetics, done with identical and fraternal twins, siblings, cousins, and other blood relations in order to factor out environmental shapings of intelligence and behavior, has caused a revolution in our thinking about the nature/nurture controversy.[20]

It is all now part of our media lore. One recent example broadcast over NBC television news programs by Dr. Dean Edel, a medical commentator, exemplifies the growing biological perception of our personality configuration. Research throughout the world with regard to divorce patterns of identical and fraternal twins, Edel affirmed, show that if one identical twin was divorced it was far more likely than in the case of fraternal twins that the other twin would also be divorced.[21]

Over a wide range of personality factors—the kind of spouse one chooses, one's career interests, avocations, taste in clothes—nature wins out decisively over nurture even when these twins are separated from each other from birth or shortly after. There is the by-now famous story from the Minnesota monozygotic twin study of the two Jims, identical twins raised apart from birth until they met at age thirty-seven, who both married first wives names Linda, married second wives named Betty, had been sheriff's deputies, vacationed in the same Florida beach resort, liked the same brands of beer and cigarettes, were avid woodworkers, and had each built a white painted bench around a tree in their yard, without knowing about each other.[22]

INTELLIGENT FARMERS EQUAL POWERFUL NATIONS

Let us examine what it is in the mental possibilities of those with high intelligence that makes them productive and often wealthy.

The modern farmer is an abstract symbolic analyst. Members of advanced societies don't often come into contact with raw subsistence reality—hunted game, the pointed stick turning the soil for the seed. The modern farmer cares for a multitude of specialized machines, consulting manuals for maintenance and repair. Constant reading of weather and climate reports, governmental publications on new seed, fertilizer, anti-bacterial and pest treatments, study of the complex price support programs, as well as decision making about whether or when to take land out of production, feed cattle, or plant other crops, are all part of a modern farmer's job.

The farmer has to plan next year's program, of necessity speculating on the commodity futures market in Chicago, prices at the storage bins in the area, as well as negotiate the usual yearly bank loans, now linked to the interest rates set on Wall Street. Add to this picture the requirement to lobby one's congressperson, or even the Department of Agriculture in Washington, D.C., and we understand that this "farmer" is more corporate technologist than classical agriculturist.[23]

The vaunted productivity of the American farmer inheres only partly in the richness of midwest soil. The farmer is now as much conservationist as exploiter of the potential plenty that lies under the surface of the land. Great and rich lands exist in the Sudan, Zimbabwe, Ukraine, Russia. The "plenty" exists within the brain of the farmer, his ability to utilize the latest scientific knowledge, the personal "p"-factor discipline of hard, rigorous, day-to-day commitment to the task.

The transformation of Israel from a desert to an agriculturally self-sufficient society is not merely the result of contributions from the Israelis' wealthy American brethren. The Arab oil sheiks have incalculably greater wealth. Examine by comparison the situation in Egypt, Jordan, and Yemen, even the West Bank. You will have to be struck by the reality of the human factor as creating the line between poverty and plenty in the lives of individuals, and thus in the destiny of their nations.[24]

Our experiences are suffused with abstract concepts, stock options, computer programs, "just-in-time" production and supply ordering systems, an avalanche of guidelines, laws, requirements, dials, formulas, symbols, reports, proposals, catalogs. It is almost as if no reality existed beyond the human symbol system, a weave and warp of ideas, hypotheses, experiments, refutations, claims. What kind of intelligence can order this world into a dynamic three-dimensional web within which individuals have to make sense of their position, possibilities, talents, and expectations?

Daniel Seligman, an editor for some forty years at America's business magazine, *Fortune*, writes about the hundreds of corporate CEOs that he met over the years:

> To get the job, executives must have tackled a fair number of complex business problems in the early and middle years of their careers and demonstrated an ability to think strategically about those problems. They must have avoided the screwups that inevitably overtake the not-so-smart. Executives also tend to need verbal reasoning skills. It helps in particular to have the ability to dominate the argument in meetings with peers and colleagues, something not possible if you keep getting your facts wrong and your logic muddled.[25]

Industrial psychologists John E. Hunter of Michigan State University, and Frank L. Schmidt and Michael K. Judiesch of the University of Iowa, have attempted to quantify the difference in efficiency between individuals of different intellectual levels, relative to different difficulty levels of their work.

They find that the top workers, in terms of intelligence, were always much more efficient than the lower levels. However, the more complex the task, the greater became the efficiency of the top workers, not merely over average or below-average workers, but over the next level down. "In the 'high complexity' area (managers, professionals, and some technical workers), the top 1 percent was 127% better than the average . . ." In a study of professional budget analysts, they estimated that the "dollar value" productivity of superior performers (defined in this case as the top 15 percent) was $23,000 a year greater than that of the low performers (the bottom 15 percent).

Hunter, Schmidt, and Judiesch believe that a switch to "g" or I.Q. testing before hiring or promotion to high-complexity jobs would yield a productivity gain two and one half times as great as it would for low complexity positions.[26]

Just imagine the ultimate results by the early 1990s of the 1980s competition of American auto corporations, had General Motors had the leadership of Lee Iacocco rather than Roger Smith, the latter still a patently intelligent person.[27]

The I.Q. profile of the Japanese gives them an overall advantage of from 4 to 7 points over American whites. Their educational profiles show an enormous advantage in mathematics, the symbol system *par excellence*.[28] Their average fiftieth-percentile high school seniors outscore our top 5 percent, and almost equal our top 1–2 percent.[29]

Fully 50 percent of our high school seniors cannot solve junior high school math and science problems. Our reading comprehension scores are just as poor. African-American students represent less than 1 percent of the students who are prepared for college-level work in science, math, and literacy. African-American I.Q.s average in the 80–85 range, at least twenty points behind the Japanese average. Less than 1 percent of the Ph.D.s in physics in recent years have gone to African-Americans.[30]

Economist Fred Warshafsky and David Kearns, head of Xerox, estimate that American businesses spend between $2 and $2.5 billion per year in remedial training for their workers.[31] And Lester Thurow, Robert Reich, and Bill Clinton speak confidently of retraining our American workers. They ought first to ask why the workers were not trained or educated to modern standards in the first place.

Where is the plethora of talents that poured forth after World War II to stimulate our nation to world leadership in a variety of technologies and services? Edwin Land of Polaroid, Ken Olsen of Digital, and Sam Walton of Walmart are examples of this older generation; Bill Gates of Microsoft, a Harvard University dropout, is perhaps an example of a vanishing contemporary breed.

Another example is Carl Icahn, a by-now classic takeover operative of USX and TWA, who has parlayed a brilliant ability to manipulate the financial markets to the tune of personal wealth in at least the hundreds of millions of dollars. Icahn began his higher educational career at Princeton as a philosophy major. This is another of the many confirmations of the concept of "g" for high general abstract intelligence.

As we noted earlier, many decades ago the psychologist Raymond Cattell warned us, using his native England as an example, that as the level of intelligence in a nation declined, and given that the curve was a regular one, in other words, not too many unabsorbed minorities with varying intellectual profiles, the nation would inevitably pay a higher premium for those rarer high intelligences necessary to maintain the civilizational functioning of the society.[32]

This may have already happened to the United States. As noted earlier, where the remuneration differential in Japan and Germany between on-the-line production workers and top executives stands at a ratio of between 12 and 15 to 1, in the United States it approaches ten times that differential, 100–150 to 1.[33]

The kind of society that we see being created around the world—a modern international information-processing culture—requires a uniformly high level of educated intelligence to maintain the functioning and coordination of all its strands. Because of the interdependence of all the national parts, a breakdown in any one area of worker competency could lead to chaos everywhere. The need for competency, indeed brilliance, of innovative ability at the more central foci of productive and even governmental efficiency, requires that a nation pay for what it gets, to the point of importing foreign talent if necessary.

What is interesting is that the Japanese understand the historic intelligence/creative talent superiority that has existed for the United States, and that the Caucasian advantage, in general, may lie in its more wide-ranging intellectual profile. This requires the Japanese to tap into this remaining American talent, also using our resident foreign students and researchers by setting up their research labs at crucial talent centers around the United States. In turn, they are paying these individuals sums that only American CEOs earn.

THE MEANING OF THE FREE MARKET

It is important that we not view high intelligence in its free market functioning as symbolizing mere crass financial accumulation. The varying combinations of talent and personality, along with "p," argue for individuals who have a variety of interests and commitments. That is the meaning of civilization. High "g" argues for a capacity to visualize experience abstractly, to see ever-new relationships arising from this three-dimensional meaning pattern of experiences.

Great civilizations spill out these individual talents, for the arts, political charisma, scientific curiosity and envisionment, religious depth of sensitivity, for an infinite variety of contributing symbol systems of meaning. The higher the national level of individual intelligences the richer the contributions in every conceivable area of human fascination, including entrepreneurship.

An important aspect of material wealth and plenty is that when a society possesses them, they flow spontaneously out into other, less materialistic areas of life. That should be abundantly clear to anyone who has ever taken a comparative civilization course. The wealthy, whether through their own interests or those of their spouses, wish to experience the fruits of their wealth. The greatest creative minds of all time, of necessity high "g" types themselves, whether in literature, painting, or science, have been the beneficiaries of the surplus wealth of the creative entrepreneurs' high "g."

Hans Eysenck, who is researching the psychology of creativity, is persuaded that creative contributions of a major sort are made by persons whose I.Q.s are not below 115. This is one standard deviation above the norm of 100, not an exceptionally high I.Q.[34] Seventy years ago Lewis Terman researched the nature and destiny of 1,540 gifted adolescents in California. These so-called geniuses had an average I.Q. of 153. Over a period of forty years their progress was studied and recorded by Terman and his successors.[35]

The conclusion was that these individuals, both men and women, led highly productive lives, and were physically, mentally, and socially above average in health. They contributed to our society as judges, teachers, and entrepreneurs. Interestingly, none achieved supreme eminence in any particular creative manner. Financially, they ended their careers far above the average.

Two young men, William Shockley and Luis Alvarez, recommended by their mothers but rejected from the study because their verbal I.Q.s were not up to their math achievement levels, did go on to win Nobel prizes in physics, evidence for Eysenck's claim about the modest level of intelligence required to push back the frontiers of today's "givenness."[36] What is required, Eysenck argues, are personality factors that dissolve the seeming fixed boundaries of the existing structure of symbolic reality, an imagination that in more fragile creatures might partake of dementia.

The ancient Greeks institutionalized such factors in the creative personalities of their people, in the Orphic and Dionysian mysteries, rituals and practices that went far beyond normal behavioral practices. Institutionalized and ritualized, such high emotional cultural events freed minds from the normal social conventions that could impede creativity.

The lesson that the mysteries of creative human behavior present to us lies in the fact that individuals with extremely high intelligence are still ordinary human beings, having the same emotional throbbing as the rest of us. But the individual of high intelligence can also transmute these juices into disciplined symbolic efforts and products.

The nation as a whole thus can reverberate to an exhilarating dynamic of creativity at all points in the cultural symbolic palette. To open up a society to any one dimension of the creative free market of entrepreneurship inevitably—if one follows this basic principle—allows for the explosive entrepreneurship of the society at all levels. Thus we create a civilization.

Chapter 9

The Tragedy of Low Intelligence

For if human social organization, including the inequalities of status, wealth, and power, are a direct consequence of our biologies, then except for some gigantic program of genetic engineering, no practice can make a significant alteration of social structure or of the position of individuals or groups within it.

R. C. Lewontin, Harvard University, 1984[1]

SILENT DISASTER

In the early 1990s about 4 million live births were recorded each year in the United States. Of these, approximately 1 million were born to unmarried women. The rate of illegitimacy in the United States has spiraled upward in the past 20–25 years, to where in 1992 it stands at about 28 percent of our yearly births.[2]

Some of these can be attributed to persons of means and tragedy such as Mia Farrow and Woody Allen, who chose not to marry. Whether the prognosis for such children as theirs when they come of age in and about 2010 is any better than for the vast majority of children born to the mostly poor unwed mothers remains to be seen.

But if the current economic, educational, and social debacle that we see overtaking the current cohort of young Americans born in the 1970s is any indication for the future of these humans as individuals, and then for our nation as a whole, we are now in a crisis situation.

What can be said of the potential of this oncoming generation of citizens is speculative. The evidence of today, however, is suggestive and should be placed before the reader and the public for any possible refutation. What it points to is a tragedy in terms of the life possibilities of a large and increasing percentage of our population. Inevitably it poses a perplexing series of questions and challenges for the nation as a whole.

These issues must be discussed. We are today, as a nation, *at risk*.

CONTROVERSIAL CONSIDERATIONS

The U.S. armed services are attempting to eliminate the lowest categories of individuals using the AFQT I.Q. tests. Individuals with I.Q. equivalents between 80 and 92 are to be refused enlistment. The services also believe that only those individuals with a reputable high school diploma are valuable.[3]

Our educational evidence argues that about 75 percent of our seventeen- and eighteen-year-olds receive a high school diploma of some kind,[4] but basic math tests given to seventeen-year-olds still in school show that less than 50 percent can do seventh-grade math.[5] Our educational system has supposedly improved in the math skill areas, given the higher math SAT scores, as contrasted with verbal understanding—the skill that most scientists believe is more highly "g" loaded for intelligence.

Given the older statistics for I.Q. levels in our society, whites score at about 100, African-Americans at 82–85, Hispanics somewhere in between, Native Americans also in the low to mid-90s. Clearly, considering the rapidly changing demographic structure in the United States in the past twenty-five years concerning who is having children, these estimates may already be too high by several I.Q. points.

Note, by way of anecdotal evidence, that not only does our first lady, Mrs. Clinton, have only one child, but in early 1993, the three female nominees for attorney general of the United States shared two-thirds of a child. Certainly these are all brilliant and highly educated women. Of course, the responsibility here ought not all be placed on the female side. There are too many millions of our most intelligent and educated citizens, male and female, without families.

Would it be too hypothetical to argue that the inability to do no better than seventh-grade math at age seventeen argues for an individual I.Q. somewhat below 100? On the recent international test of thirteen-year-olds noted in Chapter 5, in which mainland Chinese students were scoring 80 on seventh-grade math tests as compared to the U.S. 55, and given that these often rural Chinese were scoring at about 101 I.Q. even with an as yet undeveloped educational system, the above estimate for an average U.S. intelligence may not be far off the mark.[6] Other tests of Chinese I.Q. under more Western and therefore more comparable educational situations, given in Singapore and Hong Kong, show the Chinese to be scoring at a mean I.Q. of 110; English, 100; and Malays, 96.[7]

Would it be too venturesome to argue that 100 I.Q. would demonstrate itself in a true ninth grade, international level of achievement for fifteen-year-olds? Perhaps the U.S. I.Q. in the age thirty and below category, taking into consideration these equivalent seventh-grade achievement levels, and remembering that about 25 percent of our seventeen-year-olds were not included in the testing, having already dropped out of school, would be about 95 I.Q. Of course, it is important to remember that in ethnic pockets within this overall U.S. population, as, for example, within the increasing number of northeast Asians and within the fast disappearing Jewish ethnicity, the averages would be much higher.

SURVIVAL OF THE INTELLIGENT

The table of the distribution of intelligence over occupations summarizes data with regard to traditional skilled occupations during the period 1934–54. It doesn't conflict with more recent data derived from Defense Department and other sources. More important, however, are its implications for the competition amongst nations to survive and prosper in a rapidly intellectualizing techno-economic international structure. (See Table 3.)

The new technology is eliminating persons of less than 92 I.Q. from our armed services, eliminating millions of routine manufacturing jobs, through the increasing "intelligence" of roboticized and automated computer-guided machinery and processes. The modern supermarket, where clerks no longer tally the prices of goods, heralds the expansion of part-time unskilled and minimum wage labor for an increasing percentage of our population who cannot graduate into the upper level jobs requiring higher intelligence and educational accomplishment.

The intelligent are now creating increasingly dynamic conditions whereby the less skilled tasks and thus jobs are being eliminated by "cheaper" machines or cheaper labor. Mexico, with a population of 80 million and an increasingly efficient educational system, is rapidly becoming a satellite industrial center for U.S. and other developed nations' industries. The wages are one dollar an hour, and at a mean I.Q. level of about 95 this nation can produce millions of highly qualified technicians and workers without ever worrying about giving jobs to the less competitive because of their ascriptive ethnic or gender characteristics.

In the 1990s in Mexico an intellectual elite is being formed that will in turn push back into the dim margins of society those Mexicans unable to master modern intellectual skills. They can soon, as we are today experiencing in the United States, expect to see the basis for their traditional subsistence existence swept away by machines and by the intelligence that invents and then oversees their use.

Table 3
Occupational Means of Intelligence Based Partly on Army Drafts (American Data and English Data)

Distribution of Intelligence over Occupations

Occupation	Mean	
Professors and Researchers	134	(C1)
Professors and Researchers	131	(C2)
Physicians and Surgeons	128	(C1)
Lawyers	128	(H&H)
Engineers (Civil and Mechanical)	125	(C1)
Schoolteachers	123	(C)
Schoolteachers	123	(H&H)
Schoolteachers	121	(H&W)
General Managers in Business	122	(C)
Educational Administrators	122	(C)
Pharmacists	120	(H&H)
Accountants	119	(C1)
Accountants	128	(H&H)
Nurses	119	(C1)
Stenographers	118	(C)
Stenographers	121	(H&H)
Efficiency (Time Engineer) Specialists	118	(C)
Senior Clerks	118	(C)
Managers, Production	118	(H&H)
Managers, Miscellaneous	116	(H&H)
Cashiers	116	(H&H)
Airmen (USAF)	115	(H&H)
Foremen (Industry)	114	(C)
Foremen	109	(H&H)
Telephone Operators	112	(C)
Clerks	112	(C)
Clerks, General	118	(H&H)
Salesmen (Traveling)	112	(C)
Salesmen (Door to Door)	108	(C)

Occupation	Mean	
Salesmen	114	(H&H)
Psychiatric Aides	111	(C&S)
Electricians	109	(H&H)
Policemen	108	(C)
Fitters (Precision)	108	(C1)
Fitters	98	(H&W)
Mechanics	106	(H&H)
Machine Operators	105	(H&H)
Store Managers	103	(C)
Shopkeepers	103	(H&W)
Upholsterers	103	(H&H)
Butchers	103	(H&H)
Welders	102	(H&H)
Sheet Metal Workers	100	(C)

Combined results on occupation means from Cattell (C, C1, C2) (1934), Harrell and Harrell (H & H) (1945), Himmelweit and Whitfield (H & W) (1944), and Cattell and Shotwell (C & S) (1954).

Source: Cattell, R. B. 1983. "The Role of Psychological Testing." In *Intelligence and National Achievement*. Ed. by Cattell, R. B. Washington, D.C.: Cliveden Press, 19–69.

Over 145,000 highly skilled Mexicans graduate each year from Mexico's best universities, technical institutes, and secondary schools. Today these Mexicans are being absorbed by the new *maquiladoras* just south of the U.S. border.[8] Soon they will be transforming the nature of labor and the economy in that nation. Without traditional forms of economic sustenance what will happen to that vast mass at the bottom of the social ladder? What is their intellectual and thus educational potential in terms of the international economy as well as their internal ecological possibilities for survival in their own country?

Already by 1994, let alone 2010, roughly half of the American population can be seen to be sinking below international levels of intellectual and educational achievement requisite to the dollar productivity of this world standard. What is to become of these individuals, and then of the formerly wealthy nation that encouraged their coming into being?

Recent scientific research into the comparative mental power of different I.Q. levels, this time coming out of Germany, lends increased weight to our personal fears for the less capable. It also should increase our concern for the evolving worldwide tragedy that is quietly engulfing us.

The research of geneticists (not psychologists or psychometricians) G. Lerle, D. Frank, and V. Weiss has begun to reconceptualize the meaning of I.Q. differences. Stemming from the puzzling fact of large sibling differences in I.Q., they view the significance of "g"—general intelligence—as constituting the product of a very small number of genes.

The older polygenic model in use for so many years saw "g" as a blending of a large number of genes, or "factors," constituting the elements that make up the numerical unity given in an individual's I.Q. score. However, the differences from one brother and sister to the other are too great to constitute a blending of many genes. Thus they view "g" as the product of a "major gene locus."[9]

The result of this analysis is to view the numerical differences in I.Q. scores as signifying very different levels of intellectual power. For example, the difference between an I.Q. of 70 and one of 94, a 24-point difference, not quite two standard deviations, and the difference between I.Q. 94 and 130, 36 points, slightly more than two standard deviations, they see as each constituting a 100 percent difference in intellectual capabilities. "In populations with a mean of 90 a decrease of I.Q. related achievements of above 10% seems to be suggested; in reality in such populations the gene frequency of M1 [I.Q.130] is zero and the achievements of such populations are accordingly meager."[10]

An I.Q. of 70 is widely considered to be borderline retarded. An I.Q. of 130 is, in a European context, thought to be in the top 5 percent. There is a vast evolutionary distance between these two respective capacities for thought. But it is not revolutionary to analyze these differences in capacity, as such.

However, it *is* a radical deviation from previous understanding to view the very normal range of 94 I.Q. as being half as powerful as that of a 130 I.Q. person. It is also radical to view the 130 I.Q. gene as a tangible reality that, in its various combinations with the "p" factor genes and with the talent and personality elements of our intelligence, constitutes the kernel unit of extremely high intelligence, perhaps genius.

But wait. Hasn't the Department of Defense already pointed to the 75 percent superiority in tank gunnery efficiency of those over 105 I.Q. compared to those soldiers in the 80–92 I.Q. range? Furthermore, Hunter, Schmidt, and Judiesch have shown that managers, professionals, and technical workers of the top 1 percent achievement levels produce at levels 127 percent better than only average persons.[11]

Because of the quiet but tangible reality of these facts of human nature, what we see around the world as well as in our country is a competitive scramble to secure a high economic, intellectual, educational position. To find and educate these highly intelligent individuals ought now to become the overriding purpose of national policy. The stakes are both personal and national survival.

For the flood of other humans now being born into a world of diminishing horizons the prognosis is decidedly pessimistic. The intelligent, on the other hand, quickly perceive the nature of this new map of natural and social reality and act accordingly.

Recall what happened in south Florida several decades ago, when the middle-class refugees from Cuba displaced tens of thousands of African-Americans in the hotel, restaurant, and other industries.[12]

Then came the Koreans to the storefronts of South Central Los Angeles, innocently creating the conditions for the violence of 1992 in that city. In the early 1980s, the Caucasian majority in British Columbia instituted new admission requirements for medical school in that Canadian province because the Chinese minority was gaining a disproportionate number of places based on purely objective intellectual and academic requirements.[13]

Some argue that this same condition occurred in liberal Weimar Germany where the Jews moved into a wide variety of prominent areas of public life: the arts, industry, politics, academia, and so forth, thence to bring the wrath of Hitler down upon them.[14] These are ethnic exemplars of the pressure that high intelligent individuals exert in the natural give and take of economic, educational, and social competition. It takes place just as starkly within ethnic groups, as is the case today in Mexico and China where, ostensibly, ethnic rivalries are not as clear.

It is one thing for the economic tide to rise and thus protect the most uncompetitive minds through the social welfare net and its redistributive functions. It is another thing for a wave of births to take place demographically within the most vulnerable segments of society, parallel with a society's slide from competitive dominance.

Considering how many good jobs in the service sector depend upon the productive functioning of the manufacturing or other internationally competitive areas of the American economy, it is not surprising that such a large number of highly educated middle-class types are receiving their pink slips and are thence reentering the marketplace in an attempt to secure other, even borderline middle-class niches.

The result is that down below, the products of that 25 percent plus illegitimacy rate and the other less educable segments of the population slightly above them, those who are reading at the fourth- and fifth-grade levels, are going to be pushed deeper and deeper into the culture of poverty.

The reason for the growth of this demographic segment, decade after decade, is that those at the top are blind or indeed lack the will to close the spigot, the economy that creates and then supports this spreading human tragedy.

The spigot is the economy of welfare that invites illegitimacy in the female, while being incapable of benefiting the fathers or the children. The collapsing educational and cultural infrastructure for our own lower classes is testimony enough to our present incapacity. What about the year 2010, or else a second generation beyond, 2044?

Does it look reasonably hopeful?

THE HIGH WALL

These intellectualized issues tend to obscure the deeply personal impact as to how modest inherent intellectual ability affects the individual. Think of intelligence in its "g" or general abstract ability dimension. Behind and within the individual's sensory intake of information from sight, sound, touch, smell, and taste exists a vast neurological processing machine. The function of this maze of "wires" and interconnections is to create a multi-dimensional map of the world, experienced as the individual encounters it from his or her earliest days of life.

The map serves individuals as a guide for further behavior or learning. The world becomes meaningful through this map, and, together with the understanding that is generated within those individuals, always through dint of further education in the skills that build a deeper, more richly complex guide to causes and consequences, individuals are thrust by their drives and interests to become a dynamic part of the outside reality of things.

The individuals of limited intelligence obtain only a dim perception of the interrelationships in this external drama. They see mostly the surface shimmer of events, rarely the deeper causes, elements of "unfinished" business that education could reveal to them in terms of an exciting and inviting vocation or profession.

If they have enough "p" factor, they can be disciplined to do a simple job day in, day out, with fair regularity, usually with limited mental energy or initiative. But the correlation of "g" with "p" is what one expects. Understanding breeds initiative and interest, then effort. The drive to succeed implies a conception of what one wants to succeed at, and usually a sense of the correct pathways to be taken to go from ambition to realization.[15]

The less intelligent are not able to profit from the usual educational instrumentalities of schooling. Because of their own inner failure to perceive what this schooling is all about, they usually fall into the path of least resistance in the menu of momentary seductions, whether the pathologies of alcohol or drugs or the easy indulgences of sex. They see a world of glitter and gold, and they perceive the advantages that money and privilege bring, especially with films and television blasting their tantalizing, if simple, messages. And they will often take the opportunity, criminal or not, to obtain these objects—big cars, jewelry, electronics, whatever.

On the other hand, many of the less intelligent exist in a state of silent panic. It is a world that has no meaning or pathways that can lead to acceptable fulfillments, and they perceive this. Some will react in self-destructive passivity, others in equally self-destructive activity, the latter constituting at the least a functional attempt at personal survival. The future as consequence might as well not exist. Many individuals have borderline intellectual and educational skills. They can work the McDonalds' type of jobs. They are steady, and live within a limited if temporarily functioning universe.

But what happens when technology catches up with them, as it has in the auto and steel industries? For these latter, it has been one enormous step down to night watchman, custodian, or some other non-skilled job, all the time dreading the inevitable "modernization" that will once more, perhaps finally, render them and their loved ones redundant. Their economic basis for life has been pulled out from under them, their intellectual and educational potentialities incapable of advancing them to keep up with a changing world standard. What happens to their children, molded from similar genetic intellectual potentiality? Is it reasonable to speak of retraining?

For those at the borders of functional educability, the present situation is an unmitigated disaster. There are those of ability—we preempt the protest—who do not profit from or thrive in a formal schooling setting. They set off on their own and become legends. Fine. A small amount of formal schooling, for example, learning to read enough to learn to access the deep and rich maps of knowledge in a book, will allow such people to make the world their apple.

They have the potential for building abstract maps of experience, and with inordinate "p"-factor drives, they do not need the assistance and credentials that formal schooling provides for many of us. They once more confirm to us the unlimited power of raw intellectual potential and the significance of the "postponement and persistence" factors, as they come together to explode into tangibility, often wealth, even well-earned fame.

OUR UNDERCLASS

In the last decade or so, a new element, the homeless, has been added to the term *underclass*. By now, all the sociological authorities agree that the problem is virtually intractable. The homeless not only do not seem to want to work, they cannot work. Our leaders seem blind to this problem. The unending billion-dollar summer "jobs" programs that they enact only serve to prevent us from facing the realities and will eventually have to be halted. Simply, the middle classes will refuse to pay for them.

Once the programs are finished, the necessary drive to seek work and the requisite skills to find jobs that are both useful and pleasurable disappear. What follows is an almost inevitable drift into the underground economy of drugs, sex, illegitimacy and welfare, crime, gangs, homelessness, eventually tragedy.

Lawrence Mead, a frustrated and sobered liberal sociologist, phrases it this way: "Over years, mandates for higher behavioral standards must be implemented and defended against challenges. The nation's identity is at stake. The majority of Americans, black and white, evidently reject the ethos of resignation that pervades ghetto areas. They continue to affirm the faith of this very Western nation that effort is meaningful and individuals can be held accountable for their fate."[16]

There is no systematic attempt to link their intellectual potential with school failures or the pathologies of mental illness and substance abuse that eventually riddle their behaviors. Nor are there longitudinal studies that will trace the lineage of these failures at the least through the mothers to discover which correlations of intergenerational dependency and pathology can be linked with which biological profiles.

The reason for this is that the established ideology refuses to accept the possibility that such behaviors might have a genetic cause. To admit the possibility of such a linkage would be tantamount to being a member of the Ku Klux Klan. It does no good to point out that there are millions of African-Americans and Latinos who do not suffer such pathologies. And, of course, there are millions of whites who do.

Beyond this type of refusal is the awareness that to admit the existence of this "elephant in the corner" can lead inexorably to the conclusion that, if we are to diminish this American plague, our overriding priority would be to slow the flow of new children born into such pain and horror. To contemporary liberals, illegitimacy is one of the lifestyle options available to Woody Allen and Mia Farrow. Why not also to the thirteen-year-olds in South Central Los Angeles?

Perhaps there is hope for sober reason. Breaking through the censorship and taboos that had blocked the Human Genome Project on "Genetics and Violence" at the University of Maryland in 1992, *Time* magazine subsequently headlined the possibility that biology might be an important dimension to the sources of individual violence and crime.[17]

INTERNATIONAL MALFEASANCE

It hasn't dawned on the international community that a great and tragic act of injustice is again being committed against a major portion of the human race. Content to live within the protected ideological membrane of innocence, this community is allowing part of our humanity to go under. It should be a lesson for our own leadership. For if those far away are slipping under, might we not be far behind?

Take Africa, for example. The radical left, once so smug about the horrors of colonialism, just as smugly trumpeted how all those London School of Economics graduates would return home to build utopia in their homelands, finally freed from the white man's heel. Now, one former colonial city after another sinks back into the forest.[18] Political and military chaos, terror served up by home-grown tyrants, now starvation and AIDS. The hint is that utopia may be postponed for at least a couple of centuries. We now even read in newspapers such as the *New York Times* that colonialism has returned to the Third World, and that it is none too soon.[19]

The United Nations was considering in late 1992 whether to institute a semi-permanent army of occupation in Somalia to avoid further starvation and chaos in that country. If Somalia, are Mozambique, Sudan, Angola, Uganda, India, Bangladesh, Pakistan, Cambodia, Brazil, Peru, and Nicaragua far behind?

Do we seriously think that these nation/tribes still have any chance of attaining a standard of living, technological and productive sophistication, or educational levels that rival Japan or Europe? None but those with the most delusionary ideological expectations dares to express such *hybris*. The people of the southern Third World are flooding north into Europe and North America to tell us about their expectations for their future lives at home.

Then why aren't more people giving some serious thought to causes and solutions, real solutions, not the continuing hallucinations of ideological and momentary political expediency? Richard Lynn, a psychologist from the University of Ulster, has surveyed the research into I.Q. from Western, ostensibly middle-class, schools in a variety of African nations. The results come in at about a mean of 70 I.Q.[20] This, of course, cannot be. Scores such as this in the United States would be labeled as those of seriously retarded children. The African-American mean is in the 80–85 I.Q. range.

These African children surely suffer from culture shock. They may be sitting and memorizing European-style knowledge, but their minds and souls are far away. What kind of potential do they have? Clearly, whether the answer is a purely biological one of genetic intelligence, or of bad testing, or of true cultural alienation, the experiential results of this educational failure can be seen in each of these now dissolving *nations* out there in the real world.

Educational non-achievement speaks clearly to the social, political, and economic dependency rapidly throwing Africa back into the rescuing colonial arms of the developed world.

SADNESS

The implications here are stark. The pathologies that afflict the citizenry of Third World nations, else in the minority *favellas* of the developed world, are not remediable through more social work philanthropies, *de rigueur* in the mentality of dogmatic liberalism. Neither will the constant outpouring of aid, either to indigenous underclass communities or to the nations of the Third World, ever be more than conscience money, a palliative that will have to be renewed indefinitely until the donor nations themselves collapse.

Low human intelligence relative to an explosively cerebralized techno-economic and cultural world community has resulted in the historical obsolescence of a vast proportion of the oncoming population of our planet.

We in the United States are deeply involved in the fate and future of the people caught in this time warp of history. The sooner we face the hard facts of our existential circumstances, the sooner we may be able to extract ourselves from the inevitable fate that faces the Third World. By first confronting the realities of our own internal domestic tragedy, we may eventually be able to extend a *real* helping hand to the rest of the human community.

Here is sociologist Lawrence Mead's sad admission of the limits of the welfare system in the United States: "People really cannot be responsible for more than a part of their fate. Yet, the belief that they can be seems essential to both personal happiness and a healthy society, at least as most Americans understand things. Society must affirm individual responsibility, at least for personal conduct, or lives lose control and collective trust decays. To exempt people from minimal standards of civility on grounds they cannot cope would tempt the poor, and others with them, toward a collective slough of despond. That way, most Americans feel, lies the abyss."[21]

Part II

RENEWAL

Chapter 10

Defensive Driving

Where the willingness is great, the difficulties cannot be great.
Niccolò Machiavelli (1513)[1]

PRIORITIES

The hedgehog knows one thing, survival. No temptations on the freeway. The exuberant foxes out there zooming along at 80 m.p.h., let them enjoy it, until the inevitable crash. At intersections, the hedgehog slows up, yields the right of way. From the red light, it is one of the last to spurt beyond the stop line. No competition to anyone out there, the hedgehog knows where it is going, what needs to be done in order to get there. It keeps its priorities clear—survival and ultimate victory over all the sporty foxes.

DESTINATION

Let us first be clear about our problem—uneven national productivity and too few well-paying jobs by international standards. But it is much more than that, economically.

It is about a formal and informal educational system, our schools and our culture. The schools have not provided our young with the skills and knowledge to make them competitive with the young of the modern world. But it is much more than that, educationally.

This is a nation in which large portions of our citizenry have been beset by social pathologies. It should concern our people that our behavioral relativism is leading us into social confusion and chaos. But it is much more than that, socially.

The problem *is* centered on the enormously variable levels of intelligence potential in the diverse population groups of the United States. Indeed, it is *not* a purely racial or ethnic issue. Those at the bottom of the intellectual pyramid come from all groups, white, African-American, Latino, and others.

Intellectually competent and potentially contributing individuals come from all the above groups and others. They are a national treasure. We need to see their numbers multiply and help reverse the dramatic slide into Third World incompetence of large segments of the residents in the United States.

The reality of variable human intelligence has been around for a long time. Until recently we were not touched by it because the basic European origins of the American people allowed for our competitive equality with the home countries. Also, our remoteness from the wars and revolutions of Europe gave us a measure of insularity, a sense of immunity from such travails.

Pearl Harbor dragged us into a wholly new situation. As Admiral Yamamoto noted, the sleeping giant began to stir, and for a brief generation we inflated ourselves with power, wealth, philanthropy, and a sense of infinite moral virtue. The efficient, if impractical, *Zero* fighters that the Japanese designed should have forewarned us. But even the Europeans in their smug postwar recovery were caught unawares of a new intellectual center of power, and a new way to fight the old wars over who is truly smarter.

That's our problem. We need to increase our intelligence levels so that we can reverse the declining state of our national profile. It is a disaster-in-the-making. Every thinking citizen knows that it is happening, but few dare to diagnose it as it really is.

For the past forty years we have been engaged in a crusade to eliminate domestic inequalities. We have wound up by widening these inequalities geometrically. Yet those who presume to serve us as political, communications, and intellectual leaders have not had the faintest insight or courage to question the nature of this social policy catastrophe.

INTELLIGENCE IS TIME-BINDING

The United States has violated an ancient principle, one that goes back in evolution practically to the beginning of multi-cellular life. This principle is based on the very nature of the animal adaptation of intelligence. *Intelligence is the defensive adaptation*. It is the last to develop in the great breakthroughs experienced by various lines of creatures in the long evolutionary hegira of the multi-cellular forms of life, which first triumphed in the gill-breathing teleost fishes some 400 million years ago.[2]

Intelligence as a biological adaptation can be contrasted with other adaptations. Some animals use size, ferocity, inconspicuousness, fecundity, or various ecological specializations. The snails and ammonites at the ocean bottoms are highly specialized animals. So are the bluebird and the mountain lion. Intelligent creatures survive by learning from experience. They are fitted with nervous systems and brains that allow them to change their behavior to adapt to changing circumstances.

Most intelligent creatures use their adaptation to stay out of harm's way. They tend to be explorers, finding ever new ways of making a living, avoiding direct conflicts with creatures with more specialized, often temporarily dominant physical adaptations.

By becoming gradually freed from the genetic instinctual rigidities of specialization, whether they be intelligent fish, reptiles, birds, or anthropoids, they survive in their various ecologies by being generalists. Given any major change in the world environment around them, their flexibility of response gives them a distinct advantage over the narrow and momentarily successful rivals.

We humans are the inheritors of the adaptation of intelligence as it has been passed forward to the mammals and then the anthropoids. The concept of "g" for general intelligence, of which the psychometricians speak, represents that evolutionary gift of natural selection to humans. If we use it well, then we will be ready for the unknown. General intelligence argues for an ability to learn new skills, try out new life pathways.[3]

Above all, intelligence is the ability to be able to look ahead. Intelligence can give one person or nation an understanding of the nature of things and thus the ability to plan ahead, to bind time, as if the future were today.

The concept of a liberal arts education has emerged from this silent awareness of the need for humans to educate for unknown possibilities. Liberal arts education connotes the education of the generalist, the learner forever reeducating him- or herself.[4]

Thus, the law of evolutionary survival that the intelligent ones are destined to obey is the law of *defensive driving*. The Germans and the Japanese have learned this principle the hard way, perhaps without being fully aware of its ancient evolutionary message. We, too, must rebuild our nation, absorbing the lessons that earlier human societies have given us.

A nation, like an individual, cannot have too much intelligence, as opposed to great size, or even fecundity. In the latter cases, creatures tend to denude their environments of resources. Inevitably, mass starvation and the decimation of the animal line occur. Look at nations that unthinkingly overwhelm their environments with people or destroy the natural ecology. Is it difficult to predict the dismal future of these nations a few decades down the line?

A wise society, like an intelligent individual, does not reject a full consideration of the meaning of events by erecting ideological barriers or taboos. That the world community has suppressed such clearly available knowledge with regard to the variability of human intelligence has to stand as the preeminent element in our incipient collapse.

In fact, such intellectual taboos, or narrow sectarian forms of thinking, violate the very *raison d'être* of intelligence. The twentieth-century totalitarian ideologies that contaminated the reason of so many ostensibly wise people and their national leadership testify to this truth. Our recent experience with the Marxist/communist world is an example of reason's failure. This world flourished momentarily because it freed deep emotional forces that ran rampant over the wisdom of history.

That this ideology has now collapsed from within should warn us of the need for open debate, the full consideration of all ideas that might clarify a nation's situation. This is the deeper significance of the democratic way of life. It should open the society to the full consideration of possibilities. It broadens the base of decision making to the intelligence of all the people. The leadership of such a nation, given high on-average education and "g," or general intelligence, will tend to reflect the wisdom of its people.

INTELLIGENCE IS SOBRIETY

Another evolutionary element in the development of both individual and national intelligence must be emphasized. This is the "p" factor. Postponement and persistence are two ways of seeing this dimension of our intellectual biology at work. The "p" factor is the power element that gives voice to "g."

Centered in the frontal areas of the cortex of the brain, the "p" factor is in humans freed from any specialized instinctual response. Now it allows humans to overrule the passionate pleadings of the mammalian sectors of our brain and personalities: sex, aggression, patriotism, ethnic nationalism, religious millennialism, all elements in the human cultural pantheon that nature has raised up so powerfully in our biology at the same time that the enormous cortical mass was created to guide us intellectually.

It can be said that the "p" factor is the element of intellectual restraint that short-circuits all those impetuous drives that could dissolve our intellectual "g"-factored considerations. We certainly have seen individuals highly intelligent and well educated, but without controls over their momentary desires and emotions.

There are nations also who have lost this "p"-factored defensive discipline. Intelligence works its way in our massive individual neurology quite slowly. We as individuals need time to think things through. That is why the wise, disciplined "p"-factored individual will say, "Let me sleep on it. I'll let you know my decision tomorrow."[5]

Perhaps America's leaders throughout the period 1945–90 should have said to its people, "Let's sleep on all this potential wealth for a few decades, to figure out how most wisely to develop and utilize it. After all, if one lives as if there were no tomorrow, in all likelihood, there will be none."

In the 1970s, after the discovery of oil off their coast in the North Sea, the Norwegians, traditionally the poor Scandinavian cousins compared to the Danes and Swedes, faced the likelihood of a radical alteration of their social structure by the sudden addition of such potential wealth. This discovery followed the outlay of enormous borrowed sums to develop this undersea treasure.

Their solution was both a "g"- and "p"-factored one. They would allow this wealth to flow into the nation in measured amounts over time. In this way, sudden individual wealth would be limited in its impact. Also, they would use this national treasure to protect their traditional way of life, their ancient institutions, crafts, industries, even social values. The wealth was civic, ethnic. Its use required the assent of the entire population. And, of course, it set a historic course for this nation that would look beyond the 1970s to a new century, to the interests of Norwegians yet unborn.[6]

The Japanese are the most blatant and challenging example, as noted previously. With a wise leadership and an intelligent citizenry, by understanding the nature of the human destiny, at the least by learning from their past mistakes, they are revealing to us the character of our own myopia.

The Japanese, having enormous trade surpluses with the rest of the world—running in the hundreds of billions of dollars each year—have both saved and reinvested this surplus in a vast satellite network of industries throughout the world, a new version of their 1930s imperialistic "co-prosperity sphere," which, in part, set off World War II.[7]

Much to the anger and condescension of the rest of the world, especially the United States, the Japanese standard of living has not advanced in tandem with this wealth. They still live in tiny matchbox houses, paying enormous amounts for beef and domestically protected rice and other foods. And they often work twelve-hour days, six days a week.

The money lies in the corporation, for sponsored tours around the world, for new top-of-the-line technologies which only the Japanese seem to have the intelligence to fabricate, and at all levels of their populace. They are now using some of this extra cash for a multi-billion dollar expansion of their domestic infrastructure—roads, waste management, housing.

They live less affluently than we do. Now! But can there be any doubt that the United States with its $4.5 trillion national debt, yearly deficits now approaching $400 billion, and with a large percentage of its population making a transition from the middle class to the working poor, that this, our own formerly wealthy nation, is inevitably heading into an era of great austerity, if not depression and poverty?

Instead of *defensive driving*, the United States plunged into gigantism, economically, demographically, and socially. Politicians and boosters call it equality, growth, and prosperity. Now, we are feeling the brunt of nature's rude "retribution" for an epochal intellectual miscalculation.

We were lured by the ideological liberalism of the twentieth century, first in believing our own patriotic rhetoric about our anointed eternal omnipotence, and second, in assuming the uniformity of intelligence of the indigenous American population, and of those around the world who were flooding under our gates to help themselves to our munificent welfare system.

STRATEGY

Clearly, all our people feel that our nation's direction must be changed. All hope that the direction will be up. More important is the still inchoate sense by the people that basic assumptions must be corrected, and critical value orientations need to be altered so that a real change in social policy can be effected.

What do I propose, in the light of today's universal American soul searching? Two critical changes are necessary. The first is to stanch our intellectual hemorrhaging. We need to slow, if not stop, the flooding of our population with low intelligence individuals. If we can create social policies that stem the flood of children from the welfare classes of all racial and ethnic groups, then we can create policies that discourage this trend.

At the same time, we must encourage the working, middle, and upper classes who can raise educable and contributing children to take up the slack. This is our national defense, a defense that goes beyond the military; it goes to the very core of our stability and viability as a nation.

The second point also has to do with intelligence, but now, in addition, it has to do with the mysterious deterioration in educational achievement from those social classes of all races and ethnicities from whom one would expect much better educational and economic results. We have to find ways, in education and family life, to improve achievement levels. We have to uncover the reasons for the *environmental* failure, if indeed there are reasons to be so identified.

If we discover, after concretely improving family, schooling, even economic structure over a period of years, that we *can't* get more than 8 or 9 percent of our high school seniors ready for college-level work, then indeed we will know that our declining international intellectual profile is real and, possibly, permanent.[8]

Today, the masking of our incipient national disaster may be due to the fact that we have accumulated much wealth from the older generations, much of it in pension funds and overvalued real estate. Many from this generation are still in the workforce, and in leadership positions. As the leadership is passed on to the generation whose SAT scores began to drop precipitously in the 1970s, the true extent of our crisis will become apparent.

Of course, if we can immediately begin to reverse the American intelligence decline, we could, a generation forward, expect some improvement. This would depend on the existing levels of high creative intelligence that have been salvaged, on possible changes in immigration patterns, and on our success in mobilizing our existing residual talent through a great reconstruction of our social, educational, even economic systems.

The bottom line is this: We have to redirect the institutional structure of the United States so that in the first place we produce more children of high intellectual potential. Then we can restructure our institutions both to stimulate the full development of these children and to reward them as rationally as possible for their contributions to our nation.

LEADERSHIP

The vision ought to extend to 100 years. A citizenry of high intelligence can be persuaded that this is the proper time frame within which, at the least, all planning should take place. In 100 years our grandchildren's grandchildren will themselves be entering a world of hopefully better prospects than their forebears. They could praise us for our vision and discipline.[9]

For this we need a highly intelligent leadership willing to sacrifice its own momentary advantages to teach us—we who have been so poorly educated about reality—that we need to account for the future. Certainly the residual intelligence exists now that could overcome the opportunists and demagogues who will conjure up a fiery assortment of demons to account for the miseries of the moment.

The power to resist will be nurtured by clear teaching about the realities of our international situation, about the manner in which high intelligence, through science, medicine, and technology, has changed our world forever.

The core of the debate over the pathway into the future will be centered on our understanding of the larger nature of our universe, our place in it, and the human context within which these decisions must be made.

If we blind and deafen ourselves with regard to the issue of variable functional intelligence levels in our world and in our nation, all decisions about the future will be as flawed in the twenty-first century as they have been for us in the past two generations. A once great nation will sink into incompetence and poverty, then chaos, finally catastrophe.

The debate must focus around issues that can be concentrated on reversing the downward spiral that the United States is experiencing at the close of the twentieth century. *Defensive driving* is a metaphor that distills the general strategy for nation building and the need to plan for the long term, in the light of the most rational description of human and natural experience that we have available to us.

The question is: Is anyone out there looking or listening?

Chapter 11

The American Family

THE CORE NATIONAL PROBLEM

The nature and future of the American family is not merely an intellectual question. It is a battlefield. The ideological left, having lost so many of its traditional fortress issues, has focused on this already riven institution. Because of the weakening social supports for the family, and with so many hostile constituencies on the attack, the family is a truly endangered phenomenon. Be clear: We refer to the traditional nuclear family.

One of the techniques of revolutionary movements is to confuse by altering the language; confuse the meaning of words and you destroy traditional centers of reason. Thus there are new families being defined and reified into orthodoxy, or so the extreme deviants of our society proclaim.

There are the single-parent families; the non-married heterosexual live-togethers; the gay families. Naturally, they all line up at the trough to extract government benefits that in more non-ideological times were directed at the traditional family, with, Heaven forbid, the male breadwinner and the mother-homemaker, plus dependent children.

This is all *passé* today, and as Pat Buchanan, erstwhile presidential candidate and perennial ultra-conservative television personality phrased it at the 1992 Republican convention, the war was between "them" and "us." Unfortunately his cohorts hit the wrong button, *right to life*, as their theme song, and lost.

Too bad, for if they had hit on the vulnerable Democrats' support for the institutionalization of *gay rights* as well as of illegitimacy and single parenthood, they might have made a stand with the heretofore silent majority. The radical extremes are confused over abortion.

Ideological liberals are pro-abortion for affluent women, and therefore are obligated to support it for the poor, at the least out of consistency. But they also idealize and romanticize single mothers of whatever age, education, or condition, including the unmarried, divorced, and separated. They will support adoptions for lesbian and gay singles and couples.

What this liberal culture is against, however, is very clear. They hate monogamy and the nuclear family. They fear and despise men as heads of household, and thus with a woman actively raising her brood of children in the home, the kids not out in day care or with illegal aliens acting as "foster" parents. The idea that males and females differ in any important bio-cultural manner, physical or intellectual, is anathema to their unisex ideology, and their despising of historical male and female values.

If this were merely one more of the interminable cultural and social political wars that the United States has undergone since its hot bath of affluence, one could shrug and go on one's way. However, we are no longer a nation of affluence. Not quite on the ropes, but the islands of poverty and degradation now are growing into peninsulas, on their way to becoming continents.

The United States has come apart, socially. This latest episode is not merely a fallout from affluence, but rather a product of our confused unraveling. If we don't save the traditional nuclear heterosexual family, our only hope to reverse the slide, then all sides in this latest cultural conflagration will find their views to be beside the point. The setting for such conflict will itself have disappeared as we know it. The United States of America will no longer be a real context for meaningful debate over lifestyle, the wherewithal for choosing and subsidizing such styles having evaporated.

CAN HISTORY TEACH US?

When the ancient Roman morality had finally collapsed in the third century under the weight of many similar high living styles among its elite men and women, a spontaneous response came from large numbers of its ordinary citizens. Centuries earlier, the Roman elite had ignored the admonishments of its first and most powerful emperor, Caesar Augustus. His speech to the senatorial classes about family responsibilities and the rearing of children took place several decades before Jesus walked the highways and byways of Galilee.[1]

Two hundred years later Christianity had become a powerful moral force throughout the Empire. Christian women, especially, were leading the Roman middle and working classes back to hearth and home, emphasizing monogamy, child rearing, devotion to their families and their religious communities.[2] It was a response to crisis, as traditional Roman social institutions were rotting away. The old Roman elite had disappeared—no children.

The new elites, from such provinces as Spain and Illyria (the former Yugoslavia), had earlier and temporarily given Rome a second wind. Rome lasted several hundred years longer than it should have because of the moral and civic glue that its philosophical and religious minorities, especially dominant Christianity, gave it.

It should be emphasized that the liberated feminist matrons of Rome were well educated, sophisticated in their intellectual stoicism, and little different than ourselves in their disdain for traditional Roman family values as exemplified in the old Republican tradition of extreme patriarchy. The pregnancies that these women could not avoid were often concluded in abortion, then a very risky affair, or else the newborn was given out for adoption to the few matrons, often from poorer families, who wanted a child. If this could not be managed, the infant was left beside the *cloaca*, the sewer system, to die, or, rarely, to be rescued by anonymous women or families desperate for a child.

This elite disappeared because it did not renew itself. Into the vacuum came the country Romans or colonists, then the political dependencies and their military aristocracies, finally the barbarians and their disciplined fecund females from the north.[3] But it was Christianity, the reviled mystery religion born amongst the ignorant Eastern masses and the Jews, which eventually taught the Romans a new ethic, a new relationship between the genders. It created an extremely stubborn and long-lived perspective on the human family.

WHY THE TRADITIONAL FAMILY?

My argument is that the traditional family is the basic source of human progress. It is through the traditional nuclear heterosexual families with their well-raised and -educated children that the survival of the larger social community is ensured. Though some may imply that it doesn't matter who has children, no one can deny that children and their nurturing constitute the woof and warp of national survival.

Contemporary radical liberals and their allies want to rationalize that it doesn't matter who has children. The population slack will be taken up by someone else as they indulge themselves in their sexual and economic freedom. By creating a taboo out of the issue of variable human intelligence, attempting to bury it, they hope that no one will discern what happens when just *anyone* has children, and under just any kind of "familial" circumstance.

The traditional family, because it derives from a lifelong commitment to faithfulness and trust, creates children as a testament to this steadiness of purpose and hope for the future. It is high intelligence that allows a man and a woman to plan and work for a generation to ensure the success of their nurturing efforts, the education of their children, even beyond the time that they leave the nest.[4]

This kind of "p"-factored persistence demands the highest form of human intelligence. The nuclear family as it has developed in the West is the greatest insurance for the stability of a society because it is structured around the ability of the mass of its citizens, all committed to this core form of familial allegiances, to survive, even prosper in the dynamic instability of change and complexity.

We in the United States have been victimized by the pseudo-liberation preached by the irresponsible. Our contemporary social chaos and degradation can be traced directly to the snowballing illegitimacy rates in our most impoverished classes, to the explosion of homosexuality as a way of socio-political life, let alone its sexual and medical perversities, to the abandonment by our most educated classes of the responsibilities of family life.

That there is literally a cultural war taking place within the United States over its social and moral destiny has to be evident in the dissolution of the social consensus, and the disastrous decline of the nation's intellectual capital, itself the only long-term possibility for social renewal.

If we don't save the traditional family, establish it as the most modern, as well as perennial source of human fulfillment, undergirded by having the most intelligent and educated men and women bearing and raising many more children than those from the bottom of the economic and educational social class structure, and thus inevitably from the less intellectually able, the nation will not survive, no less prosper.

The question that all Americans must face today is whether the nuclear family can be reestablished as the most favored, modern, and personally fulfilling pattern of life for the most intelligent and educated. My argument is that it always has been the most basic form of human attachment, relating, and living. It flows out of *Homo*'s most ancient as well as advanced evolutionary achievements. As such there can be no more fulfilling pattern of sexual, social, or psychological life. It is not a mere way station on the road toward the liberation of humans in their pursuit of new and "freer" social relationships.

ORIGINS

The line of humans, and their enigmatic predecessors who split away from the monkeys and the apes some 20–30 million years ago, was probably the most unspecialized of the various primate forms. The contemporary consequences of this evolutionary hegira argue for this assumption. As a matter of fact the Miocene apes themselves, of this period, approximately 25 million years ago, seem to have been generalists—they lived on the ground, as well as in trees, and ate a wide variety of animal and vegetable matter.[5]

Millions of years later, we hominids have the most unspecialized vocal system of all the anthropoids. Our only real specialization lies in the existence of several language areas of the brain, which allow us to articulate a wide variety of sounds for the almost infinite number of languages that humans have created or will probably create. The earliest human fossils, *Homo habilis*, reveal a Broca's language area in the frontal part of their skulls. (To determine this, scientists had latex molds made of these fossil skulls.) Despite a very small brain, they still had speech. So, too, did *Australopithecus africanus*, an even more primitive man/ape cousin.[6]

As the most physically unspecialized apes, our ancestors had to have had the wits at least to scrounge out a living. By contrast, the specialist apes rapidly developed their economic niches and flourished. The proto-human outsiders were probably pushed to the fringes of the primate economy in those early eons. The lack of proto-hominid fossils, of anything that looks as if it might have evolved into man, argues for this hypothesis.[7]

The need to depend on the ability to stay out of harm's way argues from evolutionary theory that a line of ancestral creatures would have needed somewhat better intelligence than the successful others, otherwise the game would have been up. Intelligence implies brain size, a correlation already well established in the prior several hundred million years. Isn't it surprising that scientists still debate this issue as regards modern humans? Bigger brains have signified greater intellectual power for hundreds of millions of years. Why not now?[8]

In the earliest phases of the pull away from the apes and monkeys, this trend toward intelligence probably did not alter the basic behavioral or familial patterns of these human monkeys/apes. But as the landmass of Africa became more crowded with competing life forms, a radical reconstruction took place among the hominids, including the australopithecine man/ape.

This competitive pressure put a premium on our preeminent adaptive skill, intelligence, and thus on brain size. In a creature now beginning to specialize and profit from upright posture and walking—despite a more ancient pelvic structure that females have retained from the past—a bigger-brained neonate became very adaptive.

Undoubtedly nature and natural selection pulled a number of variable combinations of creatures through the selective sieve. What came through successfully was a restructured human family. In many ways this hominid group reflects the destiny of one of the other anthropoid extremists, the great ape, the gibbon. Gibbons, who are fully arboreal, flying through the treetops out of the sight and mind of other competitors, are monogamous. The need to care for their fragile and gravity-prone young seems to have made that familial virtue out of real selective necessity.

Female humans had to give birth to increasingly fetalized neonates. The skulls of these infants had to be small enough to pass through the birth canal, to continue their growth while the infants were still in an extremely dependent state. Female humans, like the gibbons, lost their estrus (periodicity for sexual relations and insemination). They became regularly and constantly available to the male, unquestionably an adaptation that bound the males to the females for protective as well as sexual reasons.[9]

Human females, instead of birthing every three or four years, could give birth once a year. They often had at their side several dependent children and were cared for by a male who, increasingly, was out and about, not merely fending off animal and human raiders and rapers but also scrounging, often with other related humans, for sustenance. The dependent females and the children remained close to "home."

This is not to argue that males were perfect monogamists. But they certainly had to be regular and committed if the young were to reach maturity. And like "good" mammals or even "good" birds, they were promised to the task.

The interesting dimension to this equation is that those human groups who gave birth to the most fetalized young with the largest skulls—often to the limits of the mothers' physical possibilities, and very often beyond—would flourish. The added brainpower and adaptiveness that the band or tribe would accrue from this sacrifice would redound to the long-term good of the larger group, indeed to the survivors' own genetic immortality.

Sexual differences in humans owe themselves primarily to the specialization of function that male and female had to take on to enable the family to survive. Many millions of years have gone into producing a female who is bonded to her children for the long term. The Texas rancher will quickly cull out those cows who do not suckle their young with devotion. Their genes are soon out of the herd as the rancher ships the negligent mothers off to market.

So, too, in humans, those females without the psychological, intellectual, and personality structure to bear and rear children saw their genes eliminated from the ethnic gene pool. Those males without the intelligence or "p"-factored disciplines to create an economy that would defend and provide for their mates and the dependent young would see their own and the genetic heritage of their relations disappear.[10]

Until quite recently in human history, many marriages were between cousins, thus emphasizing the best in the ethnic or tribal group, but also exposing biological weaknesses, which could then be expelled from the gene pool. This closeness of biological relations in the social group, as well as the relative isolation of wandering human groups, sharpened their survival potentialities, else made them doubly vulnerable.

These shared and intimate biological affinities emphasized the groups' cultural values. Here developed a bio-cultural substitute for the instinctual glue of lower animals. Patriotism and nationalism can be seen as modern equivalent expressions of this ancient human bonding and self-defense machinery.[11]

The monogamous closeness of the human male and female created the nuclear family. Its function, to provide an economic and learning base from which the young could attain to their own sexual maturity, has for eons formed a baseline of human existence. Where deviations take place, as in retrogressive tribal cultures or in stagnant and/or degenerating civilizations—perhaps traditional China, or the religiously-sanctioned polygyny of the Muslim or Jewish cultural worlds—the defensive functions of the family can be mobilized to rescue us in times of stress.[12]

NATIONAL DISASTER I. POLITICAL FEMINISM

All advanced nations have experienced the phenomenon of political feminism. The well-bred daughters of wealthy families find that marriage and/or the hardship of bearing and raising children limits the comfort and well-being that come with being "princesses."

This was true of the Greeks after the Macedonian-imposed hegemony, and true of the Romans from the time the republican avalanche of spoils began to pour into Rome starting around the first century B.C.[13] It was a factor in France among the eighteenth-century aristocratic classes before the days of the guillotine. Even in the United States, the tough and prolific dames of the congregational churches of seventeenth-century New England towns and farms gradually evolved into the pampered ascetics of the nineteenth-century gentry—the Emily Dickinsons.

In fact, historians have noted that in times of plenty the upper-class women of all societies have to be coerced to enter into the family way. So, too, in our time. The birth-control pill, which appeared about 1960, in the flush days of American affluence, sealed our fate. The well-educated middle-class damsel would have no more of it. She would not become a brood mare, much less stay at home while her husband worked.'Twas too boring, too self-enclosing!

It was no longer a matter of many personal choices as it had been with our nineteenth-century middle-class Anglo-Saxon elites. These were political times. This new middle class of women could have their social and sexual freedom without Louisa May Alcott dependency. Yet how could one use this new freedom if the economic wherewithal was not available?[14]

The reader should not see this argument as a denial of the rights of the female. Both genders should be able to participate to the fullest in whatever human dignity requires. At our advanced historical moment, modernity opens up wholly new perceptions of the relationships of the sexes.

We therefore do not argue for a return to the enslavements of the past that women have over time suffered. Likewise, we do not wish for the male to be subject to the horrors that both sexes have inflicted on this more vulnerable sex. On the other hand, what with all the new possibilities for living mentally interesting lives, given the justified opportunities for education and personhood, there nevertheless will always exist certain evolutionary constraints on both the male and the female of the human species. These, that they may continue to enjoy their mutual liberation for more than a measly one or two generations.

If we do not have the children who will partake of the same general skills that allowed our parents and ourselves to create the conditions for "emancipation," then we will soon see these conditions disappear and a far more encapsulating set of conditions begin to dominate our behaviors, finally to efface the soft burnish of affluence, comfort, and liberation.

We are mammals, but we also have enormous cortical potencies. We can think about our personal existence in a way that can cancel out 20 million years of mammalian/primate programming when it comes to sociobiological behavior. Thus the ideological attractions of entering into an exciting new intellectual relationship of political liberation—which also provides a rationale for breaking with so many traditional moral values and behaviors—have pushed so many of our most intelligent and educated daughters into the radical feminist movement.

Certainly in a time of a diminution in the level of the national intelligence, the more middle-of-the-road abilities of women take on real economic attractiveness. The traditional creative male frontier entrepreneurship will thus have diminished. And it is this energy and creativity that previously spun off enough of the "middle"-ground jobs that offer so much opportunity for women today. Now, even these may be going off-shore to women whose educational liberation does not yet require the kind of incomes that emancipated American feminism demands for its true fulfillment.[15]

We have lost the children of almost two generations of our educated and liberated women. It has had almost the same effect as if it had been genocide. They, the sons and daughters of parents who themselves sacrificed much to bring these children into this world, have shouted a collective "no" to the future of their society, in the name of an ideological movement: liberal egalitarianism. According to this ideology, it didn't matter whose children were born; we could educate them all to an equally high level.

It did not happen. We desperately miss the talents of these unborn.

The good news is that more and more women are awakening to the fact that political feminism is an ideological creation of a small portion of radicalized, often lesbian women.

The news reports are filled with stories about fortyish women desperately racing against their biological clocks so that they can fulfill their womanhood with at least one biological child before they are forced onto the less-favored adoption route.[16]

We may be able, through wise legislation, to stanch the flood of poverty-class children. Thus, in a few years the tragic pathologies could lessen and gradually disappear. But we cannot replace the lost creativity of millions of youngsters who would have been the progeny of these generations of brilliantly educated, but sterile yuppies.

NATIONAL DISASTER II. HOMOSEXUAL PLAGUE

The explanation that has a measure of plausibility for the "why" of the explosion of gays in our society is both demographic and cultural. The doubling of the U.S. population since 1940 has produced children from all sectors of society. We are seeing the heterogeneous results of this reproductive plenitude.

The wealth that we have accumulated during these decades has also produced freedoms for individuals of various psychological profiles, including the probably small minority of homosexuals that is biologically determined. Estimates today are that 1 percent to 2 percent of the male U.S. population are participating homosexuals.[17]

The Greco-Roman culture tolerated a form of homosexual behavior, especially among its upper-class males. Most of these liaisons, whether or not stimulated by the isolation and dependency of war or the educational isolation of women, did not preclude marriage, often happy, and the raising of families.[18]

It is the plague of AIDS that has brought the behavior of the homosexual community, especially of the males, to public consciousness. It was a concrete form of sexual activity that spread the disease throughout this group before it began to spread to the heterosexual drug community here in the United States.[19] The enormous political pressure placed upon the government to give AIDS research programs priority over other diseases exemplifies the powerful political role that homosexuals and their allies have established in the entertainment, media, and liberal political communities.

The promise of Bill Clinton during the campaign to lift the ban on gays in the military in exchange for their 4–6 million votes, and then his subsequent attempt to accomplish this as president, with all the public furor over this now modified decision, reveals the enormous political power now exercised by the homosexual community and its cultural and political allies.[20]

The homosexual community has achieved a new cultural self-consciousness. It views itself in political terms as an oppressed minority. It now lobbies to dissolve discrimination against avowed gays in jobs, housing, public welfare, health, and other benefits heretofore reserved for the traditional family. And as noted earlier, homosexual couples or individuals wish to legalize such marriages as well as gain the right to adopt and educate children, and, crucially, the right of parents to inculcate their most intimate values, much as parents have in the religious sphere.

It is clear that the priority of the traditional family to receive favored political and social treatment by the state and other institutions of cultural life is here challenged. Much as with single, unmarried households, homosexuals wish to argue the case that the society should be neutral toward all such lifestyles. The argument for including homosexuals in our "rainbow" coalition of minorities that have official state legal protection against the "majority"—white heterosexual males—is that their traits are comparable to the extrinsic characteristics of African-Americans.

Not stated in this argument by homosexual advocates is the fact that behavior was never an issue in the case of African-Americans. They were to be protected from discrimination against their persons, regardless of their exemplary behavior from the standpoint of the majority patterns. The crucial issue of behavior, no less the public health and economic dimensions of such freely chosen lifestyles, seems not to be germane in this debate. Yet it *is* crucial.

Much of the power adduced in defense of the gay lifestyle derives from the higher-than-average intelligence and education of important segments of the gay community. One estimate is for an average income of over $50,000 per year. It is a mysterious but not entirely unexplainable dimension of the situation. Throughout history, some of the greatest creative minds, both male and female, were homosexual or practiced homosexuality as part of their life commitments. It is a dimension of the human supra-adaptive biological profile. And no doubt there is a "piggyback"-linked genetic relationship between high intelligence and the tendency toward admitting homosexual behavior into one's life.[21] The fact that many creative individuals have lived in two worlds, that of the traditional family, with wives or husbands and children, as well as in the homosexual culture, is evidence of this quality in human existence.

It is clear that homosexuals, keeping to their own private world of behavior, as with heterosexuals, should not suffer from general discrimination or harassment. On the other hand there are a large number of careers, such as the military, child care, and teaching, and even in certain defined cases in community life, religious life, and housing, where homosexual *behavior*, the only clear definition of homosexuality, could be a criterion for rightful discrimination.[22]

Memory Suggestion: One remembers from the history of ancient Greece that in Thebes, a city in Boeotia just north of Athens, a brief if final florescence occurred during the middle of the fourth century B.C. Under the leadership of two men, friends and lovers, Pelopidas and Epaminondas, Thebes was catapulted to dominance in Greece over once glorious Athens, and then in a series of spectacular military victories finally brought Sparta to its knees. Some attribute this surge to power to the tactical innovation of the long lance phalanx, subsequently adopted by Philip and Alexander of Macedon; Philip was a student-hostage in Thebes during this period.

Others attribute Theban greatness to the creation by these two generals of the "Sacred Band," a regiment of lovers who fought side by side with and for each other. When at last the Greeks met their Macedonian Greek match at Chaeronea in central Greece in 338 B.C., it was the Sacred Band which distinguished itself as heroic as the Spartans at Thermopylae 150 years earlier.

This defeat of allied Greek armies propagandized to fight the Macedonian Greeks by the Athenian orator, Demosthenes, saw the Athenian army reeling homeward in brave if futile struggle. The Thebans, too, had to abandon the field, except for the Sacred Band. They retreated to a small hillock, where the 400 lovers fought on to their final "glorious" annihilation.[23]

Dr. E. L. Pattullo, of Harvard University's psychology department, in a recent article, "Straight Talk About Gays," argues that many individuals are born to grow in alternative sexual directions. It is important, he argues, for society to send clear and distinct educational and behavioral signals to the young as to which route we want them to travel in their maturation.[24]

If one can be shaped one way or another to be "gay" or "straight," it becomes an issue of great importance to propagandize, to educate not merely for the personal side of the decision that an individual would make, but also for the civic issue. Gays, in the main, are highly intelligent, sensitive human beings, a high proportion of them having the potential for mixed dominance, or bisexuality.

We as a nation need the children of highly intelligent, sensitive, educated citizens. There is an unknown number of gays who have the potential to live, if not entirely heterosexual family existences, then certainly bisexual family lives to contribute their abilities, if not necessarily their homosexuality, to the next generation.

As currently structured the homosexual community is a parasitic appendage to the American present. It takes from our momentary affluence to enjoy its pleasures. What does it give to the next generation?

JUSTICE

One can question the entire structure of civil rights legislation that establishes protected communities of minorities merely by pointing to statistical differences as prima facie evidence of discrimination. Professor Richard Epstein, of the University of Chicago Law School, has created a legal stir by arguing in several books that the whole structure of "eminent-domain" and "civil-rights" laws is basically unconstitutional.[25]

His book *Takings* indicts a heritage of New Deal–inspired tax law that has served to underwrite federal legislation to redistribute wealth to those supposedly discriminated against. This book is an attack on all laws that limit individuals in the private sector from choosing employees and teachers, and making any other "people" decisions that might exclude minorities. The only exception that Epstein makes is the right of the government so to discriminate.

One can, however, support such laws when individuals are confronted by discrimination by great private enterprises, in themselves governments of power or often delegates of government. The mere ascriptive fact of color, sex, or even ethnic background ought not to exclude an individual from a job or residence when no consideration of ability, skill, or behavior is involved.

In the case of homosexuals, it *is* their behavior that distinguishes them from all other minorities. If governmental agencies such as the armed services or private enterprises have no rights to choose the behavioral components of those with whom they are associated, truly, liberty is at risk.

Such distinctions ought not to lead to witch hunts. The privacy of one's sexual orientation should be affirmed. However, if one so chooses to make one's behavior a philosophical or political demonstration, others ought to be entitled to make their demonstrative decisions accordingly.

Furthermore, no society can exist if it is divided among itself when it decides which human behaviors are to be merited and which not. The range of sexual perversions deviating from the basic heterosexual family forms is enormous. Once we admit onto the stage of normality all that is possible in humans, unconstrained as is our species by instinctual determinations, we will have abandoned a core element in the cultural unity of the nation.

Can the United States exist as a political entity when it places the nuclear family in the pantheon as merely one among many patterns of acceptable behavior that we will admit into legal protectedness?

Remember, we are struggling to survive culturally in an extremely competitive international environment. What policies and values we adopt will not be a matter of merely choosing a national lifestyle. It could be the difference between utter decadence, social disorganization, economic decay on the one hand, and the possibility for a national revival on the other.

Certainly we cannot persecute those whose sexual and lifestyle preferences are not orthodox. So, too, we cannot give the imprimatur to abnormal behavior, even if it has the current sanction of the "bright and beautiful." After all, it has been their suasion that has helped bring us to our present sorry historical state.

Sexual behavior should generally be a matter of privacy. It should not become emblematic of a messianic political movement of a pseudo-liberated class. Else it will, and must, receive political notice in kind, and eventually the full moral and legal obloquy of the people.

DESTRUCTION OF THE FAMILY

As described in Chapter 6, the disintegration of the social bond that heretofore held a very diverse and dynamic society together has its greatest impact on that institution which has served for millions of years as the glue that held humans together, the nuclear family.

One visits public schools all over our nation and finds that the schools themselves are becoming centers that provide social services formerly performed in the home by the family. The father is no longer at home, the mother often is absent, away at work, or gone. After breakfasting in school, children receive health assistance, counseling, and after-school baby-sitting; eventually someone arrives to take the children from school, to where is often not known.

In 1960 less than 20 percent of women with children under the age of six were in the workforce. In 1992 the figure was 60 percent. Not even a generation ago, in 1970, 13 percent of our eighteen-year-olds and younger lived in a single-parent home. Today the figure is 30 percent.[26] It is a snowball hurtling down the mountain. And we pretend not to notice, or search wonderingly for the causes.

The child-abuse statistics ought to have clarified our thinking about its causes and the fate of the traditional family. Together with the avalanche of reports concerning the beating of and often fatal attacks on women, the violence of the pseudo-home is today proverbial. Unsubstantiated reports of child abuse rose from 785,100 reports in 1980 to 2,025,200 in 1987. This translates from 3.5 per 1000 to 8.3 per 1,000 in only seven years. From 1976 to 1986, U.S. government reports of child neglect, maltreatment, and abuse grew from 669,000 to 2,080,000.[27]

One cannot believe that in this short period of American history such an increase in reports constitutes merely the public announcing of such events, rather than a real and substantial increase in the number of events themselves. However, Richard Wexler estimates that some 1 million Americans are accused of child abuse each year.[28]

That there is reality here is buttressed by the crime statistics for young offenders, the battered children five to ten years later. Total homicide arrests in the United States for eighteen- to twenty-four-year-olds rose from 7.5 to 16 per 100,000 people from 1977 to 1991, well over double. For fourteen- to seventeen-year-olds, there was a 50 percent rise during the same period, from 16 to 24 per 100,000 population.

For white males, the rise in homicide arrests for eighteen- to twenty-four-year-olds between 1977 and 1991 was from 20 to 23 per 100,000 population. For the fourteen- to seventeen-year-old group, the number rose from 10 to 15 per 100,000, a significant increase.

From the African-American population, where the collapse of family structure is close to total, the impact on young black males is, as expected, catastrophic. For the eighteen- to twenty-four-year-old group the rate of homicide arrests per 100,000 population went from 125 to 210 between 1976 and 1991. This was almost ten times the rate for equivalent white males. For the fourteen- to seventeen-year-old group of black males the increase went from 48 per 100,000 population to 110. This 100 percent plus increase in homicide arrests among African-American males constitutes an approximately seven-fold rate higher than the equivalent white age group of males.[29]

Can we really point to the ostensible 50 percent illegitimacy rate in Sweden to provide comfort in the ideological liberal rationalization of this new lifestyle of single parenting which they so gleefully promote and subsidize?

My argument is simply that the war against the traditional family, the rationalization that it does not matter who conceives and gives birth to the next cohort of American citizens, is a perverse crusade with unintentional and deeply tragic consequences.

Margo Wilson and Martin Daly, researchers at Macmaster University in Canada, report that the homicide rate in the home involving both children and adult victims is 70 times as likely to be perpetrated by a non-blood-related member of the household than by a blood relation.[30]

The combination of the new philosophy of "let the social service agencies worry about it," a divorce rate that is tearing the middle class apart, and, now, a falling economy that is forcing women out of the home and into the marketplace in order that some viable economic family structure might be maintained, should bring the problem of the family to the top of any list of national priorities. In 1965, the marriage rate per 1,000 Americans was 9.3; divorces and annulments, 2.5. In 1989, the rates were 9.7 and 4.7, respectively. Thus, the divorce rate almost doubled.[31]

Only from intact two-parent households in which mothers, at the least, perform some traditional child-rearing functions, will we ever be able to produce the next generation of citizens able to contribute to the maintenance, not to speak of the reconstruction, of the United States to a level equal to the heady days of half a century ago.[32]

PROPOSALS

1. Reeducation comes first. How can we teach men and women, before it is too late for them personally, that careers are only marker points, surface blips, under which surge the great tidal movements of life—commitments of love, marriage, and children? The glitter of surface excitements today comprises a delusionary snare for so many of our educated but unwary young.

Certainly the media elite are indifferent to the plight of the family, except to the extent that it provides titillating copy. The media are indifferent, that is, until they perceive the great swell from the still majoritarian middle classes demanding that they no longer be chided for their monogamous commitments, their love of children.

Money-hungry carnivores have always existed, the Madison Avenue, Rockefeller Center, and Hollywood moguls who follow the latest public trends. They will follow wherever the cash cow of the future happens to be.

Therefore, it is in the interest of the nation at large for those groups who are concerned about our national future to rally around this issue. It is an issue that will unite us, one that we can address successfully. We should not pursue the hopelessly divisive route taken in the abortion debate.

2. Another suggestion would be to reinstate the job priorities traditionally given to married men with families. Naturally this will directly oppose the quota ideology that Congress has been persuaded to support. With real political clout behind the support of families with children, one hopes from the middle classes, especially women, of all races and ethnic groups, a movement that could make family life attractive and desirable, even for the pampered and educated social classes, could develop.

One can predict that if the present economic downturn continues, in which manufacturing jobs, traditionally the jobs of working-class males with families, disappear, that women in the job market will begin to feel resistance. This may be true especially from women with children, those whose husbands have been displaced in this same job market by working women without children.

It has always been the role of the majority in democratic societies to legislate the laws guiding social policy, whether to reward or to discourage those human behaviors that benefit or hinder the larger ideals and goals of the society. The family-oriented middle class should not be afraid to use its political clout. The homosexual lobby is not.

3. How should we deal with the family tragedies at the bottom of the social and economic scale? The answer is simple, if difficult to carry out. Reduce the births. Where couples have no children, there are no broken families.

All births should require the identification of the father. DNA testing may be our great technological salvation. The child, legitimate or not, requires of society at the least a minimum chance for a decent human life. On the other hand, illegitimacy is a tragedy for all the individuals involved; it has become a curse for our nation. It must be discouraged.

Shouldn't the mother have to feel some of the weight of responsibility that bringing a child into the modern world entails? Yes. She should be helped to get on her feet, but her behavior ought not to be seen by others, who might be persuaded to take the same route, as an acceptable alternative lifestyle. If one is going to accept a governmentally subsidized lifestyle, one must accept also some of the burden, at the very least to repay the neighbors and citizens for the help received in the light of unacceptable behavior. This follows even more strongly for the fathers who today often get away scot-free for what amounts to a social crime, a dereliction of duty.

Minimal housing, perhaps even dormitory-style, given our economic straits. Never money, only food, clothing, health services, and these only in person, to ensure that they are used properly. Perhaps even the application of Norplant, the newest form of birth control, after one illegitmate child, to qualify for welfare.

Recent proposals and court cases in Baltimore and in the states of Kansas and California, mandating compulsory birth control using such contraceptives, suggest that the radical proposals of one era become, in the blink of an eye, the now de facto public response to an urgency that reflects a national crisis.[33] In a word, citizens should not be forced to pay for the dereliction of their neighbors.

Fathers should be required to work at jobs commensurate with their skills, even public works gangs, to pay for the support of their progeny. We already have an "honor court" for reforming alcoholics and other miscreants.

None of these suggestions is new. What is new should be a greater readiness by all to admit to the failure of traditional social welfare policies, policies that have incontestably worsened our nation as a decent place in which to live and raise our children.

4. At the top of the social scale is a different kind of problem. Again, it is a problem that affects all racial and ethnic groups. We need their intelligent children. We need the children to be educated to the highest levels possible, to become the potential creators, innovators, entrepreneurs of tomorrow. Without the talent at the top, there will be no economic and cultural future for those in the middle.

Persuasion and education can do much to convince those so easily seduced by the "in" trends. There came a day in many colleges when senior female undergraduates stopped showing their engagement rings to their dorm colleagues. They were denounced as "finks" to the women's movement. This could change back to normality with a strong enough stand by rational public opinion.

What about the truly highfliers, especially the female careerist at the very top, who in earlier days felt the importance of passing on their dominant genes in the name of family destiny as well as the nation at large? These traditional joys once seemed sufficient compared to the excitement of the marketplace, and the affluent, if lonely, retirements on Fifth Avenue, in Paris, or East Hampton.

Is it unfair to say that these men and women, paraded before our young as role models for their future, in reality rank as national *parasites*? They have taken for granted the sacrifices of their forebears, the heritage of high intelligence and philanthropic wealth that made their world-class education possible. In their sterility they have transformed their own private tragedy into public irresponsibility.

And we should deal with them, at the very least, through the tax system. It would be doubly persuasive to match public tax policies with public disclosure of their use of wealth. After all, the United States made this wealth possible by dint of their citizenship. Public revelation that the CEOs of Warner Communications and Coca-Cola each received yearly remuneration of over $75 million had a sobering effect on corporate America.[34]

These individuals can no longer flaunt their wealth anonymously. The public will know. We can predict fewer irresponsible boards of directors that allow such sharks to bleed their corporations, and thus their employees and the public. So, too, the selfish careerist should have to bear the public's stigma.

Thomas Hobbes, the seventeenth-century English philosopher, is thought to have been one of the first to suggest that government should not tax productive earnings; rather, it should tax consumption.[35] This would have the double virtue of increasing the savings and investment levels of the nation as well as blunting the enthusiasm of the highfliers.

FAMILY AS DEFENSE

Family life and the nuclear family have been central to the evolution of high human intelligence.[36] The chimpanzee, ostensibly our closest living relation, displays few behavior patterns that could even faintly be described as familial in the human sense. Our own familial pathway has been in progress for at least 4–5 million years and perhaps three times longer. As far as it can be rationally perceived, this pattern of human bonding and child rearing will probably continue indefinitely into the future.

We therefore have to come down hard in defense of the nuclear family. Our leaders have no other choice. Any finessing of the issue slips us faster down the slope. If we do gradually rebuild family life, we will have a chance at creating a stronger, more egalitarian middle-class American society.

Chapter 12

A Non-Hyphenated People: W.E.B. Du Bois (1868–1963)

I am inclined to think that in the light of available data and the results of fairly wide observation that at least one-third of the Negroes of the United States have recognizable traces of white blood, leaving about 6,000,000 others. (This does not mean that these 6,000,000 have no white blood— many of them have—but there are few distinct traces of it.) This, of course, is partial guess-work—it is quite possible that the mulattos form an even larger percentage than this, but I should be surprised to find that they formed a smaller proportion. . . . A word may be added as to race mixture in general and as regards white and black stocks in the future. There is, of course, no general argument against the intermingling of the world's races. "All the great peoples of the world are the result of a mixture of races." (Bryce, Jas. *The Relations of the Advanced and Backward Races of Mankind*, Oxford, 1892, 46 pp.) . . . In the United States . . . if slavery had prevailed the Negroes might have been gradually absorbed into the white race. Even under the present serfdom, the amalgamation is still going on. It is not then caste or race prejudice that stops it—they rather encourage it on its more dangerous side. The Southern laws against race marriage are in effect laws which make the seduction of colored girls easy and without shame or penalty. The real bar to race amalgamation at present in the United States is the spreading and strengthening determination of the rising educated classes of blacks to accept no amalgamation except through open legal marriage. This means practically no amalgamation in the near future. . . . At present those who dislike amalgamation can best prevent it by helping to raise the Negro to such a plane that he will never stoop to mingle his blood with those who despise him.

W.E.B. Du Bois (1906)[1]

WHAT IS AN AMERICAN?

These passionate words from a great forerunner of the civil rights movement, a man who passed his ninety-five mortal years in perennial struggle against the injustices of history and irrational humanity, are path-breaking insights into our future as a nation. Yet they were written almost one hundred years ago, giving us insight into the earliest definitions of a possible solution to one country's struggle with diversity and inequality.

W.E.B. Du Bois, himself a Son of the American Revolution, his ancestors having fought for the freedom of the Commonwealth of Massachusetts, with the blood of Holland and France as well as of Africa flowing through his veins, knew that the ultimate solution to the problem of the "Negro-American" lay in the passing of his own minority into the unity of this nation.2

Indeed, he was deeply wounded by the conditions under which his people still lived in 1906, forty years after the Civil War. He understood that no progress could be made until a new social and economic revolution would occur to free all of subject humanity, including the vast majority of the world's citizens—the dark people residing on our planet.3

The solution to the racism of his day, a racism that Du Bois observed and experienced with intellectual eyes and intelligence for almost three-quarters of a century, would not disappear through the moral purification of the dominating and corrupt overlords of the South and elsewhere. This was clearly impossible. He became a communist, eventually returning to the homeland of the people he was leading, to Africa.4

What Du Bois did not live to experience in these few years after his death were the events that led to the present amazing internationalism, and, equally, to the dismaying deterioration of the dark peoples of the world, too long after the achieved independence that Du Bois saw as the beginning of a new world morality.

The goal was correct, the perception accurate then and emblematic of the future. Then as now the Negro-American was already partially European— as was Du Bois—as was also the leadership that followed him on the march. The choice for all hyphenated Americans was either to become American, or, as we see today, suffer the multicultural quota-fracturing of the American society, to witness these dreams of nationhood disintegrate in a way that the Confederacy dared not imagine in its most exuberant fantasies.

CULTURAL PLURALISM

There was a time, early in this century, when it was thought right and possible for the United States, if not the world, to organize itself politically as well as culturally in terms of the idea of unity in difference. Given the multitude of immigrants from all over the world pouring into the United States, one solution was the amalgamation of these immigrants into the fabric of our society, the concept of cultural pluralism.5

By committing them to the ideals of our nation, yet allowing them to retain much of their cultural distinctiveness, it was thought that we would be a better nation. The newcomers would not be flattened out to fit stereotypical traditional Anglo-Saxon nationalism.[6] Nor would they have to conform to the indiscriminate blending inherent in the melting-pot vision of America.[7]

Horace Kallen, a student of William James at Harvard, as was Du Bois before him, proposed, the metaphoric separation of the two strands of our human nature into daylight and nighttime modes. Thus, during the daylight hours, the individual would participate in the work of the nation as a whole, contributing to its needs for unity. On the other hand, the evening component would allow each individual to seek the privacy and intimacy of the cultural community. Thus the United States could be both unified and free.[8]

Another way of looking at this deeper stratum of diversity in the cultural palette of *Homo* is to see the symbolism inherent in all cultural meaning as dividing itself into those universal modes, the international economies of technology, law, or scientific principle. At the same time, humans would be experiencing the plural symbols of their cultural community in its religious values, cuisine, the unique creative vision of national artists and musicians, the poetry and novelistic mystery of a national language.

Such "nondiscursive" symbolism, the meanings of the intimate group, has its roots even deeper in the souls of human communities. One cannot dissolve these ethnic allegiances. One can obscure them for a time under the press of universal political or ideological forces. Once loosed, the full eruption of repressed ethnic values demands its due.[9]

In the United States the tremendous dynamic of the technological revolution of the past several generations, the nomadic population shifts away from their home bases, have torn away the geographical foundations for a cultural or ethnic pluralism "in place." This is true of all the existing European ethnicities in this country, now even more confused by intermarriage.

The African-Americans and the various Latino minorities are certainly not "in place"; they share little with each other in their variety except in some cases a language. Their Spanish is itself shaped by various dialects and nuances. Thus the seeming upsurge of what is euphemistically called multiculturalism needs to be understood.[10] Where is all this leading us?

In the midst of this enormously dynamic world, now, as earlier, people in free societies search for "roots," identity in plurality and community. They do not want to be dissolved into an amorphous, abstract national identity, especially one so large and remote. The ethnicity being created in America today is a creation of the media and the great national institutions.

How spontaneous is multiculturalism? How much is it a product of the independent constructive efforts of communities? How much is it a reflection of the attempt to divide governmental largesse into preestablished multicultural units, to obtain a piece of the political and economic pie?[11]

The politicization of multiculturalism, in that its advocates are forever at war to obtain chunks of recognition and perquisites in state school curriculums and texts, in arts grants, in college academic departments, and in the quota system for governmental positions, argues for the death of pluralism, multiculturalism, even, and sadly, ethnicity.

As our country gets poorer and the government weaker, the wherewithal to support the pseudo-diversity of these political-action cliques will wither—the power-brokers will just go on to other and greener fields—and the need for *real* diversity and cultural pluralism will be left unaddressed. The political spoils system approach to multiculturalism, having displaced the spontaneous creation of voluntary institutions from below, will help ensure that cultural pluralism will finally disappear from the American scene.

Perhaps this is not bad. It will symbolize the reality that we need to build a totally new ethnic profile in our country, one created, independently or not, by groups of people from their own inner sense of equality and autonomy.[12]

MINORITY RECONSTRUCTION

Du Bois understood clearly that intermarriage is the key symbolic act of equality between groups. And we know from studies of I.Q. that the closest correlation of I.Q.s exists not necessarily just between regular siblings or between parent and child but also between husband and wife (about 50 percent), usually two unaffiliated humans who have come together in the mutuality of intellectual perception and a love that is both emotional and infused with a rational sense of futurity.[13]

No nation can exist without the shared sense of those symbolic values reflected in the intimacies of culture. To remain a nation we need to share a culture in much the same way that the long-time residents of Texas or New Mexico—Mexicans, Anglos, and Native Americans—have gradually melded together through intermarriage as well as through the unifying symbols of their state ethnicities.

Such subtle differences in cultural values and traditions can exist between the various states of our union. The United States is too large ever to be homogeneous in cultural values. The climate, the ecology, the various economic concentrations will create local differences throughout that are important for that political amalgam or alloy similar to that which, for instance, makes a steel rod stronger than pure iron.

To do this, the various minorities, which now suffer from disadvantage and make their claim against the majority for social and economic reparations, will have to face the real issue. They cannot continue to parade the tired mythological rhetoric of guilt and retribution that they have used in the past to shame the majorities.

The tragic pathologies that afflict these minorities are clearly self-inflictions by their weakest representatives, the tragic heritage of intellectual incapacity. Naturally, this heritage is not one that can be laid at the feet of the ethnicity per se. It only appears so, because middle-class members of those communities ally themselves with their underclass brethren, not realizing that this alliance, provoked by liberal demonology itself, constitutes a racist claim that *all* members of the minority are so tainted with a lack of requisite intelligence. It is an argument that should be summarily rejected.

It is an argument as false as that which dooms African-Americans to pathological criminal behavior or Hispanics to live in the *favellas* and *barrios* in unending poverty. Just as we make a distinction between poor white "trash," "rednecks," and "good" Anglos, so too can we make clear distinctions between minorities, of which there are millions with powerful intellectual and cultural potentials.

The Cuban-Americans in Florida clearly showed that they understood this distinction when in 1979 Fidel Castro emptied most of his hard-core prisoners and violent mental patients onto the shores of Miami. These Cuban-Americans were in the lead in helping the U.S. government hunt down this group when they turned violent again, eventually to have many of them returned to Cuba.

The Cuban-American community worked its way up to affluence and political power by dint of middle-class intelligence, great cultural pride, and educational ambition. Castro knew well who his enemies were when he allowed them to flee in the first place. Totalitarianism hates intelligence in humans, because it connotes independence of thought, creativity, enterprise, all those skills and values that Fascist regimes such as Castro's attempt to destroy in their thrust for absolute power.[14]

Minority leaders can no longer, as they have done in the post–Du Bois era, go beyond the righteous demand for full legal empowerment, full equality of opportunity, the dissolution of all governmental inhibitions on the rights of any group or individual on the basis of extrinsic physical attributes, color, or race. They should withdraw this new class of demands for welfare support and special ethnic status in the name of their membership in a registered "protected" minority.

A principle will eventually be established that the claim for recognition as a cultural minority, if not a racial one, requires that the leadership take responsibility for the internal discipline of the minority, as well as to make its case for fair play on the part of the majority.

Internal responsibility will have to entail the protection and enhancement of the intellectual and educational profiles of the community in question. The pathologies that now exist in significant portions of these so-called colored minorities argue for the malfeasance of their leadership cadres. It is they who have allowed the destruction of these minorities' intellectual profiles over the past forty years. Blaming this state of affairs on "whitey" has lost its punch.

The responsibilities, as both Booker T. Washington and Du Bois argued many decades ago, must be shared. First, true equality of opportunity and legal freedom must be obtained for all minorities. Then must come the slow tedious task of reconstruction from within, an endeavor that must eventually conclude with a truer equality of condition.

Booker T. Washington:

In what I say here I would not by any means have it understood that I would limit or circumscribe the mental development of the Negro student. No race can be lifted until its mind is awakened and strengthened. By the side of industrial training should always go mental and moral training, but the pushing of mere abstract knowledge into the head means little. We want more than the mere performance of mental gymnastics. Our knowledge must be harnessed to the things of real life. I would encourage the Negro to secure all the mental strength, all the mental culture—whether gleaned from science, mathematics, history, language or literature that his circumstances will allow, but I believe most earnestly that for years to come the education of the people of my race should be so directed that the greatest proportion of the mental strength of the masses will be brought to bear upon the every-day practical things of life, upon something that is needed to be done, and something which they will be permitted to do in the professional class which the race needs and must have. I would say give the men and women of that class, too, the training which will best fit them to perform in the most successful manner the service which the race demands.[15]

W.E.B. DU BOIS' EXEMPLARS

The following extracts are taken from the printed report of the superintendent of schools of Fulton County, Georgia, for 1909, and show something of Negro self-help in public school education.

College Park—The Negroes of this town made a deed to a half-acre lot to the board of education and besides, met them half way in the building of a $1,200 house.

Bethlehem—The following lines which appear in the *School and Home* tell the tale of this building: This school, valued at $800, was constructed by a dozen Negroes of a community, 10 miles from Atlanta, none of whom owned more than $300 or $400 worth of property. There are hundreds of schools for white children in Georgia that would suffer by comparison.

Pittsburgh—Since the beginning of the last term the Negroes here, with the aid of only $75 from the county board of education, have bought a lot worth $200 and built an $1,800 house. It has been hard to get this accomplished, mainly, because of difficulties which they apprehended from the city extension movement, but it is done at last and this work reflects great credit on the teachers and community.

Springfield—This building has been continually improved since it was constructed a year ago and it is now in very good condition. This is largely due to the leadership of the teacher.

South Atlanta—The house and lot cost $3,200 and was raised almost entirely by the Negroes of the community.

By way of summary the report says:

Our Negro schools have done excellent work in the way of improvement during the last year. But little help has been given by the county authorities, the Negroes for the most part desiring to own their buildings themselves. Building plans are furnished them, together with much inexpensive advice and insistence upon comfortable quarters for teachers and pupils. Here and there, as an incentive, some small part of the building material used has been given them, but they have met nearly all the expense connected with the new schools.[16]

The report of the U. S. commissioner of education for 1870 says: [Report of United States Commissioner of Education, 1870, page 202]:

This state [Missouri] has a larger proportion of schools for colored children than any former slave state. . . . Opposition to the education of the colored people is rapidly disappearing. Their rapid improvement and good conduct help to disarm prejudice.

The report (page 204) speaks as follows of Lincoln Institute, a school for the training of Negro youth:

Lincoln Institute owes its origin to the liberality of colored soldiers enlisted from Missouri. In the spring of 1866 a subscription of $4,000 was made by the enlisted men of the Sixty-second United States colored infantry, to aid in the foundation of an educational institution in Missouri for the especial benefit of the colored people. Afterward another colored Missouri regiment added to it the sum of $1,325; and $2,000 were subsequently received from the Freedmen's Bureau.[17]

THE DREAM

Can there be any doubt that human power is created in the struggle for self-definition and justice? The moving greatness of this people struggling for freedom, emancipation, and then civil liberty, in defense of their humanity, stands in contrast to the despair of the 1990s. What has happened to turn what was one of the great liberal struggles for right and good into such a paradoxical dependency on charity and forbearance?

Du Bois' early vision of the "talented tenth" leading the Negro masses to a higher civilizational destiny than that of their oppressors, has to be seen as the only rational goal of an oppressed people. Nourished on the thought of Thomas Carlyle as well as of William James, Du Bois saw the role of leadership in creating a peoplehood that stood independently in the struggle for the group's civilizational fulfillment. They were Americans, but more so, with a unique mission for all mankind.

Surely, he left the battlefield when it was near to being won. The 1954 *Brown v. Board of Education* decision (desegregation) was symbolic of Du Bois' ongoing demands against the supposed accommodations of Booker T. Washington in 1895, in Atlanta ("Cast down your bucket"), though Du Bois praised Washington for his words.[18] So, too, with the infamous 1896 *Plessy v. Ferguson* (segregation decision) which was handed down the same year Du Bois received his Ph.D. from Harvard (also the year Frederick Douglass died). Rather, Du Bois demanded complete civil equality.[19]

The subsequent leaders, Walter White, Paul Robeson, A. Philip Randolph, Roy Wilkins, all fought for that same goal, equality of achievement and consideration in the mind of the world community, to be won through legal parity alone.[20] The goal was always civilizational; the goal was never to commit the African-American community as a de facto ward of the state. The demand was, to paraphrase, to remove the albatross of slavery, segregation, and discrimination, and they would do it themselves, and create a better exemplification of human nobility for all who would struggle to achieve such goals.

It must be that the bloat of *hybris* that infected America in general after 1954, even if we accept the good intentions of the 1964 Civil Rights Act, has become a factor in the destruction of the African-American community, as it has gravely wounded other communities, majority and minority, leaving the nation itself in jeopardy.

It would not have been significant to the traditional leadership of the African-American community in its original struggle for legal emancipation that the community might diminish in size. The key was not how many African-American politicos could be elected to office, but rather the social condition of this community relative to other groups, including the white majority.

The "talented tenth" was a metaphor as useful in the envisionment of a future of parity as was Booker T. Washington's picture of every former slave now at work with hammer and saw, or plow and scythe: "I would set no limits to the attainments of the Negro in arts, in letters or statesmanship, but I believe the surest way to reach those ends is by laying the foundation in the little things of life that lie immediately about one's door. I plead for industrial education and development for the Negro not because I want to cramp him, but because I want to free him. I want to see him enter the all-powerful business and commercial world."[21] The image was, first, greatness in difference, and subsequently, indifference to the choices black or white would make with regard to the future hue and shape of the American visage.

What was important was that some day a Fisk, Tuskegee, Wilberforce, or Lincoln could stand equally with a Harvard, Williams, or Cornell, much as Notre Dame or Brandeis today raise the banners of their own minority communities.[22]

This is what we have to strive for: to take from the knowledge that modern civilization privileges us to understand and apply it for the betterment of all people. The minorities of color in the United States are again much in need. Their situation seems to take priority, but the demands of high intelligence in the twenty-first century beckon coercively to all our people.

A century from now we could hope for another reversal, from the precipitous decline in the condition of the "Negro American." Once more they could be on the road toward substantive equality, adding their unique timbre to the rich orchestration of our American continent; perhaps blending into an ever regenerating America as it looks toward an even newer and now inviting century, the twenty-second.

W.E.B. Du Bois, 1897–1910, on the "Talented Tenth":

The nobility of effort, long continued, wearying, never ending effort, the imperativeness of eternal strife, the divinity of sweat . . . leaven the lump, guide the Mass away from the contamination and death of the Worst, in their own and other races . . . thrift and business knowledge mean more to us today than the right of suffrage . . . educated women as mothers, not quantity but quality . . . as scientific farmers leading to an aristocracy of country gentlemen . . . as merchants rather than as mere money makers, as doctors, artists, and scientists . . . must conserve our physical powers, our intellectual endowments, our spiritual ideals; as a race we must strive by race organization, by race solidarity, by race unity to the realization of that broader humanity which freely recognizes differences in men, but sternly deprecates inequality in their opportunities of development . . . the training of a self whose balanced trained assertion will mean as much as possible for the great ends of civilization.[23]

Chapter 13

Immigration: Hot War

We also ought to ask ourselves, before we assure ourselves that we could comfortably accommodate further waves of immigration, where, if anywhere, the limits of this complacency are to be found. This is a big world. Billions—rapidly increasing billions—of people live outside our borders. Obviously, a great number of them, being much poorer than they think most of us are, look enviously over those borders and would like, if they could, to come here . . .

. . . The possibility [has] never become apparent to us that in some instances, where the disparity between what these people were leaving behind and what they were coming into was too great, the new arrivals, even in the process of adjusting to our political tradition, might actually change it. One need only look at our great-city ghettos or the cities of Miami and Los Angeles to satisfy oneself that what we are confronted with here are real and extensive cultural changes . . .

Just as water seeks its own level, so relative prosperity, anywhere in the world, tends to suck in poverty from adjacent regions to the lowest levels of employment. But since poverty is sometimes a habit, sometimes even an established way of life, the more prosperous society, by indulging this tendency, absorbs not only poverty into itself but other cultures in the bargain, and is sometimes quite overcome, in the long run, by what it has tried to absorb.

George F. Kennan[1]

THE TIDE

Imagine you are at the beach. Lying on the soft moist sand, ocean wavelets breaking just below you, gulls screeching above, the warm sun, the smell of surf, a delicious unity with nature. The tide is rising in the late afternoon drowse. An oozing of saltwater tickles your heels. The moments flow along in a dreamy doze. Suddenly, the water is there again. This time it seems to surge impatiently up your bathing suit and shudders cool water into the small of your back.

You should head up the beach to the dry crowd of umbrellas, into the cacophony of a rock beat and scolding mothers. Just a moment more. But don't wait too long. If it's a real surge, you will be pulled into the beckoning roar. The power of cosmic inevitabilities will drag you down. You may, in one unwary moment, join the eternal chaos.

The tide is immigration, a force that we do not want to confront. We are thus vulnerable to its encompassing embrace. It is an embrace that will suck us back into evolutionary history if we delay too long. Lack of perception, as always, breeds unreadiness, paralysis of action.

For several hundred thousand years, the genes of evolutionary destiny have been heading south. Also, in little wavelets, they transformed humankind.[2] They created *Homo sapiens* and then, almost everywhere, *Homo sapiens sapiens*. The work of evolution is far from complete in our very variable super-species. If it is to be completed, we must halt this uninvited tidal invasion of the genes of the south, at the least until they can be transformed into the form of high intelligence, and all over the world.

You must know. There *is* a good deal up in the north. You would take up the offer if it came your way. And the people of the south recognize a great bonanza for the immortality of their genes when they see it. All that they have to do is return the favors of the north.

These words may sound crass. They are. But the situation is crassly serious. The United States, along with other European cultures around the world, is at risk. An epochal change is in process.

For the past 35,000 years, the genetics of European intelligence, passed around the world, have laid the groundwork for what we call and treasure as civilization. Civilization in the West is now in jeopardy.[3]

Indeed, the road upward has been rocky. But we have no choice but to continue to perfect an as-yet-imperfect human setting. For the other is unacceptable, a barbarism without the bucolic quaintness of the primeval past. It certainly is our responsibility, those of us of the north, now alloyed from all the ancient races and the new ethnicities of humankind. We have caused this tidal surge from the south, desperate, decent humans searching for what all humans want, a life of dignity and security.

As they proclaim proudly in California, Mexicans, Central Americans, even refugees from the horrors of Middle East totalitarianism, can live far better than they could dream of in their homelands, on welfare, including health and social services, with a fine education thrown in. Even illegal immigrants can expect to have their children accepted in school, and they are eligible for much more. For example, in the event a woman gets pregnant and the baby is born in California, the family is home free![4]

Today, immigrants of the "proper" ethnic groups are eligible to take advantage of the job quotas established for indigenous members of those groups. Beyond being accorded restitution for prior disadvantage, these newcomers are given a unique political boost.

Our wealth is European. Our structure of science, law, philanthropy, arts, and technology, all reflect the creative and intellectual juices of Cro-Magnon, the first true *Homo sapiens sapiens*, and the initiators of that glorious cave civilization of the icy Eurasian tundras of the Upper Paleolithic, 25,000 B.P.[5]

Let us again reflect on the Dutch, indigenous inheritors of this intelligence and its potential for civilization building. As with the Venetians, but several hundred years later, the Dutch, too, found themselves in opposition to a hostile and restrictive environment. They faced up to the reality of their own tidal waters off the North Sea coast. Throughout the late Middle Ages they battled these tides by building dikes and polders, rescuing the land from the sea.

Thus, after hundreds of years of diligent and intelligent work, out of farm and village they built one of the great civilizational traditions of human history, resiliently bouncing back from every political, economic, and technological change that the larger powers had the ability and will to impose.

After the destruction of their nation by the Germans in World War II, the Dutch again re-created their nation, constructing an enviable infrastructure of high technology industries by which their large population could flourish amidst an absence of natural resources. Their capital was that hard-won intelligence and educational potential that they had inherited and nurtured from the ancient past.[6]

So what did they do? In an act of ideological subservience, they gave in to the current rhetorical denigration of this European past and of their own colonial history. They invited the Third World to share the wealth of the home country, *in situ*.

Go to Amsterdam, that once jewel-like city on the canals. Graffiti sprawl over the walls of the ancient buildings, drugs and prostitution, homelessness and general degradation are rampant. The people of the Third World, now ensconced and flourishing in philanthropic Amsterdam. Doing very well, if you please.[7]

The Dutch fought and won a difficult victory over the tides of nature only to be inundated by the myopia of their own good hearts. Will they survive this new, it is to be hoped, momentary evolutionary time warp?

PRINCIPLE

Let it be stated, and firmly, that significant portions of the various ethnic groups of the "south" are fully capable intellectually of profiting from the educational and social opportunities of the north. The problem arises because the Dutch, Germans, or Swiss, for example, are so homogeneous in intellectual and educational potential and able at such a high skill level to absorb the economic and labor requirements of the new technology that the comparison with the south has become even sharper in the last several decades.

Also, because Western medicine has made death control possible in the south, the population surge now derives primarily from the bottom of the social/intellectual classes. The leaders of the nations of the south have the ability to carve out modern power bases in their own home countries, not so the *Lumpenproletariat*. Thus the latter desperately and appropriately attempt to profit from the welfare/work philanthropic openness of the *guilty* ex-colonialist northerners.

THE PRICE

The problem of immigration for the United States is somewhat different. We have a tradition of openness, receptivity to the poor of the world, those who seek opportunity. The difficulty is that history is not like chemistry. Things happen differently over time; the elements do not remain the same. What is happening now is qualitatively different from what occurred in the first decade of the twentieth century when the United States admitted about 9 million immigrants. At that point (1900), our total population was about 76 million people.

Now we have well over 250 million, and an ecology and environment that was overwhelmed by pollution, urban sprawl, and poverty, on a scale quite different from ninety years ago. Our borders are a sieve, partially because, as with the contemporary Germans, we do not stand behind our own immigration laws. According to these, 270,000 new immigrants per year are allowed, but with all the dispensations, over twice that number arrive, 5 million in the 1980s alone.[8]

No one knows the number of illegals that have arrived in the past two decades, and who have been "grandfathered" into potential citizenship since the change of the law in 1986. It could be twice the legal 5 million in each of the last 2 decades. For example, estimates of illegal immigrants resident in the United States range from the 2–6 million of the Census Bureau to as high as 15 million. New York City is estimated as home to one million illegal aliens.[9] In our major cities, we are witnessing a phenomenon not seen since that first decade of the twentieth century, a major portion of the population being foreign-born.

Albert Shanker, president of the American Federation of Teachers, writing at the end of 1992, reported that 36 percent of the student body in New York City is from non-English speaking families, representing 167 different countries. In Dade County, south Florida (Miami), 25 percent of the student body was born outside the United States and comes from 132 countries. During the period between 1989 and 1992, over one thousand additional immigrant children have enrolled in the Dade County schools each month.[10]

There is no question that the new aliens, legal and illegal, have proved a bonanza for America's minimum wage employers. They clean buildings at night, work "off the books" for upscale yuppie families, toil in basic garment and furniture manufacturing, do kitchen work in restaurants, dominate in fruit and vegetable harvesting and laundries, even work as taxi cab drivers (in New York City, 70 percent of the applications in one recent period were from newly arrived immigrants with rudimentary English language skills).[11]

The question is whether the temporary advantages for a sector of our economy that depends on unskilled minimum wage workers to gain world-class status constitutes an important long-range contribution to the aim of our country. If the manufacturing or agricultural jobs move to Malaysia or Honduras, will the workers idled by such a move be capable of upgrading their skills to the higher symbol-using requirements of manufacture or services? Looking at it another way, if we do not have unskilled citizens or aliens available for such tasks, will we not be stimulated to find more efficient automated means of doing many of these unskilled jobs without recourse to uneducated labor?

EXEMPLAR: CALIFORNIA

The state of California is a tremendous magnet for immigrants, legal and illegal. The estimate by Leon Bouvier, writing for The Federation for American Immigration Reform (FAIR), in *Fifty Million Californians?*, is that in twenty-five years, given current immigration and births, the population of California will rise from about 32 million in 1993 to over 50 million.[12]

At present, FAIR estimates that almost 300,000 immigrants, legal and illegal, the overwhelming proportion of whom are poor and undereducated, are being added to the population each year. Will these people ever be able to rise from the poverty that they brought with them, considering their historic track record? Will the United States, having peaked in its productivity, wealth, and its ability to propel poor people into the middle class, be able to absorb this tide? Will this once affluent and beautiful land still be able to offer our new immigrants such a beneficent welfare package?

In 1992, Governor Pete Wilson and the California State Legislature had to confront a budget deficit of $11 billion brought about by the inertial increases of all such government programs, accompanied by a recession, and by additional demands on the system, such as unemployment and decreased tax revenues. The predicted result should have been seen as inevitable by anyone in the leadership not interested solely in momentary political survival—incipient bankruptcy.

The public schools and the system of higher education, once the glory of California, now shadowed by racial and ethnic quotas and slipping into mediocrity, have been savaged. Classes in the lower schools, once 20–30 pupils per class, have now risen to 30–45 per-class levels, accompanied by diminished supplies and support, including serious salary cuts for teachers.

For example, average annual teacher salaries have fallen from $44,000 to $38,700 in Los Angeles. Yearly expenditures per pupil are now $4,187, one of the lowest among American major cities. Still, the Los Angeles School District is $400 million in deficit out of a $3.9 billion budget.[13]

Thomas Sowell, the well-known African-American economist, states, in a recent book, *Inside American Education*, that the racial quota system initiated by the University of California, using the SAT composite scores, 400–1600, allows for the admission of black freshmen having scores almost 300 points below those required for admission by white admittees.[14]

California, like other sections of the United States, has opted to join the Third World. Why? Because the political, intellectual, and media leadership were intimidated by the myth of intellectual uniformity, the obligatory American acquiescence to virtually unlimited immigration, legal or illegal. Why should it risk the stain of being labeled a bigot?

ECONOMICS OF IMMIGRATION

The stagnation in the production of high-paying frontier technology jobs that has overtaken the United States since the early 1970s, becoming an ongoing crisis in the employment market since 1979, has not usually been attributed to uncontrolled illegal immigration. However, it is becoming axiomatic that the United States increasingly is represented on the world marketplace as a nation of "easy" wage rates.[15] Some attribute this to the flight of industry offshore, and the resultant fears by workers for their jobs, and thus the dampening down of union and other demands for wage and benefit increases.

There is also internal competition from the "illegals." These individuals, fearful of deportation, will work for a pittance and without benefits. The example of the Peruvian aliens who worked for Zoë Baird, President Clinton's first choice for attorney general, and her law professor husband is a case in point. Baird, a millionaire corporate attorney, with a yearly family income of well over $600,000, naturally could have found qualified citizens for such work. But they would have cost her more money, plus benefits, which would have included social security payments.

From 1979 to 1992, manufacturing lost 15.6 percent of the total non-farm national employment pie. These non-supervisory manufacturing jobs now pay an average of $23,500 per year. Service jobs, which increased 40.8 percent at an average of $17,500 for non-supervisory positions, and retailing jobs, which increased 21.7 percent during this period and which now pay the average clerk $10,500 per year, show the greatest expansion in the national employment picture. In addition, of the 108.4 million now in our workforce, fully 40 percent are part-time employees.[16]

The relative decline in income of the average American worker over the past twenty years, noted in Chapter 7, has been linked by Vernon Briggs, a Cornell University economist, to this influx of poorly educated and weakly skilled people now entering our country. As both Briggs and Lawrence Harrison have noted, these pools of labor are too tempting for employers not to use for the reduction of labor cost, by far the largest item in the cost of producing goods and services. They therefore do not invest in frontier labor-saving technology.[17]

On the other hand, formerly developing nations such as South Korea and Taiwan, blessed with ever advancing levels of skilled workers, are expending their product capital and their high-end profits in creating such machinery, and this despite a proportionately large workforce. The result for these nations is real economic growth for their respective economies and an ever-increasing level of personal income for the average worker, as compared to the stagnation experienced here in the United States.

POLITICAL RESPONSIBILITY

It is the radical ideological blackmail and intimidation that needs resisting. We stand on a rampart from which should come the battle cry of reform. What rights do the citizens of any nation have in asserting the demographic, economic, and ethnic integrity of their nation? Dare a citizen make such a claim without being labeled a racist?

Someday, we will look back in horror at the power of such leaders as Prime Minister Harold Wilson of Great Britain (1964–70) and Helmut Kohl of Germany (1980s–90s), who, ignoring the voice of the people, insinuated millennial changes in the ethnic and demographic composition of their nations. These political power plays not only affected the lives of the current inhabitants of these nations, but, far worse than incurring any major defeat on the battlefield, created national repercussions for many generations down the line.

No wonder that irrational vigilantes have taken up the issues of immigration and the subversion of their respective nations' historic ethnic heritages. Whenever the responsible authorities, intellectual and media groups, fail to present such issues for public political debate, subject them to the will of the people, these public perceptions and feelings will go underground, where they will be vulnerable to manipulation from the Fascist left or right.

It is now happening in Europe. It could happen in the United States. One example of this dangerous manipulation of reality by ideological power groups exploiting our judicial system is exemplified in the situation in Haiti. The right of the U.S. government to interdict these boat people before they land is now entangled in the subtleties of our legal system, and stems from the question of the Haitians' status as economic or political refugees.

The original laws exempting political refugees from immigration regulations were passed in the United States and in various European countries at a time of real persecution during the Cold War and the accompanying political ferment throughout the world during that period. It rightly should have specified sanctuary for small numbers of the leadership of the respective nations and peoples. It was never meant to apply to massive transfers of populations, as it did with the Vietnam boat people, as well as the Cambodian refugees.

As expected, the political tumult in Haiti, as in the above-mentioned nations during the 1970s and 1980s, has dredged up refugees. It is a good time for people to get out; they have nothing to lose, and they hope that they will land in beneficent arms. Four billion people are living in the poverty and chaos of the Third World. To think of any but a tiny minority as political refugees stretches credulity to the exploitable limits of our legal system.

The citizens of the nations of the north need a clear intellectual mandate that undergirds their perceptions that they, and their ancestors who have brought these respective nations to prosperity, be assured that their elected representatives will not destroy this heritage, thus undermining the future of generations to come.

A nation's decisions concerning its future should be determined by an explicit mandate from its citizens. Immigration policy set by unauthorized political decree or political negligence must be halted immediately, permanently.

POLICY

1. Armed forces exist to protect the viability of a nation. Threats vary in immediacy as well as in methods of countering and eliminating potential dangers. We have recently seen the satisfactory and bloodless conclusion to an almost forty-five-year-old Cold War threat from the various communist empires. We defeated them because we held them at bay militarily until the internal contradictions of their fraudulent ideology finally consumed and disintegrated their political, economic, and military integrity.

We understood that threat because it was so similar to traditional military challenges. In addition, however, we inchoately perceived the wrongness of their socioeconomic ideology, and the inherent rightness of our social and economic system. Still we do not understand fully the meaning of this ability of our system of social and economic life to release human initiative and intelligence. Otherwise we would better understand the nature of the even greater threat to our national integrity by the tide of immigration sweeping over us and the rest of the north from the south.

It needs to be stopped and rolled back. What better use for our armed services than to be redirected to stop the leakage in the dikes? No more illegal immigration. Over and above that, we must return to their homelands those who are here in violation of our laws, along with the children that have been born here in the interim. These children ought not to be candidates for citizenship.

No more grandfathering by law, nor the political opportunism of ethnic politics. No matter what one's ethnicity, there should be a realization that the short-term interests of political opportunists ought not to take precedence over the safety of the nation. And it *is* clear from every opinion survey that Latin Americans born in the United States today oppose immigration from south of our border.

If it is not wartime, it is close to it. The motto should be: *Remember California!*

2. A simple law. Children born of mothers who are present on our shores illegally or who are on temporary work or student visas have no claim to citizenship. Those who marry to evade our immigration laws should be deported after due process.

3. Family unification and political refugee citizenship should be applied rarely, probably only by Congressional petition. The U.S. Labor Department reported that between 1985 and 1987, of the approximately 591,000 legal immigrants admitted to the United States, only 4 percent were work- or talent-related admissions. The rest were mostly family unifications. David Francis has estimated that out of approximately 700,000 immigrants to be

legally admitted between 1992 and 1994, only 55,000–60,000 visas will be issued "for the talented immigrants sought by business."[18]

4. Talented people are always sought by forward-looking nations. The wily tyrant of sixth-century B.C. Athens, Pisistratus, made a career of inviting the most creative artists and thinkers from all over the Greek world. No barbarians needed to apply for Athenian refugee status.[19] The criterion for immigrants and future citizens was "What can you do for us if we let you in?" Why not apply this motto today? After all, we want to survive and prosper, don't we? Or *do we*?

How many? That is a practical question that depends on our ability to bring the "illegals" under control. The Korean business people who were burned out in the 1992 Los Angeles riots had taken their own savings and those from relatives in South Korea, invested them in the United States, in Los Angeles, and worked like slaves to build successful businesses. In a generation, their children, had the businesses not been burned out, would have become medical doctors, scientists, and business people, contributing to the prosperity of the United States. Obviously, their track record merits our invitation to more of them.

5. Poor people. Are we turning our back on the Statue of Liberty and the meaning of the American dream if we shut out the poor from our shores? Answer: Believe it or not, the world changes and so does the United States. To go from being an empty country, with seemingly unending vistas, to one choking on its waste and smog, crime and plague, homelessness and drugs, in but a century, is a *remarkable* achievement. It should make us humble in recognizing the merited judgment that perhaps we may now have more than just our share of poor people; we may have permanent poverty!

6. Avoiding racism. There is no question that those few slots for legal immigrants that we should want to invite to our shores because their talents may be valuable to us should be chosen from all racial and ethnic groups. Whether they be from Nigeria, Ethiopia, Brazil, Ireland, China, or Russia should depend on judgment as to their objective skills as adults or extremely successful students. Naturally, all should be allowed to come with their immediate families.

7. Nation building. The United States is unique. Unlike the Netherlands or Germany, we have created our ethnicity over a much shorter period of time, and from a much wider ethnic spectrum. We are a multi-racial and multi-ethnic society gradually melding into a unity. Still, we will need a measure of cultural pluralism to maintain internal stability.

Therefore, we should not blindly oppose whatever level of immigration responsible social policy decides is proper, or restrict it to any particular racial or ethnic mix. Prudence would argue, however, that immigration ought to continue to reflect, to a degree, the existing composition of the peoples of the United States, always given the essential requirement—every immigrant applicant has the intellectual potential for contributing to the prosperity of our nation at the highest civilizational levels of contemporary life.

However one cuts it, the question is not whether there are limits to this country's ability to absorb immigration; the question is only where those limits lie, and how they should be determined and enforced—whether by rational decision at this end or by the ultimate achievement of some sort of a balance of misery between this country and the vast pools of poverty elsewhere that now confront it.

George F. Kennan[20]

Chapter 14

Disestablishing State Schooling

BASICS

It's not that the businesses are leaving. That's to be expected. In certain industries the workers in any developed country would be noncompetitive. In principle there are areas in which Mexican and Thai workers could displace Germans and Japanese, no less Americans. Their current skills match their education, which reflects the world standard of their salaries— very low.

And, in fact, the Japanese and the Germans have their low-wage, low-education satellites around the world. The disturbing news is that corporations, once wholly American, now international, do not stay in the United States to create enough other jobs that require high intellectual/educational levels and thus pay the kind of wages that once we were privileged to receive.

Something has happened to us, and in only twenty-five years. At first, the loss was hardly noticed, so much else was manufactured and built in the United States. But as other nations began to push our relaxed attitude about jobs to the boards, our workforce began to increase its percentage of underemployed or unemployable poor—some homegrown, but many others invited to slip over our borders—the pinch began to be felt.

Overseas, better educated and more reliable workers were being produced all the while we were beginning to decline. The rhetoric from our leadership was supportive, even as the nation became at risk. Education would improve, officialdom reassured us. Just add a few more government aid programs and we can do it. A few of us wondered whether more money was really the answer, for the United States already spends more per capita than any other nation of comparative wealth.[1] What have we been getting for it?

THE MYTH OF PUBLIC EDUCATION

The greatest barrier to the reform of education in the United States is the belief that the so-called public school as an institution has hallowed status, equivalent to that of the Supreme Court. The truth is that, as presently constituted, a mixture of local and state tax support, with about 8 percent of the total expenditure coming from the federal government by way of specific programs such as Head Start, the public school has existed in its present form for little more than a century.[2]

American education can be traced from the early colonizations from Europe. The beginning of this American tradition, from the first quarter of the seventeenth century, has seen much educational diversity in the past 350 years.

In fact, for a period of about 125 years, especially in New England, a tradition of church/state education was firmly in place. Each community had its own homogeneous patterns, not too different from those that were developing in the European homeland at that time. The great difference was the high level of literacy that was established in the various colonies, epitomized by institutions such as the New England dame schools for girls, Boston Latin, Harvard, and then Yale, also William and Mary in Virginia.[3]

From about 1750 to 1830, a new tradition began—semi-secular independent secondary school and then colleges, such as King's (1754) in New York City (Columbia) and the College of Philadelphia (1755) (now the University of Pennsylvania), the latter founded under the influence of Benjamin Franklin, and Jefferson's University of Virginia, in 1825. Americans always placed great emphasis on education, regardless of the ideology that stimulated their education-building passions.[4]

But in the revolutionary period, the great tradition was liberty, independence from the interfering grasp of government. The schools were central to this passion for free thought beyond the control of the state. Therefore, the Constitution lacks any reference to schooling or education per se. The reason was not disinterest in education, rather the belief that individuals, local voluntary communities, or perhaps the several states should take the initiative.[5]

A reading of the ninth and tenth amendments to the Constitution clarifies the right of citizens to take educational initiatives into their own hands as a power reserved to the people.[6] In 1925, the Supreme Court, in the so-called Oregon Decision, upheld as a right of property the parochial and independent schools of that state, freeing them from a law that would have forced all children into the public schools.[7]

The involvement of local communities and the state in education began in the 1830s when the rapidly expanding frontier began to dissolve communities, industrialism began to challenge the more leisurely pace of farm life, and new groups of immigrants arrived having differing educational traditions.

The so-called Common School was an answer that seemed to balance liberty with civic responsibility. The theme of the Common School was that the local community should have the responsibility for the education of all the children, given the will of the parents.[8] This was a time of minimal compulsory education laws. Such laws would come later, with the creation of the public schools.

The public schools, offering schooling to all our children from kindergarten through high school, began to take shape in the 1870s and 1880s. Immigration was in high gear, the explosion in scientific knowledge, now linked to industrialism, argued for a more active state role. The present mix of local real estate taxes and state regulation and support builds from this period.

Those of us who have grown up in cities recognized the great stereotyped factory-like high schools as the medium that would lead us onto the high road of democratic participation and preparation for the knowledge and skills of tomorrow. The United States won World War II with a largely high school–educated work- and armed force.[9]

But there were Catholic and other parochial as well as many private schools that also did the job for the United States. And a great part of higher education was independent of governmental involvement. The private colleges and universities also provided much opportunity to students from all social and ethnic backgrounds. The particular American mix, then and now, was the key to balance and stability in our educational system.

WHAT HAPPENED?

Institutions age. That is why the Supreme Court is constantly put to the task of interpreting a Constitution, now over 200 years old, albeit much amended, to fit new circumstances. As noted above, the public schools have no constitutional sanction. State initiative is necessary for any action in the domain of public education. What the federal government could do through the tax system in the way of tuition tax relief for private or parochial schooling, or voucher appropriations that may be used in any kind of school—the G.I. Bill model—would have to involve extras or legislative action, and, of course, special appropriations of tax monies.

Real change will have to come out of the states, as in Colorado in 1992, where a citizens' initiative (subsequently defeated) was on the ballot to give a partial tuition voucher to every child of school age in that state. In theory, any state has the right, given the voice of the people and its constitution, to dissolve the existing publicly-supported system of education. It can create any system of education that its state constitution allows, conceivably even turning the education of its children back to parental responsibility.[10]

Up until the early 1960s the public schools retained their traditions of upward mobility, despite the ferment of the court-mandated desegregation of the state-enforced racial separations of the American South.[11]

Factors in our educational collapse include: (1) the accumulating wealth in the United States, coupled with (2) the slow pace of social equalization of African-Americans, (3) the growing student and teacher ferment about our military involvement in Vietnam, (4) the dissolution of the popular consensus as to what the public schools ought to teach and how, (5) strikes and union militancy by teachers, (6) a bloated educational bureaucracy both at the school district level and in the state capitals overseeing certification of teachers and other state mandates. These factors all combined to produce a very different public education system than had existed even in the 1930s and 1940s.[12]

The remarkable thing is that the system has held together throughout a twenty-five-year free-fall of academic standards and the opting out of larger and larger proportions of the various communities—Catholics, many minority parents, home schoolers, free schoolers.[13] This abandonment took place at a time when parents were bearing the economic burdens both of supporting the existing state school system through local and state taxes and of paying to send their children to schools of their choice.

Perhaps the most profound, though unstated, cause of the decline can best be understood by considering the evidence given in Chapter 5, the overall disappearance of highly gifted children from the school population, and conversely the seemingly endless increase in the numbers of children with serious learning incapacities or disabilities. The great growth industry in the education of teachers is special education. In this field is combined all that new professionals are supposed to know when dealing with problem learners.[14]

There are many other examples of academic fragmentation and decline, including what is now being used as a substitute for the traditional international academic disciplines, "multiculturalism," a new form of intellectual and educational segregation to which white and black liberals have given their imprimatur.[15]

What happened? As with so many of our institutions, we became fat with money and self-satisfaction. In addition, the schools were politicized to serve every conceivable social cause and complaint. Eventually the decline that was being experienced in other social institutions began to be concentrated within formal schooling. No longer could it serve even the basic functions for which it was originally created. The young left our bureaucratized schools ignorant and numbed. In the meantime, the world had walked away from them.

CRISIS MANAGEMENT: NATIONAL TESTING

Can it be that only 9 percent of white high school seniors are prepared to do college-level work in reading comprehension, mathematics, and science?[16]

Can it be that less than 1 percent of the high school seniors who achieve such college preparedness are African-Americans, when this minority constitutes about 12 percent of our population?[17]

Can it be that only 50 percent of our seventeen-year-olds still in high school cannot pass eighth-grade junior high school tests in reading, math, and science? Remember, I said these seventeen-year-old kids are the ones "still in high school," not the ones who have already dropped out.[18]

Few would believe that such dismal educational achievement levels are entirely due to our declining intellectual profile. And probably you, also, cannot believe this to be the case. If it were not true, our question would be: How can this unpardonably low level of educational achievement be turned around?

The solution to this mess has been a loud call for national testing. Almost everyone is for it except the educational bureaucracy and some of the civil rights groups. The former drag their feet because testing would reveal the true dimensions of our national calamity and would put great pressure on it to acquiesce in a national restructuring of the public schools. It fears any change.[19]

The civil rights groups have also contributed to the educational disaster in that they have heedlessly acquiesced in the liberals' "welfarism" destruction of the African-American community. The educational results, clearly visible, not covered up by affirmative action and quota smoke screens, would reveal the full scope of the tragedy suffered by this community since *Brown v. Board of Education* (1954) and the Civil Rights Act (1964).

But would national testing do anything in the short or long term to remedy the situation? We have known the full truth of our universal decline in educational competency for ten years, since "A Nation at Risk" was published in 1983.[20] Much chest thumping and financial expenditure have occurred since then, which have only given further confirmation that the decline is unstanched. Now, the money is rapidly disappearing as the changing U.S. demography and the consequent declining economic profile seems to be sealing our fate as a once-developed, now essentially Third World nation in the making.

CRISIS MANAGEMENT: THE VOUCHER

This is the only straw that we can grasp in the foreseeable future. The "voucher," with federal as well as state support, must be unconditional. It must be offered to all children within a state or throughout the country, and for any state-registered and academically acceptable school. This should include public, private, or parochial schools. If such a voucher is to be a real solution, a real choice, it must not be restricted to the current state establishment, the so-called public schools.[21]

A radical structural move ostensibly to improve educational achievement should necessarily provide a scenario of prediction by which we could begin to evaluate the move. It should predict what might reasonably be expected to occur. Also, it should predict what will *not* happen, in terms of school achievement and social segregation, for example. The voucher has become politically acceptable to Republican-type conservative groups in the last several years. Thus liberals have opposed it with recitations of "doomsday" fears, predictions-before-the-fact, damning it as a proposal having no redeeming virtues.[22]

In its basic format, the voucher is a simple idea. Take an average of the monies spent on each child for its education in the public schools of each state, or an overall average of the fifty states, if one wants to go to a national system immediately. (I wouldn't. There are too many bureaucratic and ideological dangers in any national system.) Shade the distribution of money in terms of grades, perhaps giving a little more to the secondary school youngsters than to those in the elementary grades.

In many cities and states the classroom teacher salaries, room supplies, building, heat and electricity receive barely half the tax monies supplied for educational purposes; the bureaucracy gets the rest. We should expect to see a voucher pie of, let us say, $4,000–$5,000 per child, per year divided in many new and interesting ways. Just imagine: even at $4,000 per child, a classroom of twenty children would have $80,000 available for teacher, supplies, room rental, and utilities. Expand the class size a bit, and we are speaking about $120,000–$160,000 available for the education of the children in each class.[23]

The struggle within the states exemplified by the attempt to amend the Texas Constitution in 1993 to allow for a more equitable redistribution of funds for education, from more wealthy school districts to poorer ones, or else creating one vast statewide school district, would not be necessary. The process of educating one's child would become depoliticized.

For example, in Texas the students in the wealthiest 5 percent of school districts averaged one-year support of $11,801 per pupil. Those in the poorest 5 percent saw $3,190 expended on each pupil. By coming up with a reasonable voucher for each child in Texas, at perhaps $5,000 per year, one suspects that the poorest children would be better educated, the taxpayers much happier, and wealthy parents free to do as they do today, expend their personal wealth on their children as they see fit.[24]

For comparison, note that in 1993 New York City public schools, made up of largely poor children, many of them aliens, expended $7,800 per pupil. How much of this money will ever go into the classroom is a reasonable question. Evidence is that if $3,000, a bit more than one-third, was actually expended on instruction and supplies it would constitute a miracle.[25]

Contrast this $7,800 per year spent on each child in New York City with the $10,500 per year tuition that President Clinton is spending on his daughter, Chelsea, in an exclusive Washington, D.C., private school.[26] What is an inner-city parent in New York City getting for the money, as compared with the president?

With class sizes of over forty, the Japanese produce achievement levels that are unsurpassed. The myth that children need a low teacher-to-pupil ratio has too long been accepted by the public. It is strictly "union talk," with a bit of child development romanticism thrown in. This larger teacher/pupil ratio might be utilized during the actual instructional ages, not necessarily in intimate nursery or pre-school settings.[27]

A school should have absolute freedom of choice in terms of which children it will admit, just as a family should have the same freedom to choose the schools for their children. An unjustified fear exists that some children, minority and poor, will be passed over by most schools. To the extent that many youngsters do not belong in ordinary schools, this may be true. It is inconceivable, however, that for a child carrying a voucher worth $4,000—perhaps more if there is a bona fide need for additional help—both at the gifted as well as the special education levels—there would not be schools established to vie for these students and their vouchers.

The need for flexibility probably requires that there be differing voucher dollar amounts in each state as well as regulations that would allow for the most innovative sharing of facilities. The state imposition of class size, salary, and other possibly inhibiting regulatory strictures should be prevented. Of course, state or public supervision is both necessary and desirable. The principle ought to be to allow almost any sort of educational experiments. Make the state "inspector" prove the negative, after the fact of experiment, as is done in Great Britain.[28]

The argument against the voucher idea also uses foreign state education models, such as in France or Germany, to warn against the possible wholesale privatization which the voucher idea could auger. For one, however, both France and Germany up until the present have been culturally and socially homogeneous nations and much smaller than the United States. The federalist nature of German political organization has carried over into their educational structure. In a way somewhat similar to our states, the Germans use the available funds in differing ways throughout their varying states. Yet there is a traditional sense of what is orthodox, educationally. This pattern has been constructed from the perspective of a traditionally homogeneous intellectual and thus educational profile, that is, until the country feels the full impact of the children of its "guest workers," and now its millions of additional "political" refugees.

It may be possible for a state such as North Dakota or Vermont to develop a true voucher choice plan and still retain most of the existing state school facilities and structure. For instance, Vermont today uses the voucher in many areas to give students freedom of choice in the private and public sectors. It is cheaper for certain mainly rural school districts to go this route, at the least for the high school level.

The great power of the voucher is the possibility that, as, for example, in Milwaukee, Wisconsin, it offers to the poorest segments of our population to provide their children with an education at a cost no greater than what could be obtained in the public schools of their state, but an education that will fit the needs of these children. Choice. There is no greater empowerment than the ability to make decisions that can affect your own life destiny.[29]

It is this power of choice that gave the American automobile industry, indeed the entire U.S. corporate establishment, a cold chill. It illustrated that in a free market the people will pick the better product, non-American or not. That choice of automobiles remade our public awareness. Perhaps it saved corporate America, now finally competitive in the world.[30]

Finally, the terrible condition of education in the inner cities could be alleviated. Today, African-American children of potentiality are bullied within the schools by court- and ACLU-protected gangs to reject the learning of "whitey." The level of violence both within the schools and around their precincts has shocked the world, no less then the ordinary American parent.

Such children should be given access to schools where learning is serious and disrupters excluded. There are fine teachers and schools who will come to the inner city, as they have to the Catholic schools and to the new "Beta" schools in Wisconsin for deeply troubled youth. All schools, including potentially non-sectarian institutions, would have an economic basis of survival now secured by the state-funded voucher.[31]

RESULTS

Many reasons argue for the voucher. In today's context, a sharply declining intellectual, educational, social, and economic national profile—cause: more illiterates, pathological behavior, only unskilled government and private jobs available—the voucher may be the only immediate way to uncover the talent now submerged by an incompetent state educational bureaucracy.

The thrust of the voucher, and the inevitable state and federal regulation that accompanies any government largesse, will have to center on the discovery and education of a larger leadership cadre than is presently being produced.

The leadership may not be there. We simply do not know for sure whether the precipitous decline in our educational achievement levels and the concomitant decline in the creation and prospering of new frontier industries are due to the actual drying up of talent in our society or simply to its burial under a dying educational system.

This is the reason that we must direct all efforts to assisting and support-ing those educational leaders who will develop programs for the talented and gifted from all segments of our population, black or white, rich or poor. No constraints except the fundamental market arbiter—if it is good, it will sell; if spurious, eventually the clientele will wise up and the school will disappear. If only people were free at this very moment to vote on the efficacy of their children's educational institutions—even giving some of the older children (14 and over?) the right to choose the schools that will mobilize their voluntary energies to learn.

The scenario that I would predict for an evolving voucher system would be one that does not see a wholesale abandonment of the state schools by the people. The voucher will never be large enough in dollar terms to provide for massive building programs by new experimental schools. Of necessity, there will be much sharing of space by compatible existing state schools and more independently sponsored institutions.[32]

The principle is emulation as well as experimentation. Just as most great institutions are modeled after a Harvard at the university level, or after an Amherst or Williams at the collegiate level, plus other more specialized and/or experimental-type institutions, the lower schools will develop their own hierarchies based on the alert perceptions of parents and teachers.

It might be a Phillips-Andover or a Bronx High School of Science at the secondary level, a Smith College Campus School, a Harambee in Milwaukee, or any of a wide variety of excellent elementary schools, many in the inner city, run by community groups or churches, for younger children. The point is that when they have the power of *choice*, parents, as well as the children themselves, will become extremely knowledgeable about what should be valued in an education, and what should be rejected.[33]

Above all, there will be the challenge of excellence to be emulated. Schools may decide that they can do without a football team, even basketball competition, instead using their monies for a music program, perhaps chess and computers. Other schools might show the way by encouraging the judicious use, or possibly even the rejection, of television, even two hours of real homework each night. Above all, schools might once again become palaces of learning where police and metal detectors, layers of assistant principals and guidance counselors, become distant memories of the "bad old times" of American education.

Current theory by the teachers' unions and the educational bureaucracies argues that ordinary citizens are too naive to be able to make intelligent choices concerning their children's schooling. Their hands need to be held as they are guided through the hallowed and sacred halls of our public schools by the unionized teachers and their administrative and civil service confreres, the priests and priestesses of an untouchable secular churchly tradition.[34]

We can well be delivered from such an establishment. For the majority of teachers, dedicated and under-appreciated, it could be a liberation that would professionalize them light-years beyond the power-exulting September strikes of yesteryear.

We should be prepared to see two results as products of the voucher experiment. The first is an absolute increase in the number of top students, measured by SAT and achievement scores at the junior high school and 17–18-year-old levels. These should be world-class scholars and talents. They should be achieving at a level better than the mean of Japanese students in math and in the sciences. These individuals, given the continuation in the quality of our best colleges and universities, now under siege by "politically correct" feminists, homosexuals, and multiculturalists of the *loose-cannon* left, could become the entrepreneurs and creative thinkers of an early twenty-first-century renaissance.[35]

The second result would be that we should see that the mid-level on-the-line worker now be a fully schooled, technically trained individual who has been educated to learn how to learn in tandem with the day-by-day modern technology and knowledge advances. It may be that these individuals would profit from a new kind of vocational training. This training, so different in vigor and academic challenge from current expensive state and federally funded programs (Smith-Hughes Act, 1917), could be located by use of the voucher within an industry, in a quasi-apprenticeship program that still requires rigorous language, math, and science studies. Were the industry given free reign in its hiring policy—and not limited by quota—the chances are good that many industries would remain in the United States and sign up for such a plan.[36]

The key test of the voucher idea would always be, Is it producing a world-class product, a serious student, a citizen innovator who can return this nation to its once prosperous and responsible leadership in the world?

Finally, in regard to these new experimental, productive schools, I predict that great philanthropic support would follow the voucher and create a schooling renaissance throughout the country.[37] I believe that our citizens are good and would sacrifice for what is worthy.

REGULATION

The voucher with strings attached? How much should government regulate schools that receive voucher monies from the state or federal government? Answer: Not much.

Certainly schools should be subject to the same fire, safety, and health regulations that apply to independent and parochial schools today. In addition, it is fair to say that a school ought not receive public monies if it excludes members of other races, merely on the basis of race. In the case of ethnicity—an educationally valid category of behavior and learning—the test would be somewhat different.

For example, a school devoted to the Italian Catholic cultural tradition should have the right to ask of all prospective students that they be willing to commit themselves to a curriculum that reflects this tradition, plus the within-the-school mores and patterns of behavior that reinforce the values of this tradition.

Therefore we could expect the admission of African-American students or those of Jewish background, if such students show that they are willing to participate in the learnings and culture of the school. Purely racial factors, being physical, ought to have no bearing on whether or not a student is admitted to a school. This principle should be used as a criterion that cuts in various directions, as there will be many kinds of ethnic schools, some, for example, that might emphasize Latino or African-American traditions.

If a school chooses to deemphasize academics, let us say, for sports or arts, and the students and parents are made fully aware of the long-term implications of such a program, so be it. The regulatory test will have to be made on the overall impress of the school, whether or not it is a legitimate institution, and not run by charlatan teachers or proprietors. Permitted, of course, will be "schools-for-profit," such as the system developed by Chris Whittle.[38]

The British have long employed a system of senior educational inspectors to accredit or discredit schools for the awarding of the various local and national grants. The burden of proof ought always to fall on the authorities, to say "no," rather than for the school to have to argue for its existence, slogging through the red tape of yet another bureaucracy.

The voucher, furthermore, should have no means test. Give the same amounts of government money to all. If the wealthy want to spend extra for horseback riding, let them be free to do it.

It will soon be found that great educational achievement is not necessarily a product of material wealth. The key is *seriousness*.

EDUCATIONAL FREEDOM

Does the above argument really entail the disestablishing of governmental control over and running of schooling? Answer: Only partially. The voucher is the problem. True, it is a return of taxes. But as in the practices of the Mafia, both the cut that the government takes and the original price in taxation have to be too high. No question that, as with food and drugs, water and air quality, there is going to have to be a governmental, thus a public presence in schooling, at the least to ensure that the fire escapes are clear in emergencies.

E. G. West, an economist at Carleton University in Ottawa, Canada, delved deeply into the origins of English state education during the mid-to-late nineteenth century. He concluded, after much analysis, that it was all a great political, social, and educational mistake. Prior to the adoption of the first public education laws in the 1870s, the private sector, including church and philanthropic schools, were making great progress in spontaneously filling a need for an educated industrial proletariat.[39]

West concluded that this institutional development was more a case of political power-brokering by aggressive ideological elements in the society the better to control the lives and destinies of its citizens than a disinterested concern for its citizens' educational needs for access.

Certainly John Stuart Mill in his 1859 essay *On Liberty* viewed government-sponsored schooling as a great threat to the freedom of mind of the people:

The objections which are urged with reason against State education do not apply to the enforcement of education by the State, but to the State's taking upon itself to direct that education; which is a totally different thing. That the whole or any large part of the education of the people should be in State hands, I go as far as anyone in deprecating. All that has been said of the importance of individuality of character, and diversity in opinions and modes of conduct, involves, as of the same unspeakable importance, diversity of education. A general State education is a mere contrivance for molding people to be exactly like one another; and as the mold in which it casts them is that which pleases the predominant power in the government—whether this be a monarch, priesthood, an aristocracy, or the majority of the existing generation—in proportion as it is efficient and successful, it establishes a despotism over the mind, leading by natural tendency to one over the body. An education established and controlled by the State should only exist, if it exist at all, as one among many competing experiments, carried on for the purpose of example and stimulus to keep the others up to a certain standard of excellence.[40]

Inevitably, government control of schooling leads to a state educational system whose basic thrust is control of the minds of the children and the families who are required by economic status to send their young to such schools. This was certainly the case in Bismarck's Germany where a powerful grouping of state educational systems served perfectly to undergird the thrust for military and industrial power, even imperial expansion, that purportedly would serve German national interests.

The French under Napoleon had perceived long before this the importance for an imperial and powerful political and military stance. They established a national educational system under the direct rule of the state from Paris. In Paris, an educational bureaucrat could look at his watch and know what was being taught in whichever grade, anywhere in the nation.[41]

Those believers in state-run and -controlled education will point to the successful achievement levels that characterized the homogeneous institutions of France and Germany. But, as noted above, these countries are also ethnically homogeneous. They are also subject to destructive politicization in the universities and in the lower schools, thrusts for total control by various fascisms, and Nazism.

In the more decentralized setting of education in the United States, Japan, and Great Britain this will be less likely. The Japanese educational environment is far more diversified in institutional control, if not in the curriculum and examination systems. Neither the voucher idea, nor any more radical conception of decentralization, would prohibit the voluntary use of nation-wide exams such as the SAT or achievement exams to be used as a guide to the comparative placement of our students in terms of the necessary international achievement standards.

ULTIMATE FREEDOM

The United States has been a leader in so many areas of social and political freedom, including our fifty state-based public schools, that it behooves us to look more futuristically at the needs and possibilities of tomorrow. Simply, it is reactionary to allow the indefinite continuation of fixed governmental forms of life that are mandated from the center.

There is nothing more flexible, responsive, or progressive than the initiatives and voluntary activities reflected in the individual behaviors of a free people. In education, which connotes value choosing, new knowledge forms, responding to the challenges of tomorrow by parents, children, and their teachers, choice in schooling can only result in the highest standards of what our people want, and what they are able to muster.

Ultimately, schooling and education for freedom in the broadest sense will have to be privately undertaken by individuals who will themselves decide what proportion of their income and capital will be invested in the education of their children. As always, a free people will individually make considered decisions as to how much of their earned wealth they will expend on liquor, cigarettes, sports, entertainments, or vacations in Palm Beach.

The disestablishment of state-run schooling depends centrally on the creation of an independent middle class. Such a development will never occur with the continuation and growth of social dependency, today increasing, perhaps tomorrow dominating.

Here lies our educational tragedy in the making. The poorer we get, the less able to compete intellectually and educationally with the middle classes of the world, the more our public schools will become *official* charity and remedial institutions. They will fit the young for no modern responsibilities, economic, civic, or cultural.

Chapter 15

Middle-Class Economics and the Social Contract

PROSPERITY

Civilization is middle class. It is the values of the literate that have under-girded the creation of those institutions of social life that we fight to defend. These values have flowed beyond the boundaries of tribes and nations. They are now inseparably joined to our world civilization.

We have evidence from early in the post-Pleistocene Ice Ages, from about 10,000 B.C., that the tin of Spain and Cornwall, the ceramic beakers of unknown West European craftsmen, were being traded throughout western Europe as part of a tradition that began the upthrust of modern complex urban communities, soon, the beginning of literate civilizations.

Today the conception of middle class is international, with populations from all parts of the world vying to produce and consume those material and cultural symbols that will maintain a middle-class style of life. Everywhere peoples and nations are struggling to upgrade their productivity so that it will win the allegiance of the international middle class. This means that the middle class will pay for that extra value produced by a nation's citizens out of which come profits, salaries, dividends, taxes, all required for a civilizational lifestyle.

The French produce wines, and Paris prospers with tourists. Italy has fine shoes and textiles; Florence, Rome, and Venice attract millions of worshipers of the beautiful. The list can go on. The point is that it is not merely computers and machine tools that make for a middle-class way of life for a people, but also culture, tourism, the financial wherewithal of London's City. All these contribute to that accumulation of international wealth that distinguishes the First World from the Third.

INTERNATIONAL ECONOMIC LESSONS

In the 1930s, "Made in Japan" meant shoddy and cheap. In the 1980s, "Made in the U.S.A." also meant shoddy to many, but it also came to mean expensive. Thus the industries moved to the ambitious developing countries whose workers had the intellectual and now the educational levels to produce decent goods at exceptionally low cost. The leadership of these countries persuaded the people, as in Mexico and Thailand, to work for $.50–$1.00 per hour with the idea of learning to master the industrial manufacturing techniques of the First World, thus working their way up on the skill/quality/education hierarchy.

This strategy had worked remarkably well for the Japanese, South Koreans, and Chinese throughout eastern Asia and now on the mainland, and in a blink of time's eye.[1] In that same blink we in the United States have fallen dismally in our ability to meet the demands for a wide variety of goods and services that would allow a majority of our population in the twenty-first century to have middle-class lives.

In the 1980s we confronted this crisis by living on borrowed monies: federal, municipal, and corporate debt and bonds financed mostly from the accumulated wealth of the older generation, earned in more productive times, but partially from the benevolence of our international friends. The Republican propagandists speak of millions of new jobs created in the 1980s. They don't deny that we lost 2 million factory jobs as we added 10–14 million other jobs, many part-time.[2] Of course, those jobs and the supposed prosperity that they engendered were built out of this mountain of debt, which financed the entire charade.[3]

It will be interesting to see what happens to our standard of living once we can no longer accumulate budget deficits, at the risk of sinking our basic financial foundations or the value of the dollar, setting off inflation, then massive unemployment, ameliorated never again by the year-plus of unemployment payments that are keeping so many going, and are adding to the deficit.

The contrast with Taiwan during these past ten or twelve years is both instructive and frightening. First, remember that these Chinese people were under colonial Japanese rule for fifty years before being liberated by the United States in 1945. Then, in 1949, well over 1 million bedraggled and defeated troops and their families of Chiang Kai-shek and his Nationalist Army came ashore on Taiwan and set up their government under U.S. protection from the victorious Maoists on the mainland.

By the early 1960s this still-autocratic government had its basic agricultural development well enough in hand in terms of electric water pumps, motorized plows, and so forth, to relieve the United States from giving all but military aid. At the same time, the Taiwanese were inviting corporations from all over the world to set up on a partnership basis with local business-men and the government to develop industries using the cheap but increas-ingly well-educated students. The schools were dilapidated, under-funded. The students, extraordinarily intelligent, serious, extremely hard working.

In 1980 the Chinese in Taiwan produced about $8.5 million of computer products along with their other more basic manufactures. Already, their high school students were moving into the upper ranges of science, math, and language achievements in the international educational sweepstakes. The beginnings of a world trade surplus that would give them $100 billion in surplus cash by the mid-1980s were under accumulation.

And so was the gentrification of their productive ambitions. By 1992 they were producing, in one year, $7.6 billion of computer products, ninety times what they produced twelve years earlier. They were also third in the world in the value of their personal computer production, and the world leader in components such as system boards and monitors.[4]

The next phase of their technological competitive upgrade is targeting semiconductors, disk drives, and software. The latter is especially signifi-cant because of the unique requirements of the northeast Asiatic languages, which make Western-designed programs inapplicable in this region of expanding computerization.

The educational achievements of Taiwanese Chinese high school stu-dents, the basic workforce of a nation, are now at the top of the international scale. Many of these students will be going to the local universities or overseas to the remaining world-class graduate institutions in the West.[5] This nation is already run by a meritocratic cadre of Western-educated Ph.D.s. Today it has made its inevitable turn, considering the middle classification of its citizenry, to a democratic political and social system.

The Taiwanese have had no other obligation to their own people than to pick the best for their workforce without regard to external racial or ethnic considerations. There is a small population of Malayo-Polynesian hill people, but they do not figure prominently in the drive for economic advance and prosperity.

In Taiwan the economic success can be traced to Taiwanese educational competency. Total educational expenditure in Taiwan is a small fraction of our own: in 1991, 3.6 percent, as compared with the United States' 7.5 percent of gross national product.[6] The key to this awesome educational advance is, of course, the Han Chinese intellectual potential, evidenced in their I.Q. scores. In addition to the above are the family and social behavioral

profiles, work intensity, ability to discipline themselves for future satisfac-
tions, all "p"-factor (postponement) elements of their intellectual profile.

The American people, perhaps the most outward looking and philanthropic in the history of civilization, made the prosperity of such nations as
Japan, South Korea, Germany, and Taiwan possible in the first place by
opening up its ports and consumers to this flood of foreign goods. Some say
that we should now look out for ourselves, to reconstruct our internal
technostructure, and stop the hemorrhage caused by our enormous trade
deficits.

The Japanese have been racking up $100-billion per year trade surplus
with the world, $130 billion in 1992, $48 billion of it with the United States.[7]
Simultaneously, the United States has been experiencing a series of approximately $100 billion trade deficits. Remember, this surplus is a result of the
intelligence, education, and work productivity of 122 million Japanese, less
than 50 percent of the U.S. population.

In 1992 the Japanese bought from the United States the value of goods
per capita equal to what the United States bought from Japan. However,
their population is half the size of ours.

We can't close our borders now. Over half our oil is imported. Even with
massive conservation and an ongoing recession, there will be much that the
United States needs from abroad just to keep our indigenous industries
going. With a collapsed dollar, how would we pay for these imported raw
materials and parts?

In the past ten years, this trade deficit has hovered around $100 billion
per year. If it has decreased in the last several years, it is because of the price
competitiveness and efficiency of our more frontier industrial and cultural
products, aerospace and Hollywood films, for instance. Our exports have
grown by 85 percent since 1985, from $312 billion to $576 billion in 1991.[8]
Our imports have also grown accordingly.

Imagine what the picture would be were the dollar even cheaper. This
would cause our industries to have difficulty paying for the imports necessary for their functioning. The trade deficit has been buffered by the sale of
our assets at an increasing rate both to the Europeans and the east Asiatics.[9]
Today economists utilize figures that calculate our gross *domestic* product
rather than our gross *national* product, since so much of the latter flows out
to the foreign owners and investors. Add to this the bonds and stocks of our
government and corporations that we sell to foreigners, who thus become
our creditors.

At present, even given a dollar that is relatively inexpensive in the world
markets and therefore proving American products of quality to be competitive, the existing trade deficit, along with the governmental and private

accumulated debt, constitutes a real and momentary threat to our existing middle-class lifestyle. The pressure to loosen banking controls put into place after the savings-and-loan debacle is now casting a cloud over the entire banking and investment community.[10]

Economist Walter Williams of George Mason University estimates that when social security, bank obligations, retirement benefits, and other guaranteed payments are added to the official national debt, it looks more like $6–8 trillion than the official $4.5 trillion.[11] Currently our political leaders are wont to brag about the current American lifestyle. The edifice, however, stands on a very fragile foundation.

What it comes down to is a simple principle. A people, in order to maintain a high standard of living, must sell nearly as much of the good things of life as it buys. Certainly, for most of its citizens, part of the oncoming collapse of the American standard of living will be caused by the fact that the current international middle class appreciates Japanese, Taiwanese, German, and French goods more than it does equivalent home-grown American products.

Japan has an astonishing surplus of about $130 billion per year over the past several decades. Yet the Japanese consume less per capita than we do. When they do consume, except for foreign travel, they mostly prefer their own home-produced goods. At least, that is what the Japanese leadership told Carla Hills, our former trade negotiator.

Be clear as to my meaning. I do not argue that all 250 million people presently within the borders of our fifty states will become less than middle class in their lifestyle. As long as our present intellectual profile produces well educated people at about 25–35 percent of our population, we will still be able to support a fraction of the productive and service institutions that constitute a civilizational life.

But this fraction of those who can afford an international lifestyle will contrast with the many more millions of Americans who will be working in marginal jobs, or else supported by a growing, if probably ungenerous welfare system that will have to sustain our people at a marginal safety net level of survival. No more beefy benefits that once attracted so many to California.

Just look at the prosperous, classless nations of Western Europe and Japan, and soon to be added South Korea, Taiwan, Hong Kong, and Singapore. Their classlessness and prosperity derive from the fact that they are ethnically homogeneous, and thus intellectually and educationally homogeneous. It is no surprise that the economic differentials are relatively small between the rich and the poor. There is little or no intergenerational poverty. And there is much intergenerational fluidity in economic and social positions.

These nations are able to generate across their respective territories a rich diversity of products and services that are in demand both at home and abroad. As a result, in both the private and public sectors, the resources exist for a full range of individual consumption as well as state services in health, education, infrastructure, and investment. They are prosperous, all.

THE IMPORTANCE OF NATIONHOOD

It is clear in late 1993 that the hopes for European unification are beginning to lag. The national interests of citizens are being aroused, fear of being a poor cousin bereft of control. There will be trade and more open boundaries for this trade. But the nation will continue to be the unit.

That's the way it's going to have to be for us, if we are to survive as a viable transcontinental society. The way is open, however, for de facto secession and the inevitable fracturing of this nation geographically into social class enclaves, as George Kennan has suggested.[12] States will act as New Hampshire has, providing little or no welfare as well as putting into effect a long residency waiting time before any benefits become available.

We can't let that happen to us. Our potential power and recovery as a middle-class society depend on maintaining that notable American mobility and fluidity of social class and residency. There is no real nationhood until we dissolve the hyphenated multiculturalism that appears to be breaking us up today.

I am not arguing for a purely homogeneous American ethnicity, one stretching whole-cloth from Maine to Miami, Washington, D.C., to Walla Walla, Washington. Cultural differences will forever be generated, even in a twenty-first-century context of intercommunication and social mobility. A measure of cultural pluralism throughout the fifty states could constitute the social glue of self-determination. It would keep us together, stronger.

Today our ethnic differences are largely built from our intellectual, educational, and economic differences. It would be straining one's imagination to argue that the average Harvard-educated African-American is very different from fellow graduates named Gonzales, Kelly, or Silverstein when it comes to tastes, values, lifestyle. Take a look, for example, at the Clinton cabinet.

What we need to do over a period of 100 years is to effect a permanent disassociation of race and ethnicity from social, cultural, and economic differences. In turn, the great disparities in culture between the three great ethnic groups—whites, Latinos, African-Americans—will disappear or shift to the intimate zone of private enjoyment and relationships.[13]

This requires that we take that intellectual potential today found in varying proportions in all of our ethnic groups and make it the model for a new American ethnicity, in its genetic diversity an intellectual profile of enormous creative potential.

To do this will require frontier-like statesmanship and education of the citizenry. The factual and rational character of the program will lend it substantial credence. One glimmer of success, and we would see a snowball effect of public enthusiasm. The people would realize the power that inheres in a nation that moves with nature, not against the trends of the last 10 million years of human evolution.

Today we have a crazy quilt of laws on the books that attempt to rectify the sins visited upon *this* victimized group or gender or *that* persecuted minority. Now, the evil object is the white heterosexual male. The intimidated white males in the legislatures and courts are rushing headlong to be first to rule against themselves. That this irrationality is destroying the natural ability of the internationally competitive industries to determine abilities and talents, to pick the very best people without regard for external appearances, has to be apparent from the manner in which our frontier industries are fleeing the madness of a nation determined to destroy itself. Pity the luckless who have to stay behind and witness the shameful denouement.

In an analysis published in *Forbes*, Peter Brimelow and Leslie Spencer estimate that in 1991, the direct and indirect costs of quotas, of imposing them and complying with them, amounted to between $112 and $115 billion. The "opportunity cost," what the economy might have achieved without the misallocative effect of quotas, amounted to an additional $236 billion, totaling at least 4 percent of the 1991 GNP.[14]

One nation, one set of rules by which we all will live. One set of criteria, the best only will be chosen. In this way, our nation will work. Those who live and work within its borders now and in the future will be the beneficiaries of the productivity and justice of the present generation. To achieve this goal, we need to create a society in which the intelligence and education of our citizens are equal more in reality than in our dreams.

ECONOMIC TURNAROUND

We have an immediate problem. In 1993 a new American president was inaugurated. He was chosen because he promised to take dramatic steps, informed by the wisest and most rational economists, to change the direction of the long-declining economy of the United States. The key criteria by which we will judge this heroic effort will be jobs. Not merely minimum wage jobs, temporary summer jobs, or those momentarily created by debt financing, speculation, government pump priming, or pork barrel "make work." Eventually the budget for "unemployment insurance" will have to be shifted to the welfare side of the ledger.

It is good that we can see beyond our borders to the successful nations as well as to the disasters of state "planning." President Clinton spoke about the active role of government in expending tax monies on infrastructure, roads, bridges, railroads, and pollution control.

These jobs will be temporary, and mostly unskilled. Ross Perot, in 1993, called these jobs "bubble jobs," here today, gone tomorrow. The funds needed to produce these jobs will have to come through more deficit spending, at a time of fragile international assessments of our financial stability. Not much room to maneuver there. Many military contracts will be canceled, military bases shut down, service men and women forcibly returned to the civilian job market, all to pay for this investment, perhaps a productive choice but not one to make a radical long-term change in the job market.

Thus far, despite low interest rates, the banks have not been lending money to the entrepreneurs who are supposed to "invest us" out of our doldrums. Is it that the banks don't want to lend money, because they are content to live off the spread between the low interest they pay savers and the somewhat higher interest they get from government backed securities? There is evidence that the bond and equity markets have taken up some of the slack.[15] However, as economist David Levy has noted, investment in new productive enterprises, 6–7 percent of the GNP between the late 1940s and 1980s, has since then fallen to 2–3 percent per year.[16]

Or is it that there are not enough attractive and hopeful entrepreneurs with ideas and potential to be called good risks in a very questionable investment environment? The big corporations have at their elbows the large commercial paper corporations—General Motors, Ford, General Electric—but their borrowing involves progressively fewer jobs. With efficient downsizing, computers, robots, and now practical software programs, all leaner and meaner strategies, they can compete in a tough international marketplace.

The working survivors, when all the personnel cuts have been made, will be the lucky ones, for they will benefit from their relationship with world-class operations. But if the small entrepreneur isn't there to borrow, with good prospects for paying back loans or mortgages, jobs will be scarce. How many tens of thousands of jobs, of any kind, were lost due to the Los Angeles riots of 1992? If you were a bank officer, would you loan monies to a Korean or even an Hispanic shopkeeper who wanted to rebuild in that area, especially remembering that there was once a Watts that burned in that same Los Angeles?

No matter how it is viewed, what it comes down to is what all the economists are saying, and President Clinton agrees. The new jobs should flow out of the frontier technologies, products, and services of our middle-class private sector. From the actual products and services will develop the restaurants, theaters, colleges, parks, and all the other institutional values of middle-class life. These also will produce good jobs. It all flows together. Before long, if we can produce such an economic and cultural mix, we will behold a tangible realization of that dream that we all have for the vast majority of all our citizens, whatever their race or ethnicity, the international middle-class dream: house, family, amenities, vacations, education—a future.

Lester Thurow and others have enumerated these frontier productivities with which the nations of the world are earning cash on the barrel: autos, consumer electronics, high-end textiles, machine tools, optics and telecommunications technologies, computers and software, memory chips and processors, metal fabrication including steel, drugs and biotechnology, aerospace, plus the *new*.[17]

Each of these industries incorporates a myriad of satellite industries, both small and large. But each requires a workforce, from the top executives down to the sanitation engineers, that can participate in a continuous obsolescence-and-renewal environment of mega-change. Thurow talks about process technologies, the *application* of the idea being more important today than the invention of the idea itself.[18]

So many basic ideas and inventions were floating about in the decades after World War II that it was possible to take and adapt these inventions for one's nation's own use. By remaining flexible and innovative it was possible for the mega-Japanese consumer industries to stay ahead, especially as their main competition, including the Europeans, either declined or stagnated. But we can't be sure the ideas and inventions of other nationals will be so easily expropriated in the future.

The future may well reveal far more serious attempts to control both the invention and application of new technologies, especially now that the time frame for development, manufacture, and distribution has become so short. In addition, we are likely to see stricter enforcement of international patent and copyright agreements.[19]

STEEL: EXEMPLAR OF THE FUTURE

As reported by Walter Wriston in a recent book, *The Twilight of Sovereignty*, a combination of advances in material technology, computerization, and steel fabrication has permanently altered the nature of labor in the steel industry, once the fount of industrialization in the world.[20]

The so-called mini-mill, a product of this technological revolution, now requires much less investment than traditional steel mills, $15,000–$25,000 per employee as compared to $30,000–$45,000. These mills can remain profitable with production from about 7 million tons per year, in some cases as little as 200,000 tons per year.[21]

The old-style integrated steel mills, into which were poured literally billions of dollars in modernization in the 1970s—and that were promptly lost, along with 500,000 jobs—have become dinosaurs almost overnight. The new mills depend on computerized production that is specialized rather than generic in terms of ingots and rolling mills. Their needs are now not coal or iron mines, but highly skilled workers and engineers as well as ubiquitous scrap metal.

To manufacture a product in 1988, as compared with in 1977, 40 percent fewer workers were required. This is paralleled by a reduction of about 60 percent in the manufacturing space required, as compared with our needs just two decades ago.[22]

An important concrete example of this vast economic and technological change in our industrial landscape is exemplified by Kenneth Iverson of Nucor Steel Corporation. Head of one of the few profitable steel operations in the United States, Iverson has invested in automated rolling steel equipment made in Germany. It requires only 400 workers per one million tons of output compared with 2,200 workers at USX, the largest American steel operation.

The key to Nucor's success is the requirement of high educable backgrounds in all workers so that they can integrate into an efficient production team, complete dedication of the members of the production team in terms of absenteeism, health, and a merit structure of pay based on efficient productivity, without union interference. The 1991 mean salary of $36,000 per year per worker is average in the industry, but it is here accompanied by a no-layoff policy.

In addition, the headquarters of Nucor, in Charlotte, North Carolina, are located on the first floor of a three-story building. These comprise the entire central office operation—including secretaries—totaling twenty persons. All employees answer their own phones, are on their own in the parking lot, eat in the employee cafeteria, and fly coach. Nucor produces at four plants from South Carolina to Indiana to Texas.

By contrast, the USX headquarters, located in Pittsburgh, comprise the top twenty floors of a glass-sheathed skyscraper. USX has lost millions of dollars per year over the last several years and is rapidly shrinking in size as a steel company.[23]

It is clear from this one comparison that even a basic industry such as steel can be maintained by a developed country as a profitable and contributing productive enterprise. But it means that the overall corporate enterprise must be streamlined to meet the competition of developing nations whose workers and executives know the spindle of necessity and are thus willing to reward themselves with a fraction of the income acceptable to most U.S. workers and executives.[24]

The key may be the Iverson solution, one which many nations, including the already advanced societies of Germany and Japan, but also nations such as Taiwan, Spain, Italy, and South Korea, wish to try. Leave behind the cheap labor technologies and industries and develop technologies that require high levels of research and labor productivity, but also yield high value-added profits, capital that cannot be squeezed out of $.25- or even $5-per-hour production and labor.

Question: What proportion of the U.S. labor and corporate scene is capable of upping the education, production, and management efficiency levels so that they can move into world-class technologies and services? These could produce the profit levels that might maintain our world-class standards of living, not merely individual incomes, but a national tax base that could support the enormously extensive and expensive network of education, transportation, health and hospitals, museums, cultural, and recreational institutions?

Answer: Bureau of Labor Statistics and Data Resources/McGraw-Hill forecasters see no net additions to the 18 million manufacturing jobs in the United States before the year 2005. The prediction is that there will be 20 million new jobs in the United States by that time. Therefore, given present structural trends, manufacturing should then be absorbing less than 15 percent of the workforce. Both Paul Krugman of MIT and Richard Freeman of Harvard agree that the Clinton administration's plan to increase manufacturing jobs is probably chimerical. One hopes that good jobs will be created out of the service sectors—transportation, finance, wholesale trade, construction. How such high-paying jobs will be created without appreciable growth in manufacturing employment, ultimately in exports to pay for such service jobs, is not explained.[25]

COMPETITION OF NATIONS

Unquestionably, international competition in terms of generally free trade will be the rule of international relations. But just because the international corporation will increasingly dominate scientific/technological enterprise does not mean that the nation-state will wither. The nature of competition in the international marketplace will change—many more regional alliances, satellite networking of nations and regions, all connected by the great innovative corporate conglomerates and their allies.

The nation and the well-being of its people will still constitute the "stuff" of this competition. Woe to a government that subordinates the interests of its own people to the benefits of any international structure, political, military, or business.

Robert Kuttner phrased it well in his book, *The End of Laissez Faire*.[26] By observing the active construction of the last twenty years by Germany, Japan, France, and other nations of a great national economic profile, it becomes clear that these nations actively protected their frontier industries. While we twiddled our thumbs, expecting that new industries would arise to fill the gaps created by the departure or failure of the home-grown dominant industries, these nations exerted the full power both of the public and private sectors to assist their own yet nascent frontier industries to become established, to compete efficiently, first at home against the restricted foreigners, then out in the world, especially in the forever vulnerable and open U.S. market.

The agent of Japanese strategic development and trade penetration and expansion was the Ministry of International Trade and Industry (MITI). The Japanese did not give free rein to any one of their corporate combatants, whether in electronics or autos. Rather, these industries were financed and assisted to ascertain their competitive mettle in productive efficiency and quality. The pricing, the loss leaders, the pacing of the international expansion, including its financing, the restricted home markets to maintain the savings and investment support, all constituted a veritable "military" campaign of expansion and struggle. It was so well planned that the outcome was predictable.

It is interesting to note that only the finest students graduating from the University of Tokyo were considered as possible employees of MITI. Here, too, as with the French, no affirmative action. Only the best were employed.

The Germans accomplished the same results through a partnership between the various industries and the banks, especially the *Bundesbank*. Thus the development of Germany's more diversified industrial productivity was accomplished through a freely replenishable stream of bank credit investment. This took place in an environment of high rates of saving, as well as a conscientious overseership of investments—the banks themselves invested in these industries and thus monitored, if not controlled, the destiny of their corporate allies.

Sematech in Austin, Texas, a consortium of major computer companies, constitutes the closest example of protection that we have in this country. It is our own version of developing a computer memory chip industry. And apparently, with some governmental backing, it seems to be working. As Robert Reich, now the secretary of labor, has noted, our interstate highway system, NASA, the Defense Education Act, among other federal governmental initiatives, not to mention the G.I. Bill, represent the same kind of governmental initiatives that have contributed to the material and social uplift of our nation.[27]

In similar cases, Japan and Germany contributed credits as well, as we did with Chrysler in the 1970s. In contrast, the United States has poured enormous sums of tax monies, but no credits, into each of these public projects. Now, with a $4.5 trillion debt, the United States can no longer expend such vast amounts without placing at risk the stability of our financial system, and thus our economic hopes for a truly prosperous private sector.

Our choices in terms of governmental intervention, *industrial policy*, or strategic trade, if you will, may come down to imitating the simple decisions of the Japanese and the Germans—provide seed monies and thus financial discipline to the process of development in the private sector, to encourage those frontier industries that will eventually repay the government and the nation, triply: in jobs, profits, and taxes. The role of such an "industrial policy" may lie principally in facilitating and coordinating research, directing both private and public investment capital into areas that have a reasonable chance of succeeding at the high end of the productive/profit equation.

It is unreasonable to expect success with the present confrontational legal structure, which precipitates litigation at the flick of a wrist. Product liability, affirmative action, gender and racial discrimination laws, sexual harassment litigation, overzealous environmental regulation, inflated health costs and workman's compensation, do much to stifle entrepreneurial enthusiasm and send jobs overseas where advancing educational levels and willing workers are increasingly attractive inducements.

Most important for our future is the creation of a world-class workforce, uniformly educated to the highest achievement levels in the world. For this, we must have a very different population than we have at present.

PROGNOSIS

Hypothesis: If the current proposed policies of President Clinton's Democratic administration aimed at job creation do not, in the next four years, revive the entrepreneurial genius of the American tradition and begin to reproduce those high-paying jobs lost earlier for our working and middle-class citizens, we will be forced to pause and think.

The Reagan-Bush years saw an artificial prosperity built out of high-tech weaponry and financial and real estate speculation (junk bonds and the savings-and-loan debacle). What remains of our frontier industrial output, not including the raw materials, junk metal, and wood pulp that are sold to the developed world, has become lean and competitive in these years. Its leanness did not alleviate our chronic under- and unemployment problem, which seems to worsen each year in the 1990s.

Redistribution failed. Trillions of dollars have been expended domestically and abroad in a futile attempt to graduate the poor into the middle class. Few optimistic sociologists exist anymore. What hopes sociologists such as Christopher Jencks had previously mustered must now be shattered as they gaze at the wreckage overseas in the Third World, and then at the ever-increasing tragedies of the American poor.[28]

The proportion of poor grows; the ranks of the middle class grow thinner. The poor have doubled in size since 1979; now they are over twenty percent of our people. What else can be done to improve the condition of the American economy so that the proportion of middle-class citizens will grow, not decrease as at present?

Proposal: Try to establish a long-term social policy that will "encourage" the birth of 50 percent more children from the upper half of the social and income brackets than from the lower. As economic conditions improve, if they do, over a period of thirty years, maintain this "50 percent principle," thus producing an ever-larger birth cohort from the upper economic/intellectual/educated classes, does the reader think we would have fewer, the same, or more creative entrepreneurial types in sixty years? Would we have more or fewer high-paying jobs that would be filled by ever more highly educated employees?

A NEW SOCIAL CONTRACT: ITS FABRIC

In the world of tomorrow, as of yesteryear, the nation-state will remain the coinage of world political and economic competition. Hopefully, we will be playing on a peaceful playing field. International contact and the blurring of ideological, even cultural differences, among the ruling middle-class elites may dampen the traditional militaristic rampages of national power.

Our goal throughout the twenty-first century should be to transform the United States, from a nation increasingly polarized economically and socially by ethnicity and race, to a classless society, in which racial and ethnic divisions based on intelligence, education, and social class will disappear.

Let us return to our discussion about the United States' immigration problems. We are a large nation, geographically and demographically. However, as noted earlier, we, along with most of the nations of the developed world, have been besieged by indiscriminate immigration, both legal and illegal. As a result, the ethnic profile of the United States, having digested the late nineteenth- and early twentieth-century immigrants from all over the globe, has now been challenged by a new composite.

This new element will be difficult to absorb in this day and age. These immigrants, mostly from Latin America, are the products of a mid-twentieth-century population explosion produced by a medical revolution that was created by the nations of the north. This uncontrolled avalanche of people, mostly from the lowest classes, new "beneficiaries" of the "death control without birth control philanthropy," has flooded over our borders.

The Mexican immigrants, for example, seem to be quite different in educational potential from their predecessors, the mostly indigenous Mexican-Americans of the pre–World War II era often long resident in the southern United States. These new "illegals" crossing into the border counties of Texas, California, Arizona, and New Mexico are not comparable to the elite Mexicans of their home country, now attempting to turn Mexico into a modern nation. They are much like the Central-American and Caribbean "illegals," that is, from the poorest strata of society. They are very different from the Cuban middle classes who escaped from Fidel Castro. The prospects for the absorption of the Latin-American poor into a middle-class technological society of the twenty-first century is very questionable.

W.E.B. Du Bois would probably make a similar assessment with regard to the changing socio-intellectual composition of his own people. Even in his early writings, Du Bois was looking to an elite African-American community that was chosen from the talented tenth.[29] Progress would be tangible in all ethnic and racial groups were we to aim for demographic dominance in each generation from the top 50 percent.[30]

It would be interesting to hear Du Bois's assessment, as a convert to communism, of what the fellow travelers in the liberal community (including the mainstream African-American leadership) have done, through the welfare "plantation," to the African-American community, to its corporate ability to compete educationally and economically with other ethnic or racial groups.

A NEW SOCIAL CONTRACT: PRINCIPLE

Our national challenge is to create one standard of social excellence by which any individual may be measured regardless of ethnic, religious, or political allegiances. The social contract has to be constructed from as nearly homogeneous a national intellectual profile as possible. This means that the society guarantees protection to individuals and their dependents roughly equal to one's contribution to the society's welfare.

No individuals are owed a livelihood by their neighbors. We earn these protections, as minors, through our parents' contributions to the well-being of society. As adults, we ask to be protected by our fellows—police, fire, emergency medical, disaster relief—and by the fact and principle that we are productive citizens.

It is essential to emphasize that in a rapidly changing international culture no society can exist at the pinnacle of efficiency and prosperity unless all of its citizens are capable of contributing to the competitive edge. Today, an increasingly large percentage of our citizens is slipping below this international measure of intellectual potential. Such citizens will never be able to find work on the skill levels that would bring them to a middle-class livelihood and the ability to share in the responsibilities of contributing to the corporate national survival.

On the contrary, composed of all ethnicities, these citizens exist as permanently indigent classes. And yet our leaders continue to encourage them to pass down their intellectual incapacities to their children. The cost to American society has been devastating. Each year, the national tab, not merely in money, but in basic livability, rises. Many of our central cities are being abandoned. New diseases, new pathologies, from the AIDS pandemic to drug violence, homelessness, child and female abuse, seem to be expanding without limit. Crime rises to fever pitch levels, and we are going broke attempting to pay for it. Still, so-called liberals cry out "Evermore."

Let me repeat. In the world of the future, the rules of the social contract calculus will be computed starkly: As a citizen, you are entitled to all the protections of society. As a citizen, to earn this protection, you and yours will be required to function intellectually and socially at a level commensurate with society's cost in guaranteeing you its "safety net."

Simply, the moving line of intellectual competency, daily being ratcheted up by the clever ones at home and abroad, will necessitate that each generation upgrade its intellectually superior cohort. We must persuade the potentially parasitic classes at the top and at the bottom of society to act appropriately. The wealthy educated will have to validate their socially acquired assets by bearing their own offspring or adopting needy children. Those at the bottom should be humanely persuaded, with generous gifts if deemed appropriate—but for one generation only—to refrain from conceiving and having children.

The welfare state, the safety net, social security, are all highly sophisticated humanitarian solutions to the complexity and unpredictability of modern dynamic societies. We need such guarantees against catastrophe. But these guarantees have to be earned by dint of one's potential to contribute to the society that provides for this insurance.

We are making such adjudications all the time. We make them in our tax laws, our educational programs, our social welfare legislation. What we need to do now is to add a crucial heretofore-ignored factual element. Humans vary in their hereditary biological intelligence, their educability, their economic productivity, their overall potential contributions to the well-being and prosperity of their fellow citizens.

If a nation wants to survive as a First World society, it needs to choose carefully the values that will help to achieve this goal. Next, it must take steps to populate itself with individuals who can be educated to achieve those values. If it is unwilling and thus unable so to discriminate because of ideological obstinacy, it deserves to reap its historical desserts.

Chapter 16

Natality: World War III

The fact is that the people of Hellas had entered the false path of ostentation, avarice, and laziness, and were therefore becoming unwilling to marry, or, if they did marry, to bring up the children born to them; the majority were only willing to bring up at most one or two, in order to leave them wealthy and to spoil them in their childhood; and in consequence of all this the evil had been spreading rapidly before it was observed. Where there are families of one or two children, of whom war claims one and disease the other for its victim, it is an evident and inevitable consequence that households should be left desolate and that states, precisely like beehives, should gradually lose their reserves and sink into impotence. On this subject there is no need whatsoever to inquire of the gods as to how we are to be saved from the cancer. The plain man will answer that, first and foremost, we must save ourselves, either by changing our obsession or alternatively by making it illegal not to bring up every child that is born.

Polybius (202–120 B.C.), *Histories*[1]

On this occasion Hellas suffered what was not a "misfortune" at all, but a "disaster" of the most odious and dishonorable kind conceivable. She displayed a combination of disloyalty and cowardice, and committed acts so monstrous as to disgrace her name. Therefore, she forfeited everything that had ennobled her existence, and in this fateful hour her sons—with their backs to the wall, if not in mere cowardly passivity—voluntarily admitted the Rods and Axes [Rome] into their countries. They were overcome with terror at the enormity of their individual sins—if it is fair call them "individual." Personally, I should say that the majority had strayed from the true path in ignorance, and that the sin lies with the politicians by whom an ignorance of such profundity had been fostered. (146 B.C.)

Polybius (202–120 B.C.), *Histories*.[2]

The warm bath was delicious, the colonel mused. Soon he would be out and away with his contingent. War starts at midnight and it was imperative for his boys to be up and at 'em, at the stroke. War games or no, British efficiency and preparation had to show itself, even in practice.

The door to his club room suddenly burst open. Armed soldiers ran through the doorway pointing rifles at him even as he soaped the back of his bald pate. "You are under arrest, sir, a prisoner of war. We represent the Greens."

"You are mad, soldiers," roared the indignant and outraged colonel, "war begins at midnight!"

So Colonel Blimp assumed, in this wonderfully climactic scene of an old British film. But this was the time of Hitler and Rommel, World War II, and the era of the blitzkrieg. The rules of war always change. The wars of today or tomorrow are not won by employing the verities of yesterday.

Americans must absorb and internalize this principle. In applying it to the twenty-first century, we may thus be prepared for free market competition, the nature of which our current intellectual and political leaders have not the faintest awareness. They still both gloat and weep over the collapse of the communist empire.

Gloating, because free market conservatives interpret the disintegration of socialism as a vindication of capitalism and the principle of freedom and competition. The weepers are the "liberal" egalitarian levelers for whom the plebiscite and self-determination have a value, only if they lead to gray totalitarian uniformity, the "happy" price for supposedly eliminating economic and social differences between classes.

The weepers lost the war of the mid-twentieth century. Socialism had failed long before the wall came tumbling down around East Berlin in 1989. It had been only a matter of time before the final disintegration. Now we see the complete wreckage that this system wreaked upon the backs of these long-suffering hundreds of millions of people.

The gloaters ought to hold off a bit. Indeed, their system of market economics, national competition, and democratic political forms will always constitute the core of European civilizational achievements. But this way of life is presupposed on the basis of the maintenance, if not the enhancement, of a form of intelligence that is at the heart of these achievements. In sharing these institutional forms of social existence—market economies, scientific technologies, and free intellectual access to advanced forms of knowledge—we must assume the ability of the rest of the 4 billion humans on this planet to be able to reproduce and advance this civilizational style. But it doesn't necessarily have to happen.

In the past, ideological competition was wedded to force, sometimes internal armed revolution, sometimes national military aggression. With a world united in a commitment to market economies and democratic political forms, competition between peoples will tend to lose its ideological and class modalities and now take on ethnic and national forms.

The competitive war of the twenty-first century will be very different from the wars of the twentieth century. Ideology will recede as a factor. Until the new state of international affairs is sorted out, we will indeed see more of the horrors of ethnic and national conflict, a deeper and more malignant form of human "market" competition. Hitler's National Socialism and Japan's expansive Fascism during the 1930s and 1940s are horrific precursors of what we are witnessing today amid the continued redrawing of the map of humankind.

But this is not the long-range competitive warfare that we will experience as we move into the next century. The great powers well understand that prosperity depends upon open markets and an environment of peaceful coexistence among the nations of the world. As I have reiterated in this book, the struggle will revolve around the ability of nations and their ethnic constituents to trade with other nations and ethnicities with a roughly equal balance of payments.

This means that nations that wish to savor the fruits of the high intelligence/educational productivities of other nations—as simple an example as touring the beauties of Switzerland—will themselves have to produce what other productive peoples want. Our economists are universal in affirming that great natural resources alone will not guarantee prosperity.

The United States, still a relatively thinly populated society, with vast unspoiled geographies, will need more than this resource bounty to guarantee continued prosperity. Already our urban environments are choking in pollution, congestion, and chaos. Our wealth is disappearing not because we have lost our frontier technologies and industries to other nations and peoples. Rather, basic jobs have disappeared, those which for generations gave to our working classes a modern middle-class way of life.

They have gone "south" to those nations whose populations will work at these jobs at a small fraction of what the American worker can live on in our country. On the other hand, the new frontier jobs, those that can still pay the $15–20-per-hour wages that a middle-class American wage earner needs as a minimum to pay his mortgage and send his children to college no longer exist in sufficient numbers.

There are those "free traders," committed advocates of the North American Free Trade Agreement (NAFTA), who see our present trade advantage with Mexico as chiseled in granite. Let the low-tech factories go south, they argue. We will continue to sell them our high-tech drugs, computer chips, machine tools, and airplanes. The resulting cash, along with Mexican tomatoes, will flow north.

If you speak to the Mexicans they will hint at a different scenario. Three to four generations down the line of history, 75–100 years, they foresee their high-tech institutions of education and research, in cooperation with the international conglomerates, American, German, Japanese, or whatever, beginning to utilize their now-skilled workforce to fabricate those items in which the United States feels it still has a productive monopoly.

The Mexicans, like the mainland Chinese, do not expect to demand salary levels much beyond the present $2-per-hour maximum of their best workers. The Chinese, with yearly incomes of about a realistic $1,000–1,200, would be happy to increase their wage scales to this $2-per-hour mark, which would equal a yearly wage of about $4,000. One look at their current secondary educational achievement levels would convince any reasonable observer that the Chinese should be capable of very high-tech production within the next twenty-five years.

The Mexicans, with estimated I.Q. levels of about 95, compared with the Chinese, with somewhere between 105 and 108 I.Q., will still be able to muster a large workforce of highly skilled men and women. They do not have the anchor chains of quotas and other productivity disincentives that exist on the American law books. Employers in Mexico will be free to pick the best, those who are yet content with a much more modest standard of living than we are. We have memories still as to how our grandparents lived in the heady days of affluence, when men and women thought of themselves as forever "liberated."

Not to overdo this litany of challenges, one must still note our new East European "allies." The stories of Russian nuclear scientists on contract to the U.S. Defense Department for salaries of $25–50 per week—and happy to be so salaried—should alert us to the new competition. These people have in place educational structures that have been producing secondary school graduates, crisis in and chaos out, that are far advanced in achievement levels as compared to our own averages. And, of course, the East Europeans will be willing to work hard, and for a pittance. Our industrialists are nibbling and so is the rest of the world, including formerly developing nations such as Korea, which is now looking for high skill–low wage environments for its technologies.

What is to come of our own future? Foreign entrepreneurs are less likely to see the American market as something they want to get involved in, especially with our ethnic and gender politics complicating our supposed free market enthusiasms. Also, as we get poorer, the spate of satellite plants, such as those being planned by German luxury car makers for the Carolinas, could well dry up. The consumer market may no longer be here.

In late April 1993, the *New York Times* headlined a story that Pratt and Whitney in Connecticut was demanding of its workers an immediate $2-per-hour concession. The cost of producing in Connecticut was almost $6 per hour higher than in Georgia.[3] The competition with engines now being made for AirBus in Europe throughout the world was rendering this state, with its lush workers' compensation laws and other costs, uncompetitive.

The result of this evolving intellectual, educational, and thus economic competition, whether in Connecticut, North Dakota, or Alabama, is to put enormous pressure on the once munificent middle-class salaries of all our workers, not merely those in industrial production. The solution is not to find saviors from outside the country, such as Japan or Germany. We, like the leadership of these nations, must create home-grown world-class industries and services.

A small but important example. If people feel safer in Florence, Italy, or in Málaga, Spain, they will take their vacations there instead of in cheaper but more dangerous Miami, Florida. In services as well as in productive tangibles, the ultimate solution has to come from the creative, highly intelligent middle-class citizens produced in the United States who will in turn employ Americans and use the resources, human and natural, that we have within our borders.

The name of the game of international competition, whatever they say about the unifications of the European Community (EC) or NAFTA, will still remain a matter of national achievement.

Everyone knows that the twenty-first-century model of prosperity and national dominance will be the one that the Germans and the Japanese have already established at the close of the twentieth century. This is for the nation itself to be transformed into a corporate center for frontier technologies and services, those that will command the highest value-added profits. It is also for the citizens of this nation to be transformed through their intelligence and education into a classless fabric of unity.[4]

We kid ourselves when we boast with fruitless self-absorption that we are today the only "superpower" in the world. The rest of the world smiles accommodatingly at our empty bravado, knowing full well that we were essentially a mercenary force in the Gulf War, our armed forces subsidized by the rest of the world. We are still mentally fighting the wars of the twentieth century, but now without our own wherewithal to be the world's policeman.

The Japanese and Germans and others in Europe and the Asian rim, even our own frontier corporations, are off-shoring the unskilled tasks to the cheap labor/education nations. These developed nations strive, to the extent of the capabilities of their basic high school–educated workforce and their creative elites, to retain the most valuable segments of their industries at home, to keep the wealth for their own people. Any corporation or business would be both irrational and suicidal to stay at home if it could not find in its native land a highly skilled workforce at a reasonable cost.

The Japanese and the Germans are well aware that in the future it will not be as easy to appropriate intellectual property from a foreign source for productive application in one's own country. It will become essential in the twenty-first century to develop the frontier technological innovations through a concerted education and research program at home.

But, of course, each nation will have to find the requisite talent for this need through its own family and educational institutions. Thus far we have been able to utilize our finest undergraduate and graduate colleges and universities as magnets for the talented all over the world. Many of these students stay on and add to the competency of our overall population and workforce.

Our leaders still dreamily speak of educational reform, hoping that somehow the dying state educational bureaucracies will, through some magical inspiration, regurgitate a whole new level of educational achievement. They refuse to look back ten, fifteen, even thirty years, at the prior inspirational leadership and the earlier refrains of educational reform. And, of course, as I have here reported, as the talent continues to dry up at the top, the general level of educational and thus worker competency continues to sift downward. More and more of our workforce sits at home, outclassed by the poor, deprived, but now literate peoples around the world.

The secret weapon and thus the secret word of national power, is, of course, *natality*. Those who are born today will in twenty-five years be members of a nation's potential workforce. Their children, in turn, fifty years hence, will take that nation into the future. What happens in each nation with regard to the educability of each successive cohort will constitute the armed forces of victory or defeat in a very different kind of competition, essentially World War III.

The leadership in the United States today is indifferent to this issue. It does not matter to them who is having the children. As with our academic and media elites, the politicians seem more interested in retaining their perks than in facing and communicating to their constituents the bad but necessary news.

Soon they will be gone to enjoy their still-plentiful retirement monies. They will have left a nation careening headlong into oblivion. In Western Europe the leaders are also in thrall to this ideology of disaster. Why else have they invited to their shores millions of eager but tragically incompetent humans, inadequate at the least for the intellectual requirements of the twenty-first century. These immigrants from Africa and the Near East are decent people, eager to share in this current mountain of beneficent wealth. It is unfortunate, but they are still prone to the same pathologies of degradation as our own lower classes.

Our West European colleagues, as do we, encourage their very finest minds to enjoy the fruits of the temporary affluence, to forget about family life and children, perhaps to experiment in the titillating world of homosexuality, or whatever. Their talents will have disappeared with their persons. Except for the occasional rare and extraordinary individual, a Ludwig van Beethoven, a George Washington, an Emily Dickinson, they might just as well have never lived.

The northeast Asians, in general of a more practical and realistic mentality, have been poor too long to indulge themselves with such pseudo-liberation. While not overtly fighting the inevitable attempt by females to free themselves from the perennial drudgery that is women's burden, they nevertheless drag their heels at full-scale liberation. Japanese women of all educational classes still have their equal share of the few children that they can yet fit on the islands. The Chinese try to parcel out one child per female. Fortunately, all the Chinese want to get into that privileged act. The South Koreans are deeply family oriented, and at all social class levels.

In twenty-five years, the workforce of all these peoples, and thus their prosperity, will at the least be in the world-class competitive range. In the United States, the approximately 25 percent of our children that now live in poverty will have grown to at least 35 percent. The danger will be that many more individuals of potential will be excluded from the international domestic economy because we will not have produced enough of those talents in the 115–130 I.Q. range that create new ideas and enterprises. As the economy dies from the top, many more individuals of ability will find themselves displaced. Today, they still constitute an essential middle management segment that makes our country work.

We see this happening today in the downsizing of such formerly great companies as General Motors, United Technology, IBM, and Sears. Our college graduates, unlikely as we enter the twenty-first century to match the skills of the post–World War II generation, will, as they do today in India, find themselves unemployed and deeply resentful. Will our graduate research centers in 2020 have enough of a world-class faculty to attract the talented from overseas?

There is no great mystery to our current dilemmas of economic, educational, and social-cultural decline. There is also no possibility that the policies of either of our two major political parties will stem and turn this decline around. The evidence has been clear for a long time. Simply, in every area of our leadership, cowardice abounds. It is a refusal to recognize the problem for what it is—a natality crisis. Our demography is being reshaped from its recent civilizational apogee, toward a new Third World paradigm.

Our intelligence levels are declining because more children are entering our schools from the lowest intellectual classes than from our elites. We require immediate and revolutionary policy redirection, for one, because a number of other nations are not subject to this crisis. Western Europe itself might very well awaken from its own cocoon of complacency and decide to make a conscious effort to stem its decline. Of course, Africa and other Third World areas are in worse shape today, and probably will be tomorrow, than we are. This will prove small comfort to the citizens of the United States, which was once supposed to own the twentieth century.

It is all so simple in terms of a solution. We need to stimulate our finest to form families of the traditional sort in which children are conceived, born, raised, and educated to the highest levels for which they are capable. The helpless need to be encouraged and guided not to have children that they cannot rear and educate to functional cultural levels.

The reward for our nation could be the rapid re-creation of a civilization led by individuals capable of abstract symbolic thought, creative and responsible social behavior, able to frame and live by the laws, face the ever new with secular skepticism and confidence. Humans have been doing this for many thousands of years. It necessitates living life by the ancient spindle of necessity.

The decline of intelligence in America can be justly and humanely reversed and with it the decline in our anticipation of possibility and hope.

The difficulty lies in shedding our illusions.

Notes

CHAPTER 1
INTRODUCTION: TRUTH AND NATIONAL SURVIVAL

1. Mill, J. S. 1859. In *The English Philosophers from Bacon to Mill*. 1939. Ed. by Burtt, E. A. New York: Random House, 970–71.
2. Rector, Robert. 1993. Heritage Foundation reported in *Cincinnati Enquirer* (11 October).
3. Letter to W. S. Smith, 13 November 1787. In *The Papers of Thomas Jefferson*. 1950. Ed. by Boyd, J. P. Princeton, N.J.: Princeton University Press, 12:356–57.
4. Lichter, S. R., Lichter, L. S., and Rothman, S. 1991. *Watching America: What Television Tells Us About Our Lives*. New York: Prentice-Hall.
5. Itzkoff, S. W. The Evolution of Human Intelligence, a theory in four parts: *The Form of Man, the Evolutionary Origins of Human Intelligence*. 1983. New York: Peter Lang International Publishers; *Triumph of the Intelligent, the Creation of Homo Sapiens Sapiens*. 1985. New York: Peter Lang International Publishers; *Why Humans Vary in Intelligence*. 1987. New York: Peter Lang International Publishers; *The Making of the Civilized Mind*. 1990. New York: Peter Lang International Publishers.
6. Itzkoff, S. W. *Human Intelligence and National Power, a Political Essay in Sociobiology*. 1991. New York: Peter Lang International Publishers; *The Road To Equality, Evolution and Social Reality*. 1992. Westport, Conn.: Praeger Publishers.

CHAPTER 2
NATIONS, POWERFUL AND WEALTHY

1. Needham, J. 1954. *Science and Civilization in China*, vol. 1. Cambridge: Cambridge University Press; Dawson, C. D. 1955. *The Mongol Mission*. New York: Sheed and Ward.

2. Lewis, B. 1967. *The Arabs in History*. New York: Harper & Row; Said, E. 1973. *The Arabs Today: Alternatives for Tomorrow*. Columbus, Ohio: Forum Associates.

3. Jaeger, W. 1945. *Paideia: The Ideals of Greek Culture*. New York: Oxford; Bowra, C. M. 1971. *Periclean Athens*. New York: Dial.

4. Bury, J. B. 1945. *History of Greece*. London: Macmillan, 505; Xenophon. 1922. *Hellenica* II, ii, 21–23. Loeb Library.

5. Thompson, E. 1948. *A History of Attila and the Huns*. Oxford: Clarendon Press; Maenchen-Helfen, O. 1973. *The World of the Huns: Studies in Their History*. Berkeley: University of California Press; Dawson, R. 1978. *The Chinese Experience*. New York: Scribners.

6. Day, M. H. 1971. *Fossil Man*. New York: Bantam, 44, 138; Tattersall, I., and Delsen, E. 1984. *Ancestors*. New York: American Museum of Natural History.

7. Howell, F. Clark. 1965. *Early Man*. New York: Time, Inc., 109–19; Pilbeam, D. 1972. *The Ascent of Man*. New York: Macmillan, 167–69.

8. Leakey, R. 1977. *Ancestors*. New York: E. P. Dutton, 148–77.

9. Trinkaus, E. 1983. *The Shanidar Neanderthals*. New York: Academic Press; Coon, C. 1962. *The Origin of Races*. New York: Knopf; Brues, Alice M. 1977. *People and Races*. New York: Macmillan.

10. Trinkaus. *The Shanidar Neanderthals;* Solecki, R. 1975. "Shanidar IV, a Neanderthal Flower Burial in Northern Iraq," *Science*, 990:880–991; Solecki, R. 1960. "Three Adult Neanderthal Skeletons from Shanidar Cave in Northern Iraq," *Smithsonian Report Publication for 1959*, 44141:603–635.

11. Clark, G. 1967. *The Stone Age Hunters*. New York: McGraw-Hill, 55–64; Howell. *Early Man*, 158–63; Bibby, G. 1956. *The Testimony of the Spade*. New York: Knopf.

12. Marshack, A. 1972. *The Roots of Civilization*. New York: McGraw-Hill; Marshack, A. 1979. "Upper Paleolithic Symbol Systems of the Russian Plain.... " *Current Anthropology*, 22, no. 2 (June):271–311.

13. Clark. *The Stone Age Hunters*, 56–57; Clark, G., and Piggott, S. 1965. *Prehistoric Societies*. New York: Knopf, 165–70.

14. Simeons, A.T.S. 1962. *Man's Presumptuous Brain*. New York: Dutton, 276.

15. Oakley, K. 1957. *Man the Tool Maker*. Chicago: University of Chicago Press. Oakley emphasizes the mixing of the mainstream (Neanderthal) and Chatelperronian (Cro-Magnon or predecessor) cultures. "It was in France, notably in the Perigord region, that their culture reached its full flowering" (95); Phenice, T. W. 1969. *Hominid Fossils*. Dubuque, Iowa: William C. Brown Co., 47–48. Phenice quotes Sir Arthur Keith as having stated that a mainstream (Neanderthal) scraper had been buried with the body. Also buried with the body were a variety of flints and perforated skulls.

16. Bernard Vandermeersch, in 1984, discovered two Neanderthal fossils at St. Cesaire in western France, which were associated with Chatelperronian tools, seemingly intermediary between Neanderthal and Cro-Magnon technology, but

certainly one step beyond the Mousterian: "A propos de la decouverte du squelette neanderthalien de St. Cesaire," *Bulletins et Memoirs de la Societé d'Anthropologie de Paris*, ser. 14, no. 3 (1984):191–96. Thus, why not Cro-Magnon fossils along with Mousterian tools?

17. In the case of the Greeks, the Spartans, who could not come to the defense of Greece against the Persians at Marathon because of a religious festival that awaited the full moon, lost an opportunity for glory and national leadership. See Barr, Stringfellow. 1961. *The Will of Zeus*. Philadelphia: Lippincott, 88.

18. Hamilton, Edith. 1958. *The Greek Way*. New York: Norton, 29.

CHAPTER 3
AMERICA'S GREATNESS

1. Two suggestive books centering on the sometime nostalgia of these simpler days are Kazin, A. 1951. *A Walker in the City*. New York: Harcourt Brace; Kazin, A. 1962. *Starting Out in the Thirties*. Boston: Little, Brown.

2. Books about a changing America: Brooks, J. 1966. *The Great Leap: The Past Twenty-Five Years in America*. New York: Harper and Row; Miller, D., and Nowak, Marion. 1977. *The Fifties: The Way We Really Were*. Garden City: Doubleday. A less idyllic view of that era: Zelomek, W. 1959. *A Changing America at Work and Play*. New York: John Wiley.

3. Hogan, M. J. 1982. *The Marshall Plan: America, Britain, and the Reconstruction of Western Europe*. New York: Cambridge University Press; Hoffman, S., and Maier, C., eds. 1984. *The Marshall Plan: A Retrospective*. Boulder: Westview Press; U. S. Dept. of Commerce. Bureau of Census. *Historical Statistics of the U.S. to 1970*. Washington, D.C. Total U.S. foreign grants and credits from 1945–1970 totaled $145,777 million. This was the equivalent per year of 2 percent of our then gross national product, equal in 1993 dollars to about $120 billion per year.

4. This is the generally accepted figure that one sees in the print media totaled from the Johnson administration, c. 1963 on. From 1945 to 1963, the figure would certainly approximate the above dollar amount (note 3) for foreign aid and credits.

5. Sorge, M. 1986. *The Other Price of Hitler's War*. Westport, Conn: Greenwood Press. Sorge states that by 1944 the life expectancy of a U-boat and its crew was 100 days. A total of 779 U-boats went to the bottom with their crews, totaling at least 28,000 men (33–34). Losses to the Luftwaffe airmen amounted to over 70,000 killed (40). See also Cooper, M. 1981. *The German Air Force 1933–1945*. New York: Jane's Publishing, 377; Schumann, Willy. 1991 *Being Present, Growing Up in Hitler's Germany*. Kent, Ohio: Kent State University Press. By early 1945 young officer candidates of the German Army were being lectured "that 75 percent of the Offiziersbewerber do not come back from their first combat tour," 149–50.

6. Bogart, L., and Klemmerer, D. L. 1946. *Economic History of the American People*. New York: Longmans, Green & Co.; Liddel Hart, Sir Basil. 1970. *History of the Second World War*. New York: Putnam.

7. Tocqueville, Alexis de. *Democracy in America*. 2 vols. New York: Knopf, 1945; Turner, F. J. 1920. *The Frontier in American History*. New York: Holt; Grund, F. J. 1837. *The Americans, in Their Moral, Social, and Political Relations*. Boston: Marsh, Capen, and Lyon.

8. Kristof, N. 1993. "Regulation Virtually Disappears." *New York Times* (14 Feb.). Germany's and Japan's achievements are axiomatic. Mainland China's $15 billion and $18 billion balance of payment's surplus per year with the United States in 1991 and 1992, and an economy close to 50 percent privatized, including agriculture, might herald the great comeback story as the twentieth century is ended.

9. Cohen, I. Bernard. 1953. *Benjamin Franklin: His Contribution to the American Tradition*. Indianapolis: Bobbs-Merrill; Becker, C. L. 1942. *The Declaration of Independence*. New York: Vintage Books; Bronowski, J., and Mazlish, B. 1960. Part 3 of *The Western Intellectual Tradition*. New York: Harper and Row.

10. On the relationship of the Tenth Amendment to the Constitution to the growth of public education in the States, see Butts, R. F., and Cremin, L. A. 1953. *A History of Education in American Culture*. New York: Holt, 205,255; Shalhope, R. E. 1990. *The Roots of Democracy: American Thought and Culture, 1760–1800*. Boston; Hollinger, D. A., and Casper, C., eds. 1993. Part 2 of *The American Intellectual Tradition, Vol. 1, 1630–1865,* 2nd ed. New York: Oxford University Press.

11. Epstein, R. A. 1985. *Takings: Private Property and the Power of Eminent Domain*. Cambridge: Harvard University Press; Epstein, R. A. 1992. *Forbidden Grounds: The Case Against Employment Discrimination Laws*. Cambridge, Mass.: Harvard University Press.

12. Smith, Adam. 1776. Vol. 2 of *Wealth of Nations*. New York: Everyman's Library, 118.

13. Jefferson, Thomas, letter 30 May 1790 to Mr. Thomas Mann Randolph: "In political economy, I think Smith's Wealth of Nations the best book extant." In *Selected Writings of Thomas Jefferson*. Ed. by Koch, A., and Peden, W. 1944. New York, 496; Parrington, V. L. 1930. Vol. 1 of *Main Currents in American Thought*. New York: Harcourt Brace and World, 346; Machlup, F. 1952. *Political Economy of Monopoly*. Baltimore: Johns Hopkins University Press; Burns, A. R. 1936. *The Decline of Competition*. London: McGraw-Hill.

14. Leopold, A. 1949. *A Sand County Almanac*. New York: Oxford University Press; Smith, H. N. 1950. *Virgin Land*. Cambridge, Mass.: Harvard University Press; Beston, H. 1937. *American Memory*. New York: Farrar and Rinehart.

15. See also Ekirch, A. R. 1985. "Bound for America: A Profile of British Convicts Transported to the Colonies, 1718–1775." *William and Mary Quarterly* 421, no. 2: 184–200; Shaw, A.G.L. 1966. *Convicts and the Colonie*. London: Faber.

16. Miers, S., and Kopytoff, I., eds. 1977. *Slavery in Africa*. Madison: University of Wisconsin Press; Grace, J. J. 1975. *Domestic Slavery in West Africa*. London: Muller; Uchendu, V. C. 1965. *The Igbo of Southeastern Nigeria*. New York: Holt, Rinehart & Winston.

17. For a balanced discussion, see Part 10 of Linton, R. 1956. *The Tree of Culture*. New York: Knopf.

18. Davis, D. 1984. *Slavery and Human Progress*. New York: Oxford University Press; Genovese, E., and Genovese-Fox, E. 1983. *Fruits of Merchant Capital: Slavery and Bourgeoisie Property in the Rise and Expansion of Capitalism*. New York: Oxford University Press; Fogel, R., and Engerman, S. 1990. *Without Consent or Control: The Rise and Fall of American Slavery*. New York: Norton; Frazier, E. F. 1939. *The Negro Family in the United States*. Chicago: University of Chicago Press; Stampp, K. M. 1956. *The Peculiar Institution: Slavery in the Ante-Bellum South*. New York: Knopf; Du Bois, W.E.B. 1935. *Black Reconstruction in America 1860–1880*. New York: Harcourt.

19. Crawford, F. M. 1907. *Gleanings from Venetian History*. London: Macmillan; Pirenne, Henri. 1946. *Medieval Cities*. Princeton, N.J.: Princeton University Press; Norwick, J. J. 1982. *A History of Venice*. New York: Knopf.

20. Barbour, V. 1963. *Capitalism in Amsterdam in the 17th Century*. Ann Arbor: University of Michigan Press.

21. Goudsblom, Johan. 1967. *Dutch Society*. New York: Random House; Bagley, Christopher. 1973. *The Dutch Plural Society: A Comparative Study in Race Relations*. New York: Oxford University Press.

CHAPTER 4
ECONOMICS: IS THE SLEEPER A GIANT?

1. Thurow, L. 1992. *Head to Head*. New York: William Morrow, 52.

2. Toland, J. 1982. *Infamy: Pearl Harbor and Its Aftermath*. New York: Doubleday, 252; Prong, G. 1988. *December 7, 1941: The Day the Japanese Attacked Pearl Harbor*. New York: McGraw-Hill, 109.

3. Peillard, Lonce. 1983. *Geschichte des U-Boot Krieges 1939–1945*. Munich: Wilhelm Heyne Verlag; Schumann, Willy. 1991. *Being Present: Growing Up in Hitler's Germany*. Kent, Ohio: Kent State University Press.

4. Krug, E. A. 1972. *The Shaping of the American High School*, vol. 2, 1920–1941, 337–38. Madison: University of Wisconsin Press. Chapter 13, "A Change of Climate," illustrates the enormous educational and productive potential that existed in 1941, a product of our basic public educational system. By December 1941, one year after the "National Coordinating Committee on Education and Defense" had been formed, 1,776,000 people had been trained. The motto of the schools was "We Never Close."

5. See articles on auto competition among Japan, Germany, Britain, and the United States in the *Economist*, Vol. 306 (13 Feb. 1988):65; Vol. 312 (23 Sept. 1989):19–20; Vol. 318 (23 Feb. 1991):68–70; Vol. 320 (17 Aug. 1991):62. See

also Lehmann, Jean-Pierre. 1992. "France, Japan, Europe, and Industrial Competition: The Automative Case." *International Affairs* 68 (January): 37–53.

6. Baldwin, W. 1967. *The Structure of the Defense Market 1955–1964*. Durham, N.C.: Duke University Press.

7. Two contrasting Reagan presidency views: Pro: Bartley, R. 1992. *The Seven Fat Years and How to Do It Again*. New York: Free Press. Con: Moynihan, D., and Schlesinger, J. R. 1988. "Debunking the Myth of Decline." *New York Times Magazine*, (19 June).

8. Kahn, Alfred. 1992. "Nightly Business Report." PBS (27 Nov.). Kahn is an emeritus professor of political economics at Cornell University.

9. "The Chemical-Manufacturer Merger." 1991. *New York Times* (21 July). Describes the decline of U.S. dominance in the international banking scene between 1982 and 1990.

10. Figgie, H. E., Jr., and Swanson, G. J. 1992. *Bankruptcy 1995*. New York: Little, Brown, 52, 147.

11. Pasztor, A., and Murray, A. 1991. "U.S. May Reap Windfall." *The Wall Street Journal* (25 March): A3; "Report Says Kuwait Pays." 1991. *New York Times* 141 (25 November); Jonah, Monica. 1991. "Kuwait War Payments." *The Wall Street Journal* (25 Nov.).

12. Bentsen, L. 1991. "Speech to Sematech, in Austin, Texas," *Network Newsmedia Reports* (6 July). 2.6 million industrial jobs were lost since 1979.

13. 1993. *New York Times* (31 January). Report from the Bureau of Labor Statistics.

14. Figgie. *Bankruptcy 1995*, 93, Office of Management and Budget. The 16 percent figure is from Professor of Economics Mahnaz Mahdavi of Smith College, personal communication, April 1993.

15. 1992. *New York Times* (19 July).

16. Figgie. *Bankruptcy 1995*, 70. Figgie puts the interest on the debt at 20 percent, partially because of his high estimate, $400 billion, on the 1992 deficit.

17. Insurance claims for "Hurricane Andrew" in 1992 have been estimated at $16 billion. Add to this the $7.5 billion emergency aid bill appropriated by Congress for the California earthquake (*Los Angeles Times*, 30 Oct. 1991), the $10.5 billion humane aid bill appropriated by Congress in 1992 (Rogers, David, *The Wall Street Journal*, 16 Sept. 1992), and one can see the need for a strategic emergency fund.

18. Figgie. *Bankruptcy 1995*, 95–96. Congressional Budget Office Statistics.

19. Bradsher, K. 1991. "U.S. Gap in World Investing." *New York Times* (10 June). U.S. Commerce Department estimate, Thurow. *Head to Head*, 234–35. Thurow states that the "DRI/McGraw-Hill Review of the U.S. Economy" estimates that at the beginning of 1991, the rest of the world owns about $757 billion more than Americans own in the rest of the world.

20. Garten, Jeffrey, 1992. *A Cold Peace*. New York: Times Books, 139.

21. Kuttner, R. 1991. *The End of Laissez Faire*. New York: Knopf, 52. Between 1948 and 1952, the Marshall Plan provided for $13 billion uninflated, in aid to Europe; Garten. *A Cold Peace*. In 1988, the United States spent between $150

and 200 billion to maintain its forces for NATO (163) and $50 billion per year for Asia, including wealthy Japan (166); Choate, P. 1992. *New York Times* (26 July). Choate puts the Asia military aid figure at $60 billion, somewhat more than our annual trade deficit with Japan.

22. In October 1993, the thirty-year U.S. Treasury Bond briefly touched 5.75 percent.

23. Reich. *The Work of Nations*, 203–04. "Among full time, year round workers, the number who were poor climbed [1978–87] . . . by 43 percent"; Harrison, B., and Bluestone, B. 1989. "Wage Polarization in the United States and the 'Flexibility' Debate." School of Urban and Public Affairs, Carnegie Mellon University, working paper (Fall); Thurow. *Head to Head*, 163. "Between 1978 and 1988, the U.S. generated 7.5 million new male jobs . . . On a net basis [after correcting for inflation], all of those millions of new jobs were below-average jobs"; Gosselin, P. 1992. "US Job Loss: A 640,000 Undercount." *Boston Globe* (6 June).

24. Sims, C. 1993. *New York Times* (17 January).

25. Reich. *The Work of Nations*, 43–57; Thurow. *Head to Head*, 29.

26. Bingham, R. D., and Sunmonu, K. K. 1992. "The Restructuring of the Automobile Industry in the U.S.A.: Challenge of the Japanese Transplants." *Environment and Planning* Vol. 24 (June): 833–52.

27. "Selling Cars in America: Japan Comes to Forecourt California." 1985. *The Economist* 298 (16 Nov.): 81.

28. Personal conversation, 1978.

29. Perot, R. 1992. *United We Stand*. New York: Hyperion, 88; Brimelow, P., and Viscuse, G. 1991. "Socialism by Another Name." *Forbes* (9 Dec.). Government spending and regulation creates our deficit.

30. Peterson, Iver. 1992. "New Companies Bring Research to 'Video Valley.' " *New York Times* (5 July). Japanese and Korean electronics companies setting up in area around Princeton, New Jersey.

31. Bowens, Greg. 1992. "Detroit South: Mexico's Auto Boom: Who Wins?" *Business Week* (16 March); Uchitelle, Louis. 1993. "America's New Industrial Belt." *New York Times* (31 March).

32. Garten. *A Cold Peace,* 143ff.; Kuttner. *The End of Laissez Faire,* 265ff.

33. Wriston, W. B. 1992. *The Twilight of Sovereignty*. New York: Scribners, 40, 82–83; Hobsbawm, E. J. 1990. *Nations and Nationalism Since 1780.* New York: Cambridge University Press, 174–75. Compares the expansion of trading centers, such as Hong Kong and Singapore, with the Hanseatic planting of colonies throughout the Baltic during the late Middle Ages, i.e., nothing new; Kristof, N. D. 1993. "China Is Making Asia's Goods, and the U.S. Is Buying." *New York Times* (21 March).

34. Netherlands is third ($60 billion), behind the United Kingdom ($119 billion), and Japan ($70 billion), in its direct investment in U.S. industry, real estate, etc. This does not include indirect investment in stocks, bonds, commercial paper (as of 1989).

35. Thurow. *Head to Head*, 45–51.

36. Ibid., 177.

37. Ibid., 53–55, 163–64; Reich. *The Work of Nations*, 202–06. Reich cites study by Tower, Perrin, Forster, and Crosby (1990), *Report on International Compensation* (Jan.).

38. Reich. Part 3, "The Rise of the Symbolic Analyst." *The Work of Nations*, 171–243.

39. Reich, R. 1991. Part 4, "The Meaning of Nation." *The Work of Nations*, 243–317. Emphasis added.

40. Kuttner. *The End of Laissez Faire, 158–91*. Emphasis added.

41. Prestowitz, C. 1988. *Trading Places*. New York: Basic Books; Prestowitz, C. 1993. *New York Times* (14 February).

42. Garten. *A Cold Peace.*

43. Ibid., 194, 199.

44. Figgie. *Bankruptcy 1995*, 92.

45. "Company Reports." 1992. *New York Times* (8 Nov.).

46. Nassar, Sylvia. 1993. "The Risky Allure of 'Strategic Trade.' " *New York Times* (28 Feb.).

47. Lipper, Kenneth. 1989. "What Needs to Be Done." *New York Times* (31 Dec.). "The task of the 90's is to keep the middle class from defecting."

CHAPTER 5
OUR EDUCATIONAL WRECKAGE

1. The National Commission on Excellence in Education. 1983. *A Nation at Risk: The Imperative for Educational Reform*. Washington, D.C.: U.S. Government Printing Office.

2. Broadcast over network news, report on our educational crisis—California.

3. Woodson, Robert. 1992. PBS commentary (7 Sept.).

4. A television newsmagazine report.

5. American Association of School Administrators. 1941. "An Educational Program for the Common Defense," *Official Report*; King, E. A. 1972. *The Shaping of the American High School*, vol. 2. Madison: University of Wisconsin Press, 337–46.

6. Kerr, C. 1963. *The Uses of the University*. Cambridge, Mass.: Harvard University Press.

7. Kerr, C. 1991. *The Great Transformation in Higher Education, 1960–1980*. Albany: SUNY Press.

8. Itzkoff, S. W. 1976. *A New Public Education*. New York: Longman.

9. Bailyn, B. 1967. *The Ideological Origins of the American Revolution*. Cambridge, Mass.: Harvard University Press.

10. Cremin, L., ed. 1957. *The Republic and the School, On the Education of Free Man*. New York: Teachers College Press.

11. *Pierce v. Society of Sisters*. 1925. 268 U.S.:510.

12. U.S. Department of Education. *Historical Statistics, Colonial Times to 1970*, series H598 (Oct.).

13. King, E. J. 1979. *Other Schools and Ours*. 5th ed. New York: Holt, Rinehart & Winston.

14. *National College Bound Senior*, New York: College Entrance Examination Board. Annual.

15. Stewart, D. M. 1989. "A Debate on the SAT: Pro." *Boston Globe* (5 Mar.). Donald Stewart is President of the College Board.

16. Gottfredson, L., and Crouse, J. 1986. "Validity Versus Utility of Mental Tests: Example of the SAT." *Journal of Vocational Behavior* 29, no. 3 (Dec.): 363–78.

17. Humphreys, L. 1986. "Commentary." *Journal of Vocational Behavior* 29, no. 3 (Dec.): 421–37.

18. *National College Bound Senior*. College Entrance Examination Board. Annual.

19. Stout, H. 1992. "SAT Scores Rise but Remain Near Lows." *Wall Street Journal* (27 Aug.).

20. 1990. *Chronicle of Higher Education* (5 Sept.), A33.

21. Arbeiter, S. 1984. "Profiles, College Bound Seniors, 1984." *College Entrance Examination Board*, Table 10. Arbeiter shows 67.5 percent of the white seniors scored over 400 on the Verbal SAT while 26.5 percent of the blacks did so. Therefore, 32.5 percent of the white seniors were in the lowest ranks, certainly noncollege material, while 73.5 percent of the blacks who took the SAT, presumably because they wanted to go to college, could be considered ineligible for college work on the basis of the Verbal exam.

22. Arbeiter, "Profiles, College Bound Seniors."

23. Rock, D. A. 1987. "The Score Decline from 1972 to 1980: What Went Wrong?" *Youth and Society* 18, no. 3 (March): 239–54.

24. Odom, G. R. 1990. *Mothers, Leadership, and Success*. Houston: Polybius Press, 269–72.

25. Odom. *Mothers, Leadership, and Success*; see also Shea, Christopher. 1993. *Chronicle of Higher Education* (13 Jan.). Even though more students took the SAT in 1992 than in 1972, 75,243 in 1992 scored over 600 on the Verbal, as compared with 116,630 in 1972. Selective colleges show an average Verbal decline of between 40 and 70 points; Singal, D. 1991. *Atlantic Monthly* (Nov.) Selective colleges have seen the Verbal decline 50 to 60 points. About 30 percent of entering freshmen need remedial courses. See 1993. *Chronicle of Higher Education* (24 Feb.).

26. Stout. "SAT Scores Rise."

27. U.S. Department of Education. 1986. "The Reading Report Card." *NIE-NAEP* (May): Tables 81–87.

28. Mullis, Ina V. S., et al. 1991. "The State of Mathematical Achievement, National Assessment of Educational Progress— ETS." *National Center for Educational Statistics*, 7 (June). "Fewer than half the high-school seniors (46 percent) demonstrated a consistent grasp of decimals, percents, fractions, and simple alge-

bra [7th grade] and only 5 percent showed an understanding of geometry and algebra [11th and 12th grades] that suggested preparedness for the study of relatively advanced mathematics."

29. Kirsch, I., and Jungeblut, A. 1986. "Literacy: Profiles of Young Adults." ETS for U.S. Department of Education Office of Educational Research and Improvement (Sept.). Table 280. Only 2.5 percent of black young adults were able to read and use a bus schedule; whites 24.3 percent; Hispanics 6.7 percent.

30. McKnight, C. C., et al. 1987. *The Underachieving Curriculum: Assessing U.S. School Mathematics from an International Perspective.* Champaign, Ill: Stipes Publishing Co.

31. Perot, R. 1992. *United We Stand.* New York: Hyperion, 76.

32. McKnight. *The Underachieving Curriculum,* 17. See also Hodgkinson, H. L. 1989. "The One System." *The Institute of Educational Leadership,* 13.

33. McKnight, C. C. *The Underachieving Curriculum,* 22.

34. Ibid., 16.

35. Ibid., 26–27.

36. Gilder, G. 1987. *Wall Street Journal* (2 April).

37. Lapointe, A. E. 1989. *A World of Difference.* Princeton, N.J.: ETS. (Jan.)

38. Ibid., 17.

39. Ibid., 38.

40. Ibid., 39–40.

41. Ibid., 22–25.

42. Dossey, J. A., et al. 1988. *The Mathematics Report Card: The 1986 National Assessment.* Princeton, N.J.: ETS (June). Fifty-three percent of all eleventh graders feel that they are good in mathematics, 55 percent of blacks concur. Forty percent of all eleventh graders feel that math is easy, 44 percent of blacks concur (96).

43. Holden, C. 1989. "Court Ruling Rekindles Controversy over SATs." *Science* (17 Feb.), 885–87.

44. Lapointe, A. E., et al. 1992. *Learning Mathematics,* IAEP. Princeton, NJ: ETS (Feb.).

45. Terman, L. M. 1925. *Mental and Physical Traits of a Thousand Gifted Children.* Stanford, Calif.: Stanford University Press; Terman, L. M., and Oden, M. H. 1959. *The Gifted Group at Mid-Life.* Stanford, Calif.: Stanford University Press; Stanley, J., et al., 1974. *Mathematical Talent: Discovery, Description, and Development.* Baltimore: Johns Hopkins University Press.

46. Lapointe. *Learning Mathematics,* 10.

47. Ibid., 16–17. (chart, March 1991)

48. Bishop, J. H. 1989. "Is the Test Score Decline Responsible for the Productivity Growth Decline?" *American Economic Review* 79, no. 1 (Mar.): 178–97.

49. Koretz, D. 1986. *Trends in Educational Development.* Washington, D.C.: U.S. Congressional Budget Office.

50. Kantrowitz, B. 1992. "A Head Start Does Not Last." *Newsweek* (27 Jan.): 44; Berger, J. 1990. "Dropout Plans Not Working Study Finds." *New York Times* (15 May): B1; See also Jensen, A. R. 1969. "How Much Can We Boost I.Q. and

Scholastic Achievement?" *Harvard Education Review* (June): 1–123. A prescient prediction of the ultimate failure of programs such as Head Start.

51. Vining, D. R., Jr. 1982. "On the Possibility of the Emergence of a Dysgenic Trend with Respect to Intelligence in American Fertility Differentials." *Intelligence* 6:261–64.

52. Flynn, J. R. 1980. *Race, I.Q., and Jensen.* London: Routledge, Kegan, Paul.

53. Herrnstein, R. J. 1989. "I.Q. and Falling Birth Rates." *Atlantic* (May).

54. Seligman, D. 1992. *A Question of Intelligence.* New York: Birch Lane Press, 126–27; Vining, D. F., Jr. 1983. "Mean I.Q. Differences in Japan and the U.S." Letter to *Nature*, 738; Lynn, R. 1987. "The Intelligence of the Mongoloids: A Psychometric, Evolutionary and Neurological Theory." *Personality and Individual Differences* 8, no. 6:813–14.

55. U.S. Department of Education. 1993. "News" (8 Sept.); Kirsch, I. S., et al. 1993. "Adult Literacy in America." Washington, D.C.: National Center for Education Statistics, 113–15.

CHAPTER 6
THE SOCIAL BOND UNRAVELS

1. Eight panels from commemorations of the life and work of Emperor Marcus Aurelius, A.D. 161–180, decorate the Arch of Constantine.

2. Alaric was the partially Romanized Visigoth who led his army into Rome in A.D. 410 because the ransom price of the Roman Senate was not high enough. Honorius was the incapable Roman emperor ensconced safely for the moment at the imperial palace in Ravenna. Soon he was gone, too.

3. Hacker, A. 1992. *New York Times* (29 March); Solinger, R. 1992. *Wake Up, Little Suzy.* New York: Routledge.

4. Hughes, J. 1991. *Christian Science Monitor* (11 July).

5. Shanker, A. 1991. *New York Times* (17 March).

6. Bennett, W. 1993. "The Index of Leading Cultural Indicators." *Empower America.* Washington, D.C.

7. Banninger, F. 1992. Reprinted in *New York Times* (19 July).

8. 1992. *New York Times* (23 Aug.).

9. Hodgkinson, H. 1989. "The One System." *The Institute for Educational Leadership.* Washington, D.C., 3.

10. DeParle, J. 1991. *New York Times* (12 May).

11. 1992. *New York Times* (29 March).

12. 1992. *New York Times* (12 July).

13. J. P Freeman Co. 1992. In *New York Times* (9 Feb.); crime statistics from the FBI.

14. Butterfield, F. 1992. *New York Times* (3 Jan.).

15. Rowe, David C. 1993. "Newsletter." *Human Behavior and Evolution Society* 11, no. 1 (Feb.): 5.

16. "The Sentencing Project." 1992. *New York Times* (19 July).

17. Editorial. 1992. *New York Times* (30 Nov.).

18. 1992. *New York Times* (14 June). Office of Management and Budget.

19. Bandow, D. 1992. *New York Times* (23 Aug.). Cato Institute Report.

20. Haney, D. Q. 1992. *Boston Globe* (4 June). *Associated Press.*

21. 1992. *New York Times* (18 Nov.). U.S. Public Health Service: AIDS Action Council.

22. Cronin, A. 1992. *New York Times* (18 Nov.). Harvard School of Public Health.

23. 1992. *New York Times* (30 Nov.), 1. In addition, other stories noted the increase in tapeworm and other traditionally Third World maladies, products of new immigrants, both legal and illegal.

24. 1992. See *New York Times* (23 Aug.), note 8.

25. "The Corporate Woman Officer." 1990. Boston: Heidrick and Struggles.

26. National Center for Health Statistics: HHS. In the early 1960s, the rate was approximately 3.4 children per white female.

27. 1992. *New York Times.* (18 Oct.). Council of Jewish Federations.

28. Page, E. B. 1976. "A Historical Step beyond Terman." In *Intellectual Talent Research and Development.* Ed. by D. P. Keating. Baltimore: Johns Hopkins University Press, 305–06; Gordon, R. D. 1980. "Implications of Valid and Stubborn I.Q. Differences: An Unstatesmanlike View." *Behavioral and Brain Sciences* 3, no. 3:343–44; Eysenck, H. J., and Kanin, L. 1981. *The Intelligence Controversy.* New York: John Wiley, 77.

29. 1991. *USA Today* (May).

30. Cole, J. 1989. *Columbia Magazine* (Dec.).

31. O'Hare, W. 1991. *African Americans in the 1990's.* Population Reference Bureau. Washington, D.C.

32. Butterfield, F. 1993. "Colleges Luring Black Students with Incentives." *New York Times* (28 Feb.).

33. Perot, R. 1992. *United We Stand.* New York: Hyperion, 74.

34. Woodson, R. 1992. PBS commentary (7 Sept.).

35. Wriston, W. 1992. *The Twilight of Sovereignty.* New York: Scribner. See especially Chapter 10.

36. See Polybius. 2nd century B.C. Book 20, Chapter 6 and Book 36, Chapter 7 of *Histories.* In Toynbee, A. J., ed. 1953. *Greek Civilization and Character.* New York: Mentor, 72–73; for the Romans, the writings of Juvenal, Martial, Seneca, quoted in Itzkoff, S. W. 1992. *The Road to Equality.* Westport, Conn.: Praeger, 134–35.

37. Quoted in Herrnstein, R. 1989. "I.Q. and Falling Birth Rates." *Atlantic* (May).

38. Gleick, J. 1992. *New York Times Magazine* (20 Sept.).

39. Eckland, B. K., and Wisenbaker, J. M. 1979. "National Longitudinal Study." *National Center for Education Statistics* HEW 1. (emphasis added)

40. Eckland. "National Longitudinal Study," 15. (emphasis added)

41. Vining, D. R., Jr. 1982. "On the Possibility of the Reemergence of a Dysgenic Trend with Respect to Intelligence in American Fertility Differentials."

Intelligence 6:241–64. (See Table 3.) For women 25 to 34 years of age: white— 0.18; black—0.20

42. Vital Statistics of the United States. 1988. *Natality*, vol. 1, 182ff. (Tables 1–70)

CHAPTER 7
EBB TIDE

1. Magaziner, I., et al. 1990. "America's Choice: High Skills or Low Wages." *National Center on Education and the Economy* (June).

2. Ibid., 20–21.

3. Hodgkinson, H. L. 1989. "The One System." *The Institute for Educational Leadership*, 5–7.

4. Magaziner. "America's Choice," 21.

5. Editorial. 1992. *New York Times* (19 April).

6. 1991. *The World Almanac*, 554. From the standpoint of 1993, this estimate may seem large. But all previous estimates of U.S. population growth have thus far understated the real growth. Official U.S. Bureau of Census median estimates based on 1.8 births per woman and 50,000 net immigration (legal and illegal) point to a population of 368+ million by the year 2050. The higher official estimate is thus about 419 million by 2050.

7. Lynn, R. 1987. "The Intelligence of Mongoloids: A Psychometric, Evolutionary, and Neurological Theory." *Personality and Individual Differences* 8, no. 6:813–44. The U.S. white I.Q. may still be about 100. But factoring Hispanic and African-American I.Q.s, other mixed population Native Americans, immigrants from the Near East, etc., the 4 point advantage of the Japanese over whites has to increase significantly.

8. Flynn, J. 1987. "Massive I.Q. Gain in Fourteen Nations: What I.Q. Tests Really Measure." *Psychological Bulletin* 101:171–91.

9. See Chapter 5 for documentation.

10. Cattell, R. B. 1938. "Some Changes in Social Life in a Community with a Falling Intelligence Quotient." *The British Journal of Psychology* 28, part 4 (April). Reprinted in *Intelligence and National Achievement*. 1983. Ed. by Cattell, R. B. Washington, D.C.: Institute for the Study of Man.

11. Cattell. "Changes in Social Life," 175.

12. Caesar Augustus. 18 B.C. *Lex Iulia de Maritandis Ordinibus*, the "Julian Laws."

13. Gargan, E. A. 1993. "Hindus Now Demanding the Leadership of India." *New York Times* (24 Jan.).

CHAPTER 8
THE FREE MARKET OF HIGH INTELLIGENCE

1. Santy, P. 1994. *Choosing the Right Stuff*. Westport, Conn.: Praeger.

2. Terman, L. M. 1925. *Mental and Physical Traits of a Thousand Gifted Children.* Stanford, Calif.: Stanford University Press.

3. Santy. *Choosing the Right Stuff.*

4. Itzkoff, S. W. 1983. *The Form of Man.* New York: Peter Lang; Itzkoff, S. W. 1985. *Triumph of the Intelligent.* New York: Peter Lang (vols. 1 and 2 of "The Evolution of Human Intelligence," in four parts).

5. Smith, H. 1961. *From Fish to Philosopher.* Garden City, NY: Doubleday.

6. MacLean, P. D. 1990. *The Triune Brain in Evolution.* New York: Plenum.

7. Stenhouse, D. 1973. *The Evolution of Intelligence.* New York: Harper & Row.

8. Jerison, H. 1973. *Evolution of the Brain and Intelligence.* New York: Academic Press.

9. Reich, R. 1991. *The Work of Nations.* New York: Knopf. Chapters 18, 19.

10. Gottfredson, L., ed. 1986. "The g Factor in Employment." a special issue of the *Journal of Vocational Behavior* 29, no. 3 (Dec.); also Gottfredson, L., and Sharf, J. C. 1988. "Fairness in Employment Testing," a special issue of the *Journal of Vocational Behavior* 33, no. 3 (Dec.).

11. Seligman, D. 1992. *A Question of Intelligence.* New York: Birch Lane Press, 141.

12. Ibid., 142.

13. Stenhouse. *The Evolution of Intelligence,* especially Chapter 6; Halstead, W. C. 1947. *Brain and Intelligence.* Chicago: University of Chicago Press.

14. Itzkoff, S. W. 1987. "The Executor: 'P' Factor." Chapter 11 in *Why Humans Vary in Intelligence.* New York: Peter Lang.

15. Jensen, A. R. 1986. "Intelligence as a Factor of Nature." Lecture at Virginia Tech, Blacksburg, Va., 30 September; Eysenck, H. J., ed. 1982. *A Model for Intelligence.* New York: Springer. Chapters 1–3.

16. Gravlin, W. 1992. "Aiming High." Unpublished manuscript.

17. Lindsley, O. R. 1965. "Can Deficiency Produce Specific Superiority—The Challenge of 'Idiot Savant.' " *Exceptional Children* 31:226–31; Scheerer, M., Rothman, E., and Goldstein, K. 1945. "A Case of 'Idiot Savant': An Experimental Study of Personality Organization." *Psychological Monographs* 58, no. 4.

18. Bever, T., and Chiarello, R. J. 1974. "Cerebral Dominance in Musicians and Nonmusicians." *Science* 184:41–50.

19. Eysenck, H. J. 1992. *The Measurement of Creativity.* In press; Eysenck, H. J. 1992. "Creativity and Personality: Suggestions for a Theory." Manuscript paper; Eysenck, H. J., and Eysenck, M. W. 1985. *Personality and Individual Differences: A National Science Approach.* New York: Plenum; Cloninger, C. R., et al. 1991. "The Tridimensional Personality Questionnaire: U.S. Normative Data." *Psychological Reports* 69:1047–57; Cloninger, C. R. 1987. "A Systematic Method for Clinical Description and Classification of Personality Variants." *Archives Gen. Psychiatry* 44 (June).

20. Bouchard, T. J., and McGee, M. 1981. "Familial Studies of Intelligence: A Review," *Science* 212:1055–59; Bouchard, T. J., et al. 1990. "Sources of Human Psychological Differences: The Minnesota Study of Twins Reared Apart," *Sci-*

ence 250:223–28; Lykken, D. T. 1981. "Research with Twins." *Psychophysiology* 19, no. 4:361–73.

21. Edel, Dean. 1992. NBC medical report on Springfield, MA, affiliate (7 Dec.).

22. Murray, Charles. 1992. *Commentary* (Dec.): 62.

23. The great contemporary international trade conundrum, example GATT, of national agricultural subsidies derives in the main from the overproductivity of the scientific farmer. In order to maintain its agricultural base, a nation must support this overproductivity with price subsidies.

24. Kahn, D. 1988. *Agriculture and Water Resources in West Bank and Gaza, 1967–87.* Boulder, CO: Westview Press; Weitz, R. 1967. *Agricultural Development, Planning and Implementation: Israel Case Study.* New York: Praeger.

25. Seligman. *A Question of Intelligence*, 140.

26. Hunter, John, et al. 1990. "Individual Differences in Output as a Function of Job Complexity." *Journal of Applied Psychology* 75, no. 1:28–42.

27. Moore, M. 1990. *Roger and Me.* Warner Home Video.

28. Lynn, R. 1987. *Educational Achievement in Japan.* London: Macmillan; Lynn, R. 1987. "The Intelligence of the Mongoloids: A Psychometric, Evolutionary, and Neurological Theory." *Personality and Individual Differences*, no. 6:813–44.

29. See Chapter 5, note 32.

30. See Chapter 6, note 30.

31. Various broadcast interviews, PBS: Nightly Business Review, The News Hour.

32. See Chapter 7, notes 10, 11.

33. Thurow, L. 1992. *Head to Head.* New York: Morrow, 138. Thurow claims that in 1990, U.S. CEOs earned 119 times as much as the average lineworker, as compared to Japanese CEOs, who earned 18 times as much as their own manufacturing workers.

34. Eysenck. *The Measurement Of Creativity.* Also in personal communication.

35. Terman, L. M., and Oden, M. H. 1947. *The Gifted Child Grows Up.* Stanford, Calif.: Stanford University Press; Terman, L. M., and Oden, M. H. 1959. *The Gifted Group at Midlife.* Stanford, Calif.: Stanford University Press.

36. Arthur Jensen: personal communication, 1989.

CHAPTER 9
THE TRAGEDY OF LOW INTELLIGENCE

1. Lewontin, R. C., et al. 1984. *Not in Our Genes.* New York: Pantheon Books, 18.

2. Bennett, W. 1993. "Index of Leading Cultural Indicators." *Empower America.* Washington, D.C.

3. Seligman, D. 1992. *A Question of Intelligence.* New York: Birch Lane, 141–42.

4. Romer, R. 1991. *National Education Goals Report.* Washington, D.C. Romer argues that in 1990, 83 percent of nineteen- and twenty-year-olds had reported completing high school. The high school equivalent exams have been widely discredited by employers.

5. Dossey, J. A., et al. 1988. *The Mathematics Report Card.* Princeton, N.J.: ETS, 16. "By age 17, only half the high school students demonstrated an understanding of even moderately complex mathematical procedures (material generally thought to be introduced in junior high schools)."

6. Lapointe, A. E., et al. 1992. *Learning Mathematics.* Princeton, N.J.: ETS. Graph-Statistics, 16–17.

7. Lynn, R. 1977. "The Intelligence of the Chinese and Malays in Singapore." *The Mankind Quarterly* 18:125–28; Lynn, R., Hampson, S., and Lee, M. 1988. "The Intelligence of Chinese Children in Hong Kong." *School Psychology International* 9:29–32.

8. Uchitelle, L. 1993. *New York Times* (28 March).

9. Weiss, V. 1991. "It Could Be Neo-Lysenkoism If There Was Ever a Break in Continuity!" *The Mankind Quarterly* 31, no. 3:231–53; Weiss, V. 1991. "Why Are Racial Differences in Intelligence Not Larger?" *The Mankind Quarterly* 332, nos. 1–2:133–36; Lehrl, S., Frank, S., and Papp, R. 1991. "Overcoming the Limitations of I.Q." *The Mankind Quarterly* 332, nos. 1–2:137–40; Lehrl, S., and Fischer, B. 1990. "A Basic Information Psychological Parameter (BIP) for the Reconstruction of Concepts of Intelligence." *European Journal of Personality* 4:259–86; Weiss, V. 1982. *Psychogenetic.* Jena: Fischer-Verlag.

10. Weiss. "Racial Differences in Intelligence," 135.

11. See Chapter 8 discussion and note 26.

12. Perez, L. 1986. "Immigrant Economic Adjustment and Family Organization: The Cuban Success Story Reexamined." *International Migration Review* 20 (Spring):4–20.

13. See LaPointe, A. E., et al. 1989. *A World of Difference.* Princeton, NJ: ETS. The thirteen-year-old British Columbian Students, a large proportion of which are Chinese, came in third in math and first in science over twelve other nations, and including Korea. The United States was twelfth in math and ninth in science (17, 38).

14. Lacqueur, W. Z. 1974. *Weimar: A Cultural History, 1918–1933.* New York: Putnam; Koestler, A. 1952. *Arrow in the Blue: An Autobiography.* New York: Macmillan; Zweig, S. 1953. *The World of Yesterday.* New York: Viking; Gay, P. 1968. *Weimar Culture: The Outsider as Insider.* New York: Harper and Row.

15. The "p" factor is a real psychological element in human thought and intelligent behavior. As yet, it has not been researched enough to draw any variable quantitative parameters between individuals, else in the interaction with "g" for general intelligence. Anecdotal as well as experimental evidence argues that the "postponement," persistence element in human intelligent behavior, is both real and variable. See Chapter 8, notes 13–16.

16. Mead, L. 1992. *The New Politics of Poverty*. New York: Basic Books, 260; see also Kaus, Mickey. 1992. *The End of Equality*. New York: Basic Books.

17. Taufexis, A. 1993. "Seeking the Roots of Violence." *Time* (19 Apr.): 52–53.

18. Bauer, P. 1978. *The First and the Third World: Essays on the New International Order*. Rochester, N.Y.: Center for Research in Government Policy and Business.

19. Johnson, P. 1993. "Colonialism's Back and Not a Moment Too Soon." *New York Times Magazine* (18 April).

20. Lynn, R. 1991. "Race Differences in Intelligence: A Global Perspective." *The Mankind Quarterly* 31, no. 3 (Spring): 255–96.

21. Mead. *The New Politics of Poverty*, 260.

CHAPTER 10
DEFENSIVE DRIVING

1. Machiavelli, N. 1513. *The Prince*, chapter 26 (Reprint 1940. New York: Random House.).

2. Classics on this topic include: Romer, A. 1933. *Man and the Vertebrates*. Chicago: University of Chicago Press; Smith, H. 1961. *From Fish to Philosopher*. Garden City, N.Y.: Doubleday; Jerison, H. 1973. *Evolution of the Brain*. New York: Academic Press; de Beer, G. 1958. *Embryos and Ancestors*. 3rd ed. London: Oxford University Press.

3. Spearman, C. E. 1904. " 'General Intelligence' Objectively Determined and Measured." *American Journal of Psychology* 15:201–93; Jensen, A. R. 1986. "The g Beyond Factor Analysis." In *The Influence of Cognitive Psychology in Testing and Measurement*. Ed. by Plake, B., and Witt, J. C. Hillsdale, N.J.: Erlbaum.

4. The work of the "Great Books" advocates Robert Hutchins and Mortimer Adler are examples of a curriculum instituted at the University of Chicago in the 1930s preparing individuals for an undefined future where only the ability to think and reason was necessary. See Hutchins, R. M. 1936. *The Higher Learning in America*. New Haven: Yale University Press; Adler, M. J. 1982. *The Paideia Proposal: An Educational Manifesto*. New York: Macmillan.

5. The difference between high and low success in life of Lewis Terman's 1500+ gifted children of I.Q. near 153 lay in the ability of the top 5 percent to "persist" at their life commitments and the self-admission of the lowest that they could not "stick to it." Sears, P. S., and Barbee, A. H. 1977. "Career and Life Satisfaction among Terman's Gifted Women." In Stanley, J. C. et al., *The Gifted and Creative: A Fifty-Year Perspective*. Baltimore: Johns Hopkins University Press; Sears, R. R. 1977. "Sources of Life Satisfaction of the Terman Gifted Men." *American Psychologist* 32:119–28; Fincher, J. 1973. "The Terman Study Is Fifty Years Old." *Human Behavior* 2:8–15.

6. Cook, J. 1992. "Norway: The New Kuwait." *Forbes* (6 June); Strangeland, Per. 1984. "Getting Rich Slowly—The Social Impact of Oil Activities." *Acta Sociologica* 27, no. 3:215–37. Norway, once the poorest of the Scandinavian nations, now has a per capita income higher than Sweden, partially the result of its over 16.7 billion barrels of oil reserves and another 14.7 probable.

7. Trevor, M., ed. 1987. *The Internationalization of Business: European and Japanese Perspectives*. Boulder, CO: Westview Press; Kraar, L. 1991. "The New East Asia Co-Prosperity Sphere." *Fortune* 124 (1 July): 12; Tanzer, A. 1984. "The Silicon Valley Greater Co-Prosperity Sphere." *Forbes* 134 (17 Dec.): 31–32.

8. See Chapter 5 for the statistics. But if my hypothesis presented in Chapter 9 is correct, that the overall U.S. I.Q. for the under-thirty-year-old cohort is about 95, it may now be even somewhat lower than that for the below-eighteen-year-olds.

9. See Itzkoff, S. W. 1991. *Human Intelligence and National Power*. New York: Peter Lang; Itzkoff, S. W. 1992. *The Road to Equality*. Westport, Conn.: Praeger. The former title discusses the intellectual causes for political ascendancy and the nature of dominating nations. The latter book presents a philosophical argument that only high intelligence in a national profile can lead to the kind of civilizational equality that we dream of and strive to achieve.

CHAPTER 11
THE AMERICAN FAMILY

1. *Lex Iulia de Maritandis Ordinibus*, the so-called Julian Laws of 18 B.C.

2. Brown, Peter. 1971. *The World of Late Antiquity*. New York: Harcourt, Brace, Jovanovich, 62–68.

3. Tacitus. c. A.D. 100, *Germania* 9. Loeb Library, 1925.

4. Alexander, R. D., and Tinkle, D. W., eds. 1981. *Natural Selection and Social Behavior: Recent Research and New Theory*. New York: Chiron. Defensive behavior and selection for responsibility; Roth, C. 1949. *A Short History of the Jewish People*. Hartford, CT: Hartmore House. Discusses family life and education; Lattourette, K. C. 1934. "Social Life and Organization." Chapter 17, vol. 5, of *The Chinese, Their History and Culture*. New York: Macmillan.

5. Simons, E. L. 1960. "New Fossil Primates: A Review of the Past Decade." *American Scientist* 48:179; Schultz, A. H. 1966. "Changing Views on the Nature and Interrelations of the Higher Primates." *Yerkes Newsletter* 3:15.

6. Holloway, R. L. 1972. "New Australopithecine Endocasts SK 1585 from Swartkrans, South Africa." *American Journal of Physical Anthropology* 37:173–86.

7. Hill, A., and Ward, S. 1988. "Origin of the Hominidae: The Record of African Large Hominoid Evolution between 14 MY and 4 MY." In *Yearbook of Physical Anthropology* 31:49–83. Documents a few and scattered fossils that argue for the great antiquity of the line.

8. Jerison, H. 1973. *Evolution of the Brain and Intelligence.* New York: Academic Press.

9. Fisher, Helen E. 1975. *The Loss of Estrous Periodicity in Hominid Evolution.* Ann Arbor, Michigan: University Microfilms; Jolly, Allison. 1972. *The Evolution of Primate Behavior.* New York: Macmillan; Fisher, H. E. 1992. *Anatomy of Love: The Natural History of Monogamy, Adultery, and Divorce.* New York: Norton.

10. Lovejoy, C. O. 1981. "The Origin of Man." *Science* 211, no. 4480 (22 Jan.): 341–50.

11. See the discussion and the many citations in Itzkoff, S. W. 1983. "Culture as a Biological Activity." Chapter 8 of *The Form of Man.* New York: Peter Lang.

12. Van Den Berghe, P. 1979. *Human Family Systems: An Evolutionary View.* New York: Elsevier.

13. Polybius. Second century B.C. A Greek historian who was witness to the final defeat of the Greeks and the ascent of Rome writes in his *Histories* (6 vols., Loeb Library, 1925) of the glory of Rome and the wealth that was adding by the day to its power and eventual domination—ultimately the liberation of its people from "necessity."

14. Loden, M. 1985. *Feminine Leadership: Or How to Succeed in Business without Being One of the Boys.* New York: Times Books; Cannie, J. K. 1979. *The Woman's Guide to Management Success: How to Win Power in the Real Organizational World.* Englewood Cliffs, NJ: Prentice-Hall.

15. Uchitelle, L. "America's Newest Industrial Belt." 1993. *New York Times* (21 March). Young Mexican women are eager to find *maquiladora* jobs much as in the Zenith plant in Chihuahua, which pay $1.00 per hour, plus food, health, and transportation benefits.

16. Porter, B. 1993. "I Met My Daughter at the Wuhan Foundling Hospital." *New York Times Magazine* (11 April). The sad but human story of American women searching to adopt a child, almost anywhere, now from the mainland Chinese, with their surplus of girl babies.

17. Kinsey, A. C., et al. 1948. *Sexuality in the Human Male.* Philadelphia: Saunders. Estimated 10 percent of males were active or latent homosexuals; Barnes, Fred. 1993. "McLaughlin Report." PBS program. February 13. Columnist quotes recent authorities (13 Feb.) as estimating 2 percent to 3 percent of populations are practicing homosexuals; Guttmacher Institute. 1991. Research published in the *New York Times* (15 Apr.), carried out at the Battelle Institute in Seattle, Washington, puts the figure at 1 percent to 2 percent.

18. See Plato. *Symposium*; Xenophon. *Lacedaemonium Republic*; Plutarch. *Amatorius.* All in Westermarck, Edward. 1906. *The Origin and Development of Moral Ideas.* London: Macmillan.

19. Cronin, Ann. 1992. *New York Times* (8 Nov.). The Department of Health and Human Services estimates that in the United States as of January 1992 the causes of HIV infection were: homosexual sex, 58 percent; intravenous drug use, 23 percent; homosexual sex and drug use, 6 percent; heterosexual sex, 6 percent. The latter figure is being increasingly questioned as to accuracy.

20. The mayor of New York City, David Dinkins, allied himself with the homosexual community by refusing in March 1993 to participate in New York City's St. Patrick's Day Parade because its Catholic leadership refused to allow homosexuals to parade as a distinct cultural group.

21. Westermarck, E. 1906. "Homosexual Love." From *The Origin and Development of the Moral Ideas*. London: Macmillan. In *The Making of Man*. 1931. Ed. by Calverton, B.F. New York: Random House, 529–64. This chapter documents the widespread patterns of homosexual relations amongst leadership, from a classical anthropological perspective.

22. Sam Nunn, senator from Georgia, and chair of the Senate Committee on Armed Services, sees the solution of the problem of "gays" in the military as to ask no questions and have them remain anonymous. The Democratic administration bought into this solution.

23. Bury, J. B. 1945. *A History of Greece*. London: Macmillan, esp. 728–29.

24. Will, G. 1992. *Springfield* [MA] *Union News* (7 Dec.). Discusses article in *Commentary*, December 1992.

25. Epstein, R. A. 1985. *Takings: Private Property and the Power of Eminent Domain*. Cambridge, MA: Harvard University Press; Epstein, R. A. 1992. *Forbidden Grounds: The Case against Employment Discrimination Laws*. Cambridge, Mass.: Harvard University Press.

26. U.S. Bureau of Census. 1992. Bureau of Labor Statistics.

27. Steinfels, P. 1992. "Seen, Heard, Even Worried About." *New York Times* (27 Dec.); Gutman, M. 1988. "The Hidden Child Abuse in Our Schools." *Redbook* (Oct.).

28. Wexler, R. 1990. *Wounded Innocents: The Real Victims of the War against Child Abuse*. Buffalo: Prometheus; Billingsley, K. L. 1993. "The Scientific War on Child Abuse." In *National Review* (15 Feb.), esp. 25–26.

29. 1993. *New York Times* (31 Jan.). Cites Fox, J. A., and Pierce, G., from Northeastern University in Boston.

30. Daly, M., and Wilson, A. 1988. *Homicide*. Boston: deGruyter, 20–30, 85–90.

31. National Center for Health Statistics. 1990.

32. *Bureau of the Census*. In 1960, 72 children per 1000 children under 18 were involved in divorce. In 1987, 163 children per 1000 children were so involved.

33. "Laurence Pacuin School in Baltimore Provides Norplant to Its Female Students." 1993. *The Economist*. 326 (30 Jan.): 26–27; Platt, S. 1991. "Compulsory Contraception in Courts of California—Convicted Mother Given Norplant." *New Statesman & Society* 4 (28 June): 11; "Kerry Patrick, Kansas Rep. Offers Plan to Pay Welfare Moms to Use New Contraceptive." 1991. *Jet*. 79 (4 March): 16.

34. Steven J. Ross of Time Warner is now deceased; Roberto C. Goizueta remains as C.E.O. of Coca-Cola. Recent April 1993 proposals by the national Corporate Accounting Association will soon factor in stock options for executives as part of a corporation's net worth. It will detract from their bottom line.

35. Hobbes, T. 1651. Chapter 29 of *Leviathan*. In *The English Philosophers: From Bacon to Mill*. 1939. Ed. by Burtt, E. A. New York: Random House, 204ff.

36. Mount, Ferdinand. 1992. *The Subversive Family*. New York: The Free Press. A defense of the nuclear family as the basic and natural social form from time immemorial into the present and future.

CHAPTER 12
A NON-HYPHENATED PEOPLE: W.E.B. DU BOIS (1868–1963)

1. Du Bois, W.E.B., ed. 1906. *The Health and Physique of the Negro American*. Atlanta: The Atlanta University Press, 30, 37–39.

2. Reuter, E. 1918. *The Mulatto in the U.S.* Boston: Richard Badger.

3. Du Bois, W.E.B. 1973. *The Education of Black People*. Ed. by Aptheker, H. Amherst: University of Massachusetts Press.

4. Du Bois, W.E.B. 1963. *An ABC of Color*. New York: International Publishers. Du Bois died in Ghana, the honored guest of the dictator Kwame Nkrumah.

5. Kallen, H. 1924. *Culture and Democracy in the United States*. New York: Boni and Liveright; Grant, P. S. 1912. "American Ideals and Race Mixture." *North American Review* 195:513–35; Bridges, H. J. 1959. "On Becoming an American." In *Immigration as a Factor in American History*. c. 1910–1920. Ed. by Handlin, O. Englewood Cliffs, N.J.: Prentice-Hall, 163.

6. Grant, M. 1916. *The Passing of the Great Race*. New York: Charles Scribner; Fairchild, H. P. 1926. *The Melting Pot Mistake*. Boston: Little, Brown.

7. Zangwill, Israel. 1909. *The Melting Pot*. New York: Macmillan; Mayo-Smith, R. 1890. *Emigration and Immigration*. New York: Charles Scribner's Sons.

8. Kallen, H. 1956. *Cultural Pluralism and the American Idea*. Philadelphia: University of Pennsylvania Press.

9. Itzkoff, S. W. 1969. *Cultural Pluralism and American Education*. New York: Crowell. This interpretation derives from the symbolic philosophy of knowledge in the writings of Ernst Cassirer and Susanne Langer.

10. Gollnick, D. M., and Chinn, P. C. *Multicultural Education in a Pluralistic Society*. New York: Merrill-Macmillan, 20; Schlesinger, A. M., Jr. 1992. *The Disuniting of America: Reflections on a Multicultural Society*. New York: W. W. Norton; Feuer, L. S. 1991. "From Pluralism to Multiculturalism." *Society* (Nov./Dec.): 19–22.

11. Horowitz, D. 1985. *Ethnic Groups in Conflict*. Berkeley: University of California Press; Sowell, T. 1983. *The Economics and Politics of Race*. New York: William Morrow; Sowell, T. 1990. *Preferential Policies*. New York: Morrow.

12. Berkson, I. B. 1958. *The Ideal and the Community*. New York: Harper; Berkson, I. B. 1920–. *Theories of Americanization*. New York: Teachers College

Press. A laissez-faire approach to pluralism. Keep government hands off, let the people decide their cultural allegiances, yes or no.

13. Bouchard, T. J., Jr., and McGee, M. 1981. "Familial Studies of Intelligence: A Review." *Science* 212:1055–59; Jensen, A. R. 1980. *Bias in Mental Testing*. New York: The Free Press, 338.

14. Perez, L. 1986. "Immigrant Economic Adjustment and Family Organization: The Cuban Success Story Reexamined." *International Migration Review* 20 (Spring): 4–20; "Miami Recoils: Cuban Immigrants" 1984. *The Economist* (22 Dec.): 15–16. The great social impact of Cuban immigrants.

15. Washington, B. T. 1903. *The Negro Problem*. New York: James Pratt, 9–29. In *Social History of American Education*, vol. 2. Ed. by Vassar, R. L. Chicago: Rand McNally, 62.

16. Du Bois, W.E.B., and Dill, A. G., eds. 1911. *The Common School and the Negro American*, no. 16. Atlanta: The Atlanta University Press, 58–59.

17. Report of the United States Commissioner of Education. 187. Du Bois. *The Common School*, 95.

18. Harlan, L .R. 1972. *Booker T. Washington: The Making of a Black Leader, 1956–1910*. New York: Oxford University Press, 225, 265.

19. Steine, E. G. 1971. *His Was the Voice, The Life of W.E.B. Du Bois*. New York: Crowell-Collier.

20. Walter White, head of the NAACP during the 1930s and 1940s; Paul Robeson, the great singer and political activist; A. Philip Randolph, head of the Union of Sleeping Car Porters (railways), a powerful figure in the labor movement; Roy Wilkins, head of the NAACP in the 1950s and 1960s.

21. Washington. *The Negro Problem*, 63.

22. Fisk University in Nashville, Tennessee; Tuskegee University, Tuskegee, Alabama; Wilberforce University, Wilberforce, Ohio; Lincoln University, Jefferson City, Missouri.

23. Broderick, F. L. 1959. *W.E.B. Du Bois*. Stanford, Calif.: Stanford University Press, 51–53, 71.

CHAPTER 13
IMMIGRATION: HOT WAR

1. Kennan, G. F. 1993. *Around the Cragged Hill*. New York: Norton, 152–53.

2. Itzkoff, S. W. 1987. "Every Nation Needs a Southern Neighbor." Chapter 8 in *Why Humans Vary in Intelligence*. New York: Peter Lang. The scientific research evidence, which is plentiful, is documented in this section.

3. Feuer, L. S. 1991. "From Pluralism to Multiculturalism." *Society* (Nov./Dec.): 19–22. A brief but eloquent essay in defense of "Western civilization."

4. Gross, Jane. 1991. "Poor Seekers of Good Life Flock to California, as Middle Class Moves Away." *New York Times* (29 Dec.). Welfare payment for a

family of three in California in November 1991 was $663 per month. In Texas, it was $184.

5. Marshack, A. 1972. *The Roots of Civilization*. New York: McGraw-Hill.

6. Goudsblom, J. 1967. *Dutch Society*. New York: Random House; Boissevain, J., and Verrips, J. 1989. *Dutch Dilemmas*. Maastrich: Van Gorcum.

7. Bagley, C. 1973. *The Dutch Plural Society: A Comparative Study in Race Relations*. London: Oxford University Press.

8. Bureau of Census. 1990. *Statistical Abstracts*. Washington, D.C.

9. Passel, J. S. 1986. "Estimating the Number of Undocumented Aliens." *Monthly Labor Review* 109, no. 9 (Sept.).

10. Shanker, A. 1992. "Here We Stand." *New York Times* (13 Dec.).

11. Mead, L. M. 1992. *The New Politics of Poverty*. New York: Basic Books, 91–92; Reischauer, R. D. 1989. "Immigration and the Underclass." *Annals of the American Academy of Political and Social Science* 501 (Jan.): 125.

12. Bouvier, L. 1991. *Fifty Million Californians?* The Federation for American Immigration Reform.

13. Gross, Jane. 1993. "Los Angeles Schools: Hobbled and Hurting." *New York Times* (10 Feb.).

14. Sowell, T. 1991. *Inside American Education*. New York: Morrow. Cited in *Boston Herald* (4 Feb. 1993).

15. Levin, D. 1993. "What BMW Sees in South Carolina." *New York Times* (11 April). The Spring 1993 announcement that BMW and Mercedes-Benz, German auto makers, would be locating in western South and North Carolina, ostensibly for the benefit of hard-working Southern farm boys and girls, and at relatively low wages by international standards, confirms a new trend of American wages being held down by competitive Third World workers.

16. Uchitelle, L. 1993. "Stanching the Loss of Good Jobs." *New York Times* (31 Jan.). Source: Bureau of Labor Statistics.

17. Harrison, L. E. 1993. "If Domestic Work Paid Well." *New York Times* (31 Jan.); Briggs, V. 1992. *Mass Immigration and the National Interest*. Armonk, N.Y.: M.E. Sharpe.

18. Francis, D. 1991, in *Christian Science Monitor* (12 July).

19. Toynbee, A. 1959. *Hellenism, the History of a Civilization*. London: Oxford University Press, 69ff.; Barr, S. 1961. *The Will of Zeus*. Philadelphia: Lippincott, 71–77.

20. Kennan. *Around the Cragged Hill*, 153–54.

CHAPTER 14
DISESTABLISHING STATE SCHOOLING

1. IAEP-ETS. 1992. Princeton, 16–18, from *P.C. Globe*, Tempe, AZ, 1990. Israel, at 10.2 percent of GNP, spends about $900 per person, per year. Switzerland, the wealthiest nation, spends 4.8 percent, about $1,300 per person, per year. The U.S., at 7.5 percent of GNP, spends about $1,500 per person, per year.

2. The U.S. Office of Management and Budget estimates that, in 1990, the federal government expended about $26 billion, administered through the Department of Education.

3. Cremin, L. A. 1970. *American Education: The Colonial Experience, 1607–1783*. New York: Harper Torchbooks.

4. Rudolph, F. 1962. *The American College and University: A History*. New York: Knopf.

5. Bailyn, B. 1960. *Education in the Forming of American Society*. Chapel Hill: University of North Carolina Press; Boorstin, D. J. 1958. *The Americans: The Colonial Experience*. New York: Random House.

6. "Amendment IX, Rule of Construction of Constitution. The enumeration in the Constitution, of certain rights, shall not be construed to deny or disparage others retained by the people"; "Amendment X, Rights of States Under Constitution. The Powers not delegated to the United States by the Constitution, nor prohibited by it to the United States, are reserved to the States respectively, or to the people."

7. *Pierce v. Society of Sisters*. 1925. 268 U.S.:510.

8. Cremin, L. A., ed. 1957. *The Republic and the School: Horace Mann on the Education of Free Men*. New York: Teachers College, Columbia University Press.

9. 1992. *Wall Street Journal* (9 June). See the entrance exam for Jersey City High School, 1885. A forty-question exam spanning geography, U.S. history, algebra. Few think that the top 10 percent of Jersey City high school graduates in 1985 would have passed that test that was then given to eighth graders.

10. Page, C. 1993. "PBS Education Special." *South Carolina Public Education Network* (16 April). Presents a number of nontraditional breakaways from the public school experiments.

11. Kimball, S. T., and McClellan, J. T. 1962. *Education and the New America*. New York: Random House. These authors see the schools as contributing to our corporate structure of wealth and power.

12. Kurth, H. M. 1987. "Teachers Unions and Excellence in Education." *Journal of Labor Research* (Fall). Argues that regression analysis shows teacher unionism the most significant factor in the decline of SAT scores!

13. Van Galen, J., and Pitman, M. A., eds. 1991. *Home Schooling*. Norwood, NJ: Ablex. These authors estimate that 200,000 to 300,000 children are presently being "home-schooled" (35).

14. See Section 4, "The Week in Review," of the *New York Times* on any Sunday and the reader will immediately perceive the enormous proportion of ads for special education directors and administrators in the schools, and the need for professors of special education to train the teachers.

15. Koven, Lisa. 1993. "Help Wanted: Diversity Bureaucrats." *Campus* 4, no. 3 (Spring): 2ff.

16. Mullis, I.V.S., et al. 1991. "The State of Mathematical Achievement." *National Center for Educational Statistics*. Princeton: NAEP-ETS (June).

17. Mullis. "Mathematical Achievement." See Chapter 5, note 31: Only 2.5 percent of black young adults were able to read and use a bus schedule.

18. Mullis. "Mathematical Achievement," 7. Forty-six percent of seventeen-year-olds were prepared to do seventh grade math. Only 5 percent were able to do eleventh or twelfth grade math, e.g., algebra or geometry.

19. Finn, C. 1991. *We Must Take Charge*. New York: Free Press. A bold critique of American education argues for national exams, among other reforms, see esp. 263–66.

20. *National Commission on Excellence in Education*. (NCCE). 1983. *A Nation at Risk: The Imperative for Educational Reform*. Washington, D.C.: U.S. Government Printing Office. "The educational foundations of our society are presently being eroded by a rising tide of mediocrity that threatens our very future as a Nation and as a people" (5).

21. On vouchers, see: Friedman, M. 1962. *Capitalism and Freedom*. Chicago: University of Chicago Press; Mecklenburger, S., and Hostrop, R. W. 1972. *Educational Vouchers: From Theory to Alum Rock*. Homewood, IL: Etc. Pub; Coons, J. E., and Sugarman, S. 1971. *Family Choice: A Model State System for Vouchers*. Berkeley: University of California Institute of Government Studies; Itzkoff, S. W. 1976. *A New Public Education*. New York: Longman; Chubb, J. E., and Moe, T. M. 1990. *Politics, Markets and America's Schools*. Washington, D.C.: The Brookings Institution; Lieberman, M. 1989. *Privatization and Educational Choice*. New York: St. Martin's Press.

22. Kozol, J. 1991. *Savage Inequalities*. New York: Crown Publishers. In a T.V. interview given by Clarence Page, Kozol expressed great fear that "choice" would lead to more inequalities. His solution is presumably "the general will," whereby equality is mandated by fist.

23. Note that Urban Day inner city schools in Wisconsin are doing well, at a cost of $3,300 per child. New York City, now spending close to $7,800 per child, sees only about $3,000 of this in the classroom. In Los Angeles, the seeming wave of the future in the United States, $4,187 is spent per student. Who knows how much of this gets into the classroom, especially as there is, in 1993, a 10 percent, or $400 million deficit in the L.A. system.

24. Verhovek, S. H. 1993. "Texas to Hold Referendum on School-Aid Shift to Poor." *New York Times* (16 Feb.).

25. Page, C. 1993. "PBS Education Special." *South Carolina Public Education Network* (16 April). Page's interviewees stated that about one-third of funds get into the classroom.

26. Sidwell Friends' School, in Washington, D.C.

27. LaPointe, A. E., et al. 1992. *Learning Mathematics*. Princeton: IAEP-ETS, 16–18. For eighth grade, class size ranged thus: highest, Korea (highest achievement), 49; Mainland China, 48; Russia, 22; Jordan, 27 (lowest achievement); United States, 23 (next to lowest achievement).

28. *Times Educational Supplement* (Jan. 1990). In 1988, Great Britain began one of the great experiments in education, combining national curricular exams with market choice of schools by parents. Hughes, D. 1992. "All Schools to Opt

Out in Biggest Shakeup." *The Sunday Times* (26 July). Government "white paper" proposes radical changes—opting out of local system, government-grant-maintained schools seen as key to high standards.

29. Page. "PBS Education Special." Wisconsin state legislator, A. P. Williams of African-American heritage, argues that choice in schooling could be the great freedom push for the poor in the 1990s.

30. "Japan's Car Imports: The Big Stick." 1992. *The Economist* (11 Jan.); Bingham, R. D., and Sunmona, K. K. 1992. "The Restructuring of the Automobile Industry in the U.S.A." *Environment and Planning* 24 (June): 833–52; "The Ambush Awaiting Japan." 1991. *The Economist* 320 (6 July): 67–68.

31. See Finn, C. 1991. *We Must Take Charge*. New York: Free Press, 3, 263; Led by Assistant Superintendent Sy Fliegel, the New York City public schools early in the 1980s instituted in District 4, one of the most chaotic in the city, a series of mini-schools that gave choice of school and/or specialization to students. These East Harlem schools ranged from 60 to 250 students per school, sometimes four "schools" to a building.

32. The East Harlem, District 4 example, others in Milwaukee, Wisconsin, and the "Contract Schools" in Minnesota are examples that already show an efficient use of physical facilities where there is a will, even a necessity.

33. There are now parent information centers in Boston, West Side Manhattan (NYC) District 3, Minnesota, Wisconsin, and elsewhere.

34. Albert Shanker, president of the American Federation of Teachers, in his weekly Sunday *New York Times* advertisement/column, "Where We Stand," now concedes "choice," but only within the public school sector.

35. *Academic Questions* is perhaps the leading journal countering in an academic manner the new push of the "left academy." It is published by the National Association of Scholars, *Transaction* Periodicals Consortium, Rutgers University, New Brunswick, New Jersey.

36. See Page. "PBS Education Special." On Minnesota's "Contract Schools."

37. Eugene Lang, a New York City philanthropist, in his "I Have a Dream" Foundation, wants to fund scholarships to college for successful inner city products of his old alma mater elementary/junior high school. So far, the success rate has not been high. See also *General Accounting Office*. 1990. "Promising Practice: Private Programs Guaranteeing Student Aid for Higher Education." Washington, D.C.: GAO.

38. "Major School Groups Blast Plan for Commercial T.V. in Classes." 1989. *Education Week* (8 Mar.): 5; "Channel One Television Continues to Draw Fire." 1989. *Ed Line* (25 April). Benno Schmidt, formerly president of Yale University, has taken over as head of the educational area of the Whittle empire to give it dignity and clout.

39. West, E. G. 1970. *Education and the State*. London: Institute of Economic Affairs; West, E. G. 1975. *Education and the Industrial Revolution*. New York: Harper and Row.

40. Mill, J. S. 1859. *On Liberty*. In *The English Philosophers*. 1939. Ed. by Burtt, E. A. New York: Random House, 1033–34.

41. King, E. J. 1979. Chapter 6, "France: The Central Light of Reason," in *Other Schools and Ours*. New York: Holt, Rinehart and Winston, 110–73.

CHAPTER 15
MIDDLE-CLASS ECONOMICS AND THE
SOCIAL CONTRACT

1. Kristof, N. D. 1993. "China Is Making Asia's Goods and the U.S. Is Buying." *New York Times* (2 March). China's first quarter economic growth rate was over 15 percent. The U.S. trade deficit with Mainland China in 1992 was $18.3 billion.

2. Uchitelle, L. 1993. "Stanching the Loss of Good Jobs." *New York Times* (31 Jan.). Manufacturing jobs decreased from 23 percent to 17 percent of total employment between 1979 and 1992. This was a 15.6 percent decrease in manufacturing, resulting in an average yearly wage of $23,500.

3. By mid-1993, the total national debt had risen to $4.5 trillion and going up.

4. 1992. *New York Times* report (25 Sept.).

5. Extraordinarily high Chinese mathematics achievement levels reported in Chapter 5, note 30, and in Chapter 14, as well as the high I.Q.s referred to in Chapter 8, averaging over 100, argue for a very powerful ethnic group and their nations early in the twenty-first century.

6. LaPointe, A. E., et al. 1992. *Learning Mathematics*. Princeton, N.J.: AEP-ETS, 16–18. The U.S. per capita GNP is listed as $19,789, Taiwan $4,355.

7. 1993. *New York Times* (17 Jan.).

8. Myerson, A. F. 1992. *New York Times* (12 Dec.).

9. U.S. Commerce Department. 1990. Bureau of Economic Analysis. "Foreign Direct Investment in U.S." In 1989, a total of $401 billion. The Netherlands, a nation of 16 million people, was third highest, behind the United Kingdom, $119 billion, and Japan, $70 billion, owning $60 billion of assets.

10. Meier, Michelle. 1993. "Bankers Want to Roll the Dice Again." *New York Times* (18 April).

11. Williams, W. 1992. "The Nightly Business Report." PBS (21 Dec.).

12. Kennan, G. 1993. *Around the Cragged Hill*. New York: Norton. See Chapter 4, "The Nation," and Chapter 7, "Dimensions."

13. See Kallen, H. B. 1956. *Cultural Pluralism and the American Idea*. Philadelphia: University of Pennsylvania Press; Itzkoff, S. W. 1969. *Cultural Pluralism and American Education*. New York: Crowell. Both authors see a culture divided between more intimate and more universal cultural values—Kallen's "Day and Night," Itzkoff's universal vs. plural symbolism. Itzkoff's views are infused with the philosophical perspective of Ernst Cassirer and Susanne Langer; Kallen's by William James and John Dewey.

14. Brimelow, P., and Spencer, L. 1993. "When Quotas Replace Merit, Everybody Suffers." *Forbes* 151, no. 4 (15 Feb.): 80–102; see also 1993. *National*

Review report (15 Feb.): 18; Becker, G. 1957. *The Economics of Discrimination.* Chicago: University of Chicago Press.

15. Gould, C. 1993. *New York Times* (17 Jan.).

16. Levy, D. 1993. "Firing Line." PBS (10 Jan.).

17. Thurow, L. 1992. *Head to Head.* New York: Morrow, 45.

18. Thurow. 46–48.

19. In 1993, U.S. Trade Representative Mickey Kantor was emphasizing as part of the various GATT, NAFTA, and other international trade agreements that the protection of intellectual property, not merely books, records, and, e.g., patents and copyrights in the traditional sense, had to be regulated, but now software and other technological processes as well. International transfer of such will henceforth be more difficult.

20. Wriston, W. 1992. *The Twilight of Sovereignty.* New York: Scribners, 23–28.

21. Ibid., 25–26.

22. Ibid., 32.

23. In *Fortune*'s 1989 list of largest corporations, USX is listed as a refiner of petroleum, with $17.7 billion in sales. U.S. Steel corporation is not listed with the top ten metal companies.

24. Reich, R. 1991. *The Work of Nations.* New York: Knopf, 214–15; Thurow. *Head to Head*, 180. Both authors here report on Inland Steel's 1980's association with Nippon Steel to create a state-of-the-art cold rolling mill needing only several technicians to operate this highly efficient plant. Ultimately, thousands of American steel workers lost their jobs as a result of such automation.

25. Nasar, S. 1992. *New York Times* (27 Dec.).

26. Kuttner, R. 1991. *The End of Laissez Faire.* New York: Knopf. See Chapters 4, 5.

27. Reich, R. 1992. "The Nightly Business Report." PBS (28 Oct.).

28. Jencks, C. 1992. *Rethinking Social Policy: Race, Poverty, and the Underclass.* Cambridge, MA: Harvard University Press. The entire book ranks as an apologia for a failing liberal vision of redistribution. Jencks here attempts a gentle distancing from a dissipating social ideal.

29. Du Bois, W.E.B., 1973. *The Education of Black People: Ten Critiques 1906–1960.* Ed. by Aptheker, H. Amherst: University of Massachusetts Press. See Chapter 12.

30. Itzkoff, S. W. 1992. *The Road to Equality.* Westport, CT: Praeger. This is the basic argument for a more realistic egalitarianism.

CHAPTER 16
NATALITY: WORLD WAR III

1. Polybius. 2nd century B.C. Book 20, Chapter 6; Book 36, Chapter 7, of *Histories.* In Toynbee, A. J, ed. 1953. *Greek Civilization and Character.* New York: The New American Library, 72–73.

2. Polybius. 2nd century B.C. Book 38, Chapters 1–4, of *Histories*. In Toynbee, A. J., ed. 1952. *Greek Historical Thought*. New York: The New American Library, 201.

3. 1993. *New York Times* (23 April).

4. Itzkoff, S. W. 1992. *The Road to Equality, Evolution and Social Reality*. Westport, Conn.: Praeger.

For Further Reading

ECONOMICS

Brimelow, P., and Spencer, L. 1993. "When Quotas Replace Merit, Everybody Suffers." *Forbes* 151, no. 4 (15 Feb.): 80–102.

Garten, J. E. 1992. *A Cold Peace*. New York: Times Books.

Kuttner, R. 1991. *The End of Laissez Faire*. New York: Knopf.

Prestowitz, C. 1988. *Trading Places*. New York: Basic Books.

Reich, R. 1991. *The Work of Nations*. New York: Knopf.

Thurow, L. 1992. *Head to Head*. New York: Morrow.

Wriston, W. B. 1992. *The Twilight of Sovereignty*. New York: Scribner.

EDUCATION

Finn, C. 1991. *We Must Take Charge*. New York: The Free Press.

Friedman, M. 1962. *Capitalism and Freedom*. Chicago: University of Chicago Press.

Itzkoff, S. W. 1976. *A New Public Education*. New York: Longman.

Kerr, C. 1991. *The Great Transformation in Higher Education 1960–1980*. Albany: SUNY Press.

Kirsch, I., and Jungeblut, A. 1986. "Literacy: Profiles of Young Adults." *U.S. Department of Education Office of Educational Research and Improvement: Sept*. Princeton, N.J.: ETS.

Lapointe, A. E., et al. 1992. *Learning Mathematics, IAEP*. Princeton, N.J.: ETS.

Lieberman, M. 1989. *Privatization and Educational Choice*. New York: St. Martin's Press.

Odom, G. R. 1990. *Mothers, Leadership, and Success*. Houston: Polybius Press.

Sowell, T. 1992. *Inside American Education*. New York: Morrow.

West, F. G. 1970. *Education and the State*. London: Institute of Economic Affairs.

INTELLIGENCE

Cattell, R. B., ed. 1983. *Intelligence and National Achievement*. Washington, D.C.: Institute for the Study of Man.

Gottfredson, L., ed. 1986. "The g Factor in Employment." Special issue of the *Journal of Vocational Behavior* 33, no. 3 (Dec.).

Herrnstein, R. J. 1989. "I.Q. and Falling Birthrates." *Atlantic* (May).

Itzkoff, S. W. 1987. *Why Humans Vary in Intelligence*. New York: Peter Lang.

Santy, P. 1994. *Choosing the Right Stuff*. Westport, Conn.: Praeger.

Seligman, D. 1992. *A Question of Intelligence*. New York: Birch Lane Press.

Terman, L. M., and Oden, M. H. 1959. *The Gifted Group at Midlife*. Stanford, Calif.: Stanford University Press.

Vining, D. P., Jr. 1982. "On the Possibility of the Emergence of a Dysgenic Trend with Respect to Intelligence in American Fertility Differentials." *Intelligence* 6:261–64.

Lehrle, S., Frank, S., and Papp, R. 1991. "Overcoming the Limitations of I.Q." *The Mankind Quarterly* 332, nos. 1–2:137–40.

SOCIAL

Bouvier, L. 1991. *Fifty Million Californians*. Washington, D.C.: The Federation for American Immigration Reform.

Daly, M., and Wilson, A. 1988. *Homicide*. Boston: de Gruyter.

Eckland, B. K., and Wisenbaker, J. M. 1979. "National Longitudinal Study." *National Center for Educational Statistics HEW* (Feb.), Washington, D.C.

Epstein, R. A. 1992. *Forbidden Grounds: The Case against Employment Discrimination Laws*. Cambridge: Harvard University Press.

"The Corporate Woman Officer." 1990. Boston: Heidrick and Struggles.

Jencks, C. 1992. *Rethinking Social Policy: Race, Poverty, and the Underclass*. Cambridge: Harvard University Press.

Kennan, G. F. 1993. *Around the Cragged Hill*. New York: Norton.

Mead, L. M. 1992. *The New Politics of Poverty*. New York: Basic Books.

Mount, F. 1992. *The Subversive Family*. New York: The Free Press.

Solinger, R. 1992. *Wake Up, Little Suzy*. New York: Routledge.

Taylor, J. 1992. *Paved with Good Intentions*. New York: Carroll & Graf.

Vital Statistics, U.S. 1988. *Natality*, vol. 1, 182ff. (Tables 1–70)

Index

About the Author

SEYMOUR W. ITZKOFF has been a Professor at Smith College since 1965. Trained in music, philosophy, and educational theory, he is the author of twelve earlier books, including a four-part series on the "evolution of human intelligence."